Designing & Building Business Applications: Microsoft® Access

Gerald V. Post

McGraw-Hill Irwin

Boston   Burr Ridge, IL   Dubuque, IA   Madison, WI   New York   San Francisco   St. Louis
Bangkok   Bogotá   Caracas   Kuala Lumpur   Lisbon   London   Madrid   Mexico City
Milan   Montreal   New Delhi   Santiago   Seoul   Singapore   Sydney   Taipei   Toronto

McGraw-Hill Irwin

DESIGNING & BUILDING BUSINESS APPLICATIONS: MICROSOFT® ACCESS
Published by McGraw-Hill/Irwin, a business unit of The McGraw-Hill Companies, Inc., 1221 Avenue of the Americas, New York, NY, 10020. Copyright © 2005, 2002, 1999 by The McGraw-Hill Companies, Inc. All rights reserved. No part of this publication may be reproduced or distributed in any form or by any means, or stored in a database or retrieval system, without the prior written consent of The McGraw-Hill Companies, Inc., including, but not limited to, in any network or other electronic storage or transmission, or broadcast for distance learning. Some ancillaries, including electronic and print components, may not be available to customers outside the United States.

This book is printed on acid-free paper.

2 3 4 5 6 7 8 9 0 QPD/QPD 0 9 8 7 6 5 4

ISBN 0-07-294331-9

Vice president and editor-in-chief: *Robin J. Zwettler*
Publisher: *Stewart Mattson*
Senior sponsoring editor: *Paul Ducham*
Editorial assistant: *Jennifer Wisnowski*
Marketing manager: *Greta Kleinert*
Media producer: *Greg Bates*
Project manager: *Charlie Fisher*
Manager, New book production: *Heather D. Burbridge*
Supplement producer: *Lynn M. Bluhm*
Senior digital content specialist: *Brian Nacik*
Lead designer: *Matthew Baldwin*
Cover designer: *Fuel Visual Media*
Typeface: *10/12 Times Roman*
Compositor: *The GTS Companies/York, PA Campus*
Printer: *Quebecor World Dubuque Inc.*

Brief Contents

1 Introduction 1

2 Database Design 14

3 Data Normalization 30

4 Data Queries 45

5 Advanced Queries and Subqueries 65

6 Forms, Reports, and Applications 85

7 Database Integrity and Transactions 116

8 Data Warehouses and Data Mining 143

9 Database Administration 164

10 Distributed Databases and the Internet 181

Contents

Chapter 1
Introduction   1

Objectives   1
Case: All Powder Board and Ski Shop   2
  Inventory   2
  Bindings and Boots   3
  Sales   4
  Rentals   5
Lab Exercise   6
  Project Outline   6
  Project Plan   7
  Feasibility   7
  The Database Management System   9
Exercises   11
Final Project   13

Chapter 2
Database Design   14

Objectives   14
Database Design   15
Access Data Types   15
Case: All Powder Board and Ski Shop   17
  Business Objects: First Guess   17
  Relationships   18
Lab Exercise   19
  Database Design System   19
  All Powder Design   21
Exercises   27
Final Project   29

Chapter 3
Data Normalization   30

Objectives   30
Database Design   31
Generated Keys: AutoNumber   31
Case: All Powder Board and Ski Shop   33
Lab Exercise   34
  All Powder Board and Ski
  Database Creation   34
  Relationships   38
Exercises   43
Final Project   44

Chapter 4
Data Queries   45

Objectives   45
Database Queries   46
Case: All Powder Board and Ski Shop   46
Lab Exercise   47
  All Powder Board and Ski Data   47
  Computations and Subtotals   57
Exercises   63
Final Project   64

Chapter 5
Advanced Queries and Subqueries   65

Objectives   65
Advanced Database Queries   66
Case: All Powder Board and Ski Shop   66
Lab Exercise   67
  All Powder Board and Ski Data   67
  SQL Data Definition and
  Data Manipulation   77
Exercises   82
Final Project   84

Chapter 6
Forms, Reports, and
Applications   85

Objectives   85
Applications   86
Case: All Powder Board and Ski Shop   86
Lab Exercise   87
  All Powder Board and Ski Shop Forms   87
  All Powder Basic Reports   100
  Building the All Powder Application   107
Exercises   113
Final Project   115

Chapter 7
Database Integrity and
Transactions   116

Objectives   116
Program Code in Microsoft Access   117
Case: All Powder Board and Ski Shop   117

Lab Exercise   118
   All Powder Board and Ski Data   118
   Database Cursors, Keys, and Locks   131
Exercises   140
Final Project   142

Chapter 8
Data Warehouses and
Data Mining   143

Objectives   143
Data Warehouse   144
Case: All Powder Board and Ski Shop   144
Lab Exercise   145
   All Powder Board and Ski Shop   145
   Introductory Data Analysis   154
Exercises   161
Final Project   163

Chapter 9
Database Administration   164

Objectives   164
Database Administration Tasks in Access   165

Case: All Powder Board and Ski Shop   166
Lab Exercise   166
   All Powder Board and Ski Shop   166
   Security and Privacy   170
Exercises   179
Final Project   180

Chapter 10
Distributed Databases and
the Internet   181

Objectives   181
Location, Location, Location   182
Case: All Powder Board and Ski Shop   182
Lab Exercise   183
   All Powder Board and Ski Shop   183
   The Internet   189
Exercises   192
Final Project   194

Designing & Building Business Applications: Microsoft® Access

1

Introduction

Chapter Outline

Objectives
Case: All Powder Board and Ski Shop
Inventory
Bindings and Boots
Sales
Rentals
Lab Exercise
Project Outline
Project Plan
Feasibility
The Database Management System
Exercises
Final Project

Objectives

- Identify the main elements of the case.
- Structure the work needed for the case.
- Create a feasibility analysis of the case.
- Create a new database.

Case: All Powder Board and Ski Shop

The ski industry has been through many changes in the 50 years since Bill Shimek founded the ski shop that is now run by his grandson. One of the biggest changes is reflected in the prominence of "Board" in the shop name. Snowboards revolutionized the industry in several respects. They revived youth interest in the sport, brought new designs to equipment and resorts, and increased sales dramatically. On the other hand, the increased changes in ski and snowboard equipment make it more difficult for shops to stock the hundreds of options and combinations that enthusiasts might want. Shops have become larger, forcing small firms out of business. Even large ski shops have had to identify their customers and forecast customer demands carefully to make sure the high-demand equipment is in stock. Tracking sales, trends, and buyer needs has become critical to survival.

Another factor in the industry is that the firms increasingly rely on rentals. Partly because of the rapid changes in the industry, many people prefer to rent equipment so they can avoid having to buy new boards and skis every year. Consequently, the shop buys several relatively standard boards and skis every year and rents them out. At the end of the year, the used equipment is sold at a discount to make room for next year's models.

Inventory

Monitoring inventory is a first critical step in the process of providing the selection demanded by customers. Figure 1.1 shows some of the detailed information needed, as well as the diversity of equipment available. Note that because of the variety of uses, many different types of snowboards and skis exist. Figure 1.1 also shows the importance of the skill categories. Manufacturers produce special boards and skis for each of these categories. Of course, it would be impossible to stock all of the required sizes for rental purposes.

FIGURE 1.1

Inventory

Snowboards

	Manufacturer	Mfg ID	Size	Description	Graphics	List Price	QOH
Freestyle							
Pipe							
Standard							
Extreme							

Skis

	Manufacturer	Mfg ID	Size	Description	Graphics	List Price	QOH
Slalom							
Cross country-skate							
Cross country-trad.							
Telemark							
Jumping							
Freestyle							
Downhill/race							

Rental boards and skis tend to be as generic as possible. Even for sales, some sizes of the high-end skis and boards have to be special ordered.

Within a category, manufacturers tend to sell boards and skis targeted for different levels of skiers—from beginner to intermediate to expert (Type I, Type II, and Type III skier). Even within the type classifications, All Powder salespeople evaluate customers on the basis of their aggressiveness on the slope. Because of the size of snowboards, along with the youthful image of the sport, manufacturers place a high value on the graphics (images and colors) displayed on both sides of the boards. Customers have often been known to choose a board because of the graphics. Some of this emphasis has filtered over to skis as well.

Listing the sizes of boards and skis is somewhat tricky, and definitely presents a challenge to keeping adequate inventory. The length of the ski or board is a critical number, but the customer's choice is also based on several other ski measurements. Snowboards revolutionized board and ski design by adding a narrower waist to aid in turning. This concept migrated to most varieties of skis as well, so customers often want to know the waist width, sideout depth, and effective edge length of skis. Generally, boards and skis with narrower waists are targeted for more advanced skiers. Additionally, the construction of the board or ski, in terms of materials and thickness, significantly affects its flexibility and handling. Customers generally want to feel the ski to evaluate and compare its flexibility, but measures of stance location (for boards) and the rider weight range provide some prediction of the handling characteristics. Most skis and boards are also designed for a particular riding weight. With cross-country skis it is particularly important to get the proper length for the weight of the skier.

Bindings and Boots

Bindings and boots represent another common problem for All Powder and other ski shops. Each ski and each board can technically be fitted with several types of bindings. Each binding type generally requires a matching style of boot, and some of the boots can work only with some bindings. For example, snowboards can use clincher, strap, or plate bindings. Cross-country skis can use pin, strap, or rod bindings. Most modern skis use the rod binding, but customers sometimes want boots that fit the older pin bindings. Downhill, freestyle, and slalom skis use similar bindings. Because they are the most popular, the store usually stocks several models—focusing on skill levels.

Figure 1.2 shows an example of the card system that All Powder uses to help salespeople select bindings and boots. Currently, the salespeople are supposed to change the quantity on hand whenever a boot or binding is sold. Of course, the cards are rarely kept up-to-date and the salespeople often have to go search the physical inventory to see if a size needed by a customer is in stock. Note that boots and bindings are specifically matched, and a boot for one purpose can rarely be used for a different application. For example, it would not be possible to use a cross-country boot in a downhill binding. The binding is usually listed as a type (rod, step-in, telemark/cable, etc.). On the other hand, it is possible to mount bindings on different types of skis. For instance, you could mount a telemark binding to a downhill ski. Some of the combinations should be avoided, but this knowledge will not be needed in the database.

FIGURE 1.2

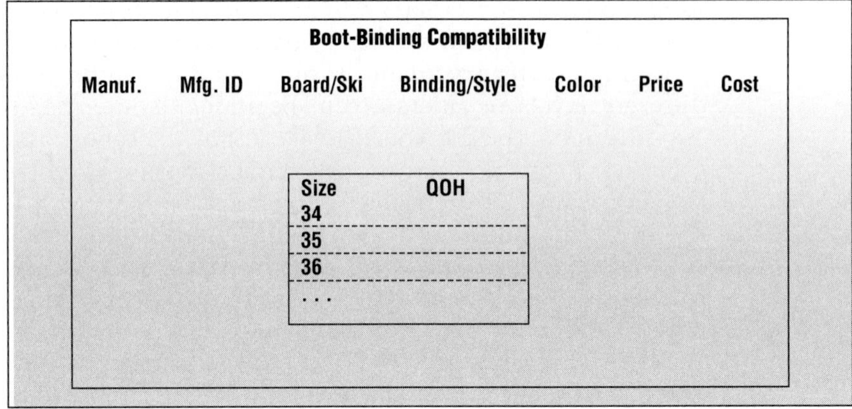

Sales

The sales form shown in Figure 1.3 is fairly standard. All of the hard work in terms of configuration was done by the salesperson. In some cases, the salesperson might ask the customer to initial some items that might present compatibility issues to make sure the customer is aware of the potential problems. The description generally includes the manufacturer's name and style. The SKU (stock keeping unit) is a special number created within the store to code each item. Returns are usually accepted on most items as long as they have not been used outside (e.g., scratched or worn boots cannot be returned).

It is important for salespeople to identify the type of boarding/skiing and the customer's skill level. This information is used to send customers mailings about special sales. The owner also has started thinking about keeping customer sizes in a database. This information would be particularly helpful in clearing out the previous year's inventory of special sizes (very small or very large), because it would help pinpoint customers who could use those

FIGURE 1.3

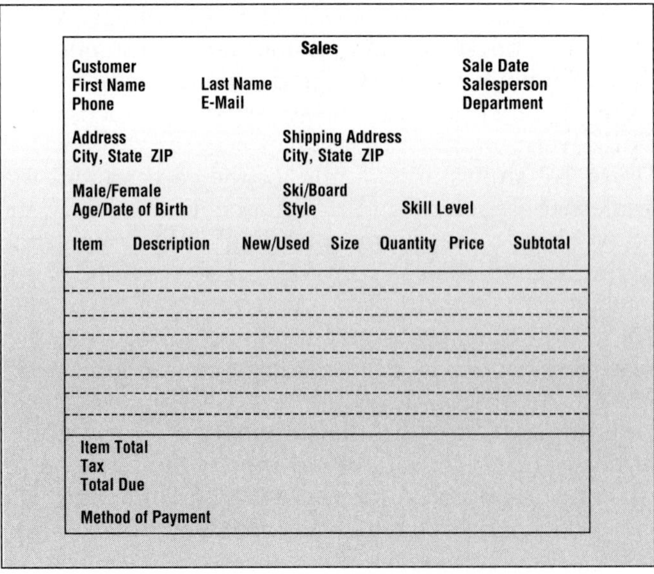

special sizes. The catch is that the owner is concerned about privacy issues and fears that customers may not want to have their sizes on file at the store. However, if a customer has already purchased items in a specific category and size, that data will be available. The difficulty emerges when salespeople ask customers for their sizes when they are not purchasing these products. For instance, it may appear rude to ask a customer who came in to buy ski wax for his or her jacket size.

The store evaluates salespeople on the level of sales they make, so it is important to track sales by each employee. Of course, the database should contain additional information about each employee, such as phone number, address, and his or her primary department assignment. Of course, clerks rarely write down the department names properly, so it makes sense to have a separate lookup table for the department names.

Also, note that some of the best customers participate in several styles, even crossing between using skis and boards. A customer who is an expert at downhill skiing might be a beginner with snowboards.

Rentals

The form to handle rentals is similar to the sales form. But notice in Figure 1.4 that columns have been added for return date, condition, and additional charges. The additional charges are imposed if an item is returned late or if it is returned damaged. Additionally, customers are required to sign the form to indicate their agreement with the skill level, rental conditions, and the release printed on the back of the form. Katy, the current manager, has talked about capturing the signatures digitally and storing them online, but it is not a high priority.

Observe that the current form requires that each rented item be checked off separately when it is returned. Although the store clerks often complain about having to mark each row separately, the store managers have determined that about 20 percent of the time, a customer forgets to return an item and has to bring it back later.

FIGURE 1.4

<table>
<tr><td colspan="7" align="center">**Rentals**</td></tr>
<tr><td colspan="7">**Customer**</td></tr>
<tr><td colspan="2">**First Name**</td><td colspan="3">**Last Name**</td><td colspan="2">**Rental Date**
Expected Return</td></tr>
<tr><td colspan="2">**Phone**</td><td colspan="3">**E-Mail**</td><td colspan="2"></td></tr>
<tr><td colspan="7"></td></tr>
<tr><td colspan="2">**Address**</td><td colspan="3">**Shipping Address**</td><td colspan="2"></td></tr>
<tr><td colspan="2">**City, State ZIP**</td><td colspan="3">**City, State ZIP**</td><td colspan="2"></td></tr>
<tr><td colspan="7"></td></tr>
<tr><td colspan="2">**Male/Female**</td><td colspan="3">**Ski/Board**</td><td colspan="2"></td></tr>
<tr><td colspan="2">**Age/Date of Birth**</td><td colspan="2">**Style**</td><td colspan="3">**Skill Level**</td></tr>
<tr><td>**Item**</td><td>**Description**</td><td>**Size**</td><td>**Fee**</td><td>**Return Date**</td><td>**Condition**</td><td>**Charges**</td></tr>
<tr><td></td><td></td><td></td><td></td><td></td><td></td><td></td></tr>
<tr><td></td><td></td><td></td><td></td><td></td><td></td><td></td></tr>
<tr><td></td><td></td><td></td><td></td><td></td><td></td><td></td></tr>
<tr><td></td><td></td><td></td><td></td><td></td><td></td><td></td></tr>
<tr><td colspan="2">**Item Total**</td><td colspan="5"></td></tr>
<tr><td colspan="2">**Tax**</td><td colspan="5"></td></tr>
<tr><td colspan="2">**Total Due**</td><td colspan="3" align="center">**Added Charges**</td><td colspan="2"></td></tr>
<tr><td colspan="2">**Method of Payment**</td><td colspan="3" align="center">**Signature**</td><td colspan="2"></td></tr>
</table>

Renting ski equipment also raises the issue of reservations. On some holidays, all of the equipment is rented out before 10:00 A.M. Some long-term customers have said that they would like to be able to reserve equipment. Currently, the rental managers will sometimes set aside equipment if a valuable repeat customer calls in advance. This process works reasonably well, but the managers have talked about creating a system that is available to everyone. One of the drawbacks is that they are concerned that the general public might reserve items and then never show up, leaving equipment idle that could be rented to someone else.

Lab Exercise

The first step in any project is to identify some basic elements of the system. What are the goals? What is the scope? What tools will be needed? What are the benefits? What are the expected costs? How much development time will be needed? All of these questions are difficult to answer, and rarely do the answers have a single value. Instead, you need to create a project plan. The plan will include a feasibility statement that describes the basic costs and potential benefits. As a real-world project, you would also include a list of developers and a statement of expected fees, so the owners can evaluate the decision to hire you.

Project Outline

As a first step in developing the project plan, you need to summarize the overall project. This summary should contain a brief description of the project, its goals, and initial lists of primary forms and reports. Ultimately, this summary will also include the scope and anticipated budget for the project.

Activity: Review the Case and Research the Industry

For the purposes of this lab, you will prepare a project proposal for developing the sales system needed by the All Powder Board and Ski Shop. The rental component will be left for another exercise. You should begin by reviewing the description of the company. You should also use the Internet to check out some of the manufacturers and some of the competitors. You need to be sure that you understand the key factors in the industry. Figure 1.5 provides a possible structure for your summary. You should review the case and enter the basic information requested.

FIGURE 1.5

Project Title: Sales System for Boards and Skis
Customer: All Powder Board and Ski Shop
Primary Contact: Katy
Goals:
Project Description:
Primary Forms:
Primary Reports:
Lead Developer:
Estimated Development Time:
Estimated Development Cost:
Date Prepared:

Project Plan

The project plan consists of a detailed breakdown of the steps needed to create the final system. A common approach is to follow the steps of the systems development life-cycle methodology: Initiation, Analysis, Design, Implementation, and Review. Some organizations have rigid descriptions of each of the steps involved in this process. Some organizations adopt a more flexible approach. Either way, this plan should outline the basic steps that need to be completed and an estimated schedule.

In the initial phase, it is also helpful to identify any potential risks to the project development. At various stages, ask what might go wrong. If you are aware of the potential problems, managers can monitor for them and can prepare solutions more quickly.

Activity: Create the Initial Project Plan

Project plans and schedules are often shown with Gantt charts to illustrate how the various steps depend on each other. If you have access to software such as Microsoft Project, it is relatively easy to create the project plan. Figure 1.6 shows the basic steps that the labs will follow in building the application. Ultimately, you would estimate the times required for each step. However, until you have read the rest of the book and worked with the databases, it is difficult to estimate the times needed for each step. For now, evaluate the steps and try to identify any dependencies between the tasks. For example, is it possible to create the forms without having the database tables and relationships? Assuming you have several people to help, reorganize the tasks so that as many tasks as possible can be done at the same time.

Feasibility

Feasibility studies are notoriously difficult. The concept is certainly simple: Identify the potential costs and potential benefits of a system and compare them. The problem is that benefits might not be quantifiable, so it is difficult

FIGURE 1.6

> 1. Define the project and obtain approval.
> 2. Analyze the user needs and identify all forms and reports.
> 3. System Design
>   a. Determine the tables and relationships needed.
>   b. Create the tables and load basic data.
>   c. Create queries needed for forms and reports.
>   d. Build forms and reports.
>   e. Create transaction elements.
>   f. Define security and access controls.
> 4. Additional Features
>   a. Create data warehouse to analyze data as needed.
>   b. Handle distributed database elements as needed.
> 5. System Implementation
>   a. Convert and load data.
>   b. Train users.
>   c. Load testing.
> 6. System Review

FIGURE 1.7

		Present Value	Subtotal
Assumptions			
Annual discount rate	0.03		
Project life/years	5		
Costs		Present Value	Subtotal
One time			
DBMS software			
Hardware			
Development			
Data entry			
Training			
Ongoing			
Personnel			
Upgrades/annual			
Supplies			
Support			
Maintenance			
Benefits			
Cost Savings			
Better inventory control			
Fewer clerks			
Strategic			
Increased sales			
Other?			
Net Present Value			

to attach meaningful numbers. Nonetheless, it is useful to at least write down the anticipated costs and expected benefits. Even if numbers are not available, managers can at least see a concise statement of the analysis.

Activity: Create the Feasibility Analysis

Figure 1.7 shows the basic elements of a feasibility study. You need to create a spreadsheet with these main categories. Use research to identify approximate costs of the various components. For example, assume that the shop will need to purchase a server to host the main database and two client computers for the sales staff. With Microsoft Access, several configurations are possible. Examine the software license to determine the number of copies you will need and the approximate cost. Other numbers, including benefits, can be estimated. Remember that annual costs and benefits should be discounted to compensate for the time-value of money. Use the present value (PV) function in Excel. Although the benefits are relatively well defined, they can still be difficult to estimate. For example, how will the system reduce the need for sales clerks? How many or how many hours? How much do clerks earn? Likewise, in terms of inventory control, how much money will be saved by not having to slash prices at the end of the season to clear the unsold inventory? You need to know or estimate the number and value of items typically left at the end of the season. In practice, the managers might have answers to some of these questions, but you will still have to do additional research. In this example, be sure that you spell out your assumptions.

The Database Management System

Activity: Explore the DBMS

Two of the features that make Microsoft Access a popular database system are that it is relatively inexpensive and easy to install. If you are working in a classroom lab, your machines should already have Access installed. If you are working on your own computer, check your startup menu to be certain that Access is available. Note that Access is not shipped with the Small Business version of Office. More importantly, you need to make certain that your system is up-to-date. You should check the three sites listed in Figure 1.8 to update your computer in terms of the operating system, Microsoft Office, and the data access components (MDAC). Microsoft often releases updates on these three sites, so you should check them on a regular basis.

To get a quick perspective of the various components of the DBMS, you need to build a simple database. Start Access and create a new, blank database. Because a database consists of tables, the first step is to create a table. Figure 1.9 shows an initial definition of a Customer table. Create a new table in Design view, and enter the names of the columns (fields) and select the data types as indicated. Then close and save the table design; name it "Customer" when asked.

Now open the table and enter some data for hypothetical customers. You can copy the data from Figure 1.10 or just create your own. Access provides several tools in the Table window to examine the data. You can sort by columns or even filter the rows to see customers that meet some criteria. However, you will rarely give users direct access to tables. Instead, you will build forms and reports for managers to use. Close the Customer table.

Access provides wizards to help build forms and reports. A common data entry form for the Customer table is relatively easy to create. Select the Forms menu item on the main Access window. Then select the option to

FIGURE 1.8

1. Windows update
   http://windowsupdate.microsoft.com
2. Office update
   http://office.microsoft.com/productupdates
3. Data access component update
   http://www.microsoft.com/data/download.htm
   Pick the highest numbered MDAC RTM.

FIGURE 1.9

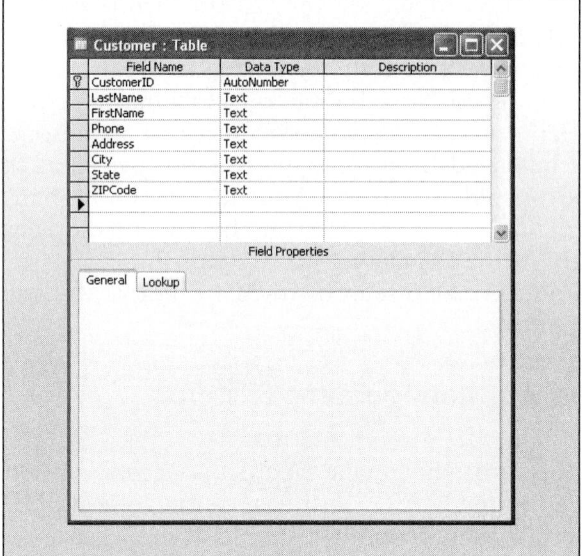

create a new form using the wizard. If necessary, pick the Customer table, then move all of the columns into the box for the selected fields. Make sure the form is a columnar form and choose a style that appeals to you. Make sure the form is titled "Customer" and tell the wizard to finish. Your form should be similar to the one in Figure 1.11, but your style choice will affect its final appearance. Notice that the form shows all of the elements for one customer. Later, you can return to the Design view of this form and modify the layout by dragging the labels and text boxes on the screen. You can resize them or change properties such as the foreground and background colors. For practice, try setting the last name field in boldface. Switch to Design view, right-click on the LastName text box, and select the Properties option. In the Properties box, change the Font Weight to Bold. Save the form and run it to see the effect of your change. Similar wizards and properties are used to build reports, but there are not enough tables and data to justify writing a report yet.

FIGURE 1.10

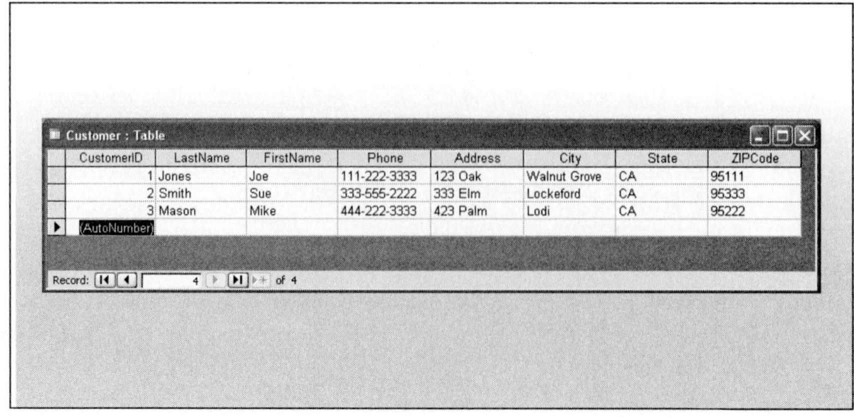

FIGURE 1.11

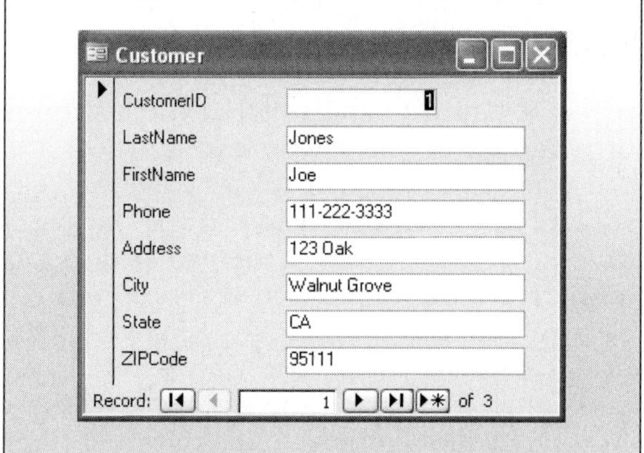

Exercises

Many Charms

Madison and Samantha, friends of yours, have a small business selling charms for bracelets and necklaces. They buy some of the charms they sell; others they make. So far, they have run the business as a hobby, selling primarily to friends and relatives. But they have recently established a website to display pictures and prices of some of the charms. You have agreed to build a database for them to track their inventory, customers, and sales. Any orders they receive through the website will be e-mailed, so the website does not have to be connected live to the database. The database is a relatively traditional sales system, but it is slightly complicated by the nature of the charms. Charms come in a variety of shapes, sizes, and materials. For example, customers who want a quarter-moon charm have a choice of 4 mm or 8 mm; and of silver, gold, gold plate, bronze, or painted ceramic. Charms are also offered in categories such as animals, hearts, birthdays, and so on. Additionally, the duo offers a variety of chains and pins to hold the charms. Eventually, they want to track the sales by all of these categories, so they will know which items are selling the best and which make the most profit. Costs and prices tend to fluctuate. If they purchase items in bulk, the per-piece cost is lower, but they need to know they can sell the entire shipment. If an item sits around too long, they find that they have to significantly cut the price just to clear out the stock. Of course, gold items are more expensive, making them more difficult to sell, and they are reluctant to tie up their money in high-priced merchandise.

1. Research similar sites on the Internet. Describe or sketch the major forms and reports that the company might use.
2. Create the initial proposal and feasibility study.

Standup Foods

Laura runs a catering company that focuses on Hollywood movie studios. Her chefs prepare hors d'oeuvres, sandwiches, and other food items that are served to the cast and crew of various movies and studios. To keep it fresh, the food is prepared each day in the main kitchens, and meals are then assembled and displayed onsite. For some clients, the company vans deliver fresh food every few hours. To hold costs down, many of Laura's employees are part time—only a few chefs and managers are full-time employees. Some of Laura's clients call at the last minute, so she maintains a large list of potential workers who can perform a variety of tasks, from driving to food preparation and display, as well as cleanup. The chefs and managers evaluate workers after each job in terms of timeliness, appearance, friendliness, and the ability to take orders and accomplish tasks. Workers often perform many tasks at a given event. For instance, a driver might also be a server. But some tasks require specific certifications. Not all workers are licensed to drive, and only a few have been trained to perform some tasks such as cutting meats. Most of the employee ratings are somewhat informal at the moment, but she would like to computerize them to help her select the best workers for future jobs. At some point, she would like to offer bonuses or higher pay to workers who routinely perform well. Another challenge Laura faces is that some clients are finicky about certain types of food. In particular, some movie clients have special preferences as well as some items that cause allergic reactions. The chefs currently keep these two lists in paper folders for some major performers and actors. But to be safe, Laura wants to computerize the lists and, ultimately, the recipe ingredients. Then when a chef plans the meals, the computer could check the list of main guests and their allergies against the recipe list to identify potential problems.

1. Research similar sites on the Internet. Describe or sketch the major forms and reports that the company might use.
2. Create the initial proposal and feasibility study.

EnviroSpeed

Brennan and Tyler are owner/managers of a consulting firm that specializes in environmental issues. In particular, the company's scientists are experts in cleanups for chemical spills. For example, if a tanker crashes and spills chemicals on a highway, the company can quickly evaluate the potential problems and identify the best method to clean up the spill and prevent problems. The company itself does not clean up the spill, but it has contacts with several crews around the globe that it can call if local emergency workers need additional help. The primary focus of the company is to provide expert knowledge in the time of a crisis. This task requires specialized scientists, good communication systems, and in-depth training and practice. Brennan wants to improve the existing information system to maintain a database of case histories. Then, if a similar problem arises in the future, the scientists can quickly search the database and identify secondary problems to examine which solutions and ideas were successful and which ones caused more problems. Tyler has explained that at a minimum, the database has to hold the contact information for all of the scientists and emergency crews. It must also list the specialties, training, and skill levels of each person in a variety of areas. In terms of actual situations, the database should track the identities and roles of the various people and the key time frames (when reported, response time, and so on). Scientists also need the ability to list all of the chemicals involved and details about the terrain (hills, water, soil composition). More subjective data must also be captured, including comments by the onsite team and a description of the problem and secondary factors. All proposed solutions should be entered into the database, along with comments regarding their strengths and weaknesses as well as the final selections and an evaluation of the result. It is important to track potential solutions that were discarded. Even if they did not apply to the original problem, they might be useful for a future event with different circumstances.

1. Research similar sites on the Internet. Describe or sketch the major forms and reports that the company might use.
2. Create the initial proposal and feasibility study.

Final Project

The main textbook has an appendix with several longer case studies. You should be able to work on one of these cases throughout the term. If you or your instructor picks one, do the following.

1. Research similar sites on the Internet. List the major forms and reports that the company might use.
2. Create the initial proposal and feasibility study.

Chapter **2**

Database Design

Chapter Outline

Objectives

Database Design

Access Data Types

Case: All Powder Board and Ski Shop

*Business Objects: First Guess
Relationships*

Lab Exercise

*Database Design System
All Powder Design*

Exercises

Final Project

Objectives

- Design the initial tables for the case.
- Create the design in the database design system.
- Determine the initial relationships for the case.
- Identify the data types needed for the attributes.

Database Design

You can design a database using paper and pencil. As you gain experience and become more skilled at the task, pencil and paper will be relatively easy to use. However, when you are learning, pencil and paper are tedious because you find that you often need to remove items from potential classes, or even alter the entire diagram. As an alternative, you might consider going directly to the DBMS and defining the tables or classes off the top of your head. This approach might work with Microsoft Access if you use the Relationships screen, but you will still find it time-consuming to continually revise the tables. With any other DBMS, trying to create tables from the top of your head is foolish because many systems do not allow you to make major changes to tables once they have been defined.

A few computer-assisted software engineering (CASE) tools remain that can help you define classes in a graphical environment. They are relatively powerful, and many have the ability to generate the final tables based on the class diagram. However, they are also expensive, hard to install, and cumbersome to learn. But if you work for a company that has invested in these tools, they are an excellent way to define the database classes.

To learn database design, there is a better tool. The database design system is an online expert system that enables students to create class diagrams graphically in a Java-enabled Web browser. The system makes it easy for you to create classes (entities) and build associations (relationships). More importantly, it provides immediate feedback on the design, which is the expert system part. The system runs on a custom Web server, and diagrams are stored in a central database. This approach means that you can access your diagrams from almost any computer. Changes you make in class or in your instructor's office are saved and are available when you return to a lab or to your own computer. From an instructional perspective, the best part is that the system contains some complex rules to provide feedback on your diagram. The system recognizes most design errors and points them out with suggestions to improve the design. Your instructor can obtain the database design system for your class. If it is available, you should use it to get the benefit of the immediate feedback. If it is not available, you can draw the class diagrams with paper and pencil, or with a graphics package such as Visio or even PowerPoint.

Access Data Types

As a database designer, your job is to define the database tables that efficiently store the organization's data and support the business rules. In this process, you will define the tables in terms of the data columns (attributes) and the table relationships (associations). You will also need to know what type of data will be stored in each column. Also, for some columns, you will want to specify constraints (for example, salary cannot be negative).

Selecting the proper data type can sometimes be a difficult step. Any DBMS supports only a limited number of domains and you have to understand the capabilities and limitations of each type. You must also understand the underlying business data—both the values collected today and the potential values that may be collected in the future. For example, workers may only use integer values to represent a quality rating. In the future, however,

FIGURE 2.1

	Name	Data	Bytes
Text (characters)			
Fixed	NA		
Variable	Text	255	Variable
Memo	Memo	64 K	Variable
Numeric			
Byte (8 bits)	Number: Byte	0–255	1
Integer (16 bits)	Number: Integer	+/−32767	2
Long (32 bits)	Number: Long Integer	+/−2 billion	4
(64 bits)	NA		
Fixed precision	Number: Decimal	+/−1 E 28	12
Float	Number: Single	+/−1 E 38	4
Double	Number: Double	+/−1 E 308	8
Currency	Currency	+/−900.0000 trillion	8
Yes/No	Yes/No	0/1	1 bit
Date/Time	Date/Time	1/1/100–12/31/9999 (1 sec)	8
Image	OLE Object	1 gigabyte	Variable
AutoNumber	AutoNumber	Long (+/−2 billion)	4

it is likely that the company will want to use fractional values as well. Although database types are becoming more standardized over time, each DBMS uses its own type names. Even more confusing, the actual values supported can be different even if the data type name is the same. The most common problem arises with the Integer data type. With some systems, an Integer is limited to 16 bits, while others default to 32 bits. With any DBMS, you should consult the help system to determine exactly which data types are provided and their limitations.

Figure 2.1 shows the main data types available in Microsoft Access. The types you will use most often are Text, Date/Time, Currency, and Long Integer. When you need to store date or time values, be sure to use the Date/Time type. It supports date arithmetic so users can subtract two dates to obtain the number of days between them. The OLE Object type can hold pictures, spreadsheets, or documents.

The numeric subtypes are generally the most confusing. To truly understand the numeric types, you need to study the way that computers convert numbers into binary format, but that study is beyond the scope of this book. The easy answer is to split types into three groups: integers, floating point, and fixed point. Integers do not contain fractions or decimal points. The difference between the three types lies in the size of data that can be held. For example, a 16-bit integer cannot hold numbers larger than 32,767. So, if you have many items to sell or customers to track, you need to use a Long Integer, which can hold values to slightly over 2 billion. If you need fractional values, you need to choose the Single or Double data type. Again, the difference lies in the size of the number and the number of digits each type can hold. Single-precision numbers hold only seven significant digits, regardless of where the decimal point falls. Double-precision numbers can contain 14 significant digits. But, be careful. Even the 14 digits could cause you problems—if you try to use the

Double type for money. Because of the way decimal numbers are converted to binary floating point, some numbers do not convert correctly and you can get round-off errors. If you need decimal point values and you need them to be exact, then you should use one of the fixed decimal types: Currency or Decimal. Currency is designed for monetary data and can accurately store 15 digits on the left side of the decimal point, and four on the right. The decimal type is both larger and more flexible than Currency. Numbers can have up to 28 total digits (specified by the precision), and you can specify how many digits fall to the right of the decimal point (given by the scale).

Although the many data types can be confusing, it is important that you choose the type carefully. In particular, for numeric types, make sure that you select a data type that will be able to hold the largest (or smallest) values that might exist in the data.

Case: All Powder Board and Ski Shop

With any database project, the first step is to understand the various elements of the organization and the components that will become part of the database application. This knowledge is critical, because the database design must reflect the business rules. In real life, you can ask workers about the processes and underlying assumptions. With a written case, it can be more challenging to determine all of the necessary rules. On the other hand, real life is messier and people often give inconsistent answers. It takes experience to learn to talk with users to identify exactly which components are the most important, and how the pieces relate to each other. Cases avoid this design complication but generally require you to make assumptions on your own. Since the goal is to make reasonable assumptions, you should search the Internet or read a few articles on snowboards and skis before you tackle the database design.

Business Objects: First Guess

One of the first steps in designing the database is to identify the business objects. In many ways, this case is a fairly typical business problem, so you would expect to see many of the traditional business objects, such as Customer, Employee, and Sale. Because the store also rents equipment, there will be a Rental object similar to the Sale object. Figure 2.2 shows initial versions of these four classes. These objects are relatively standard, but some issues arise in this case. Notice that you must also begin to think about primary keys. In each of these four tables, the primary key is a new value that will be generated by the DBMS. In Microsoft Access, it will be an AutoNumber column. This decision was made because it ensures that these values are always going to be unique, and they can be created instantly by the DBMS. In most situations, the actual key values will be hidden from the users, and they will see only the relevant names.

Notice that several attributes are missing from these initial classes. The main reason is that it is important to ensure that the columns you include at this stage are correct. If there is any doubt about a column in a potential class, leave it out and think about it. A few other classes should be relatively obvious for this case. In particular, several support tables are used to provide lookup data for other tables. Ultimately, you will have to define all of the objects, identify the columns for each table, and specify the data type for each column.

FIGURE 2.2

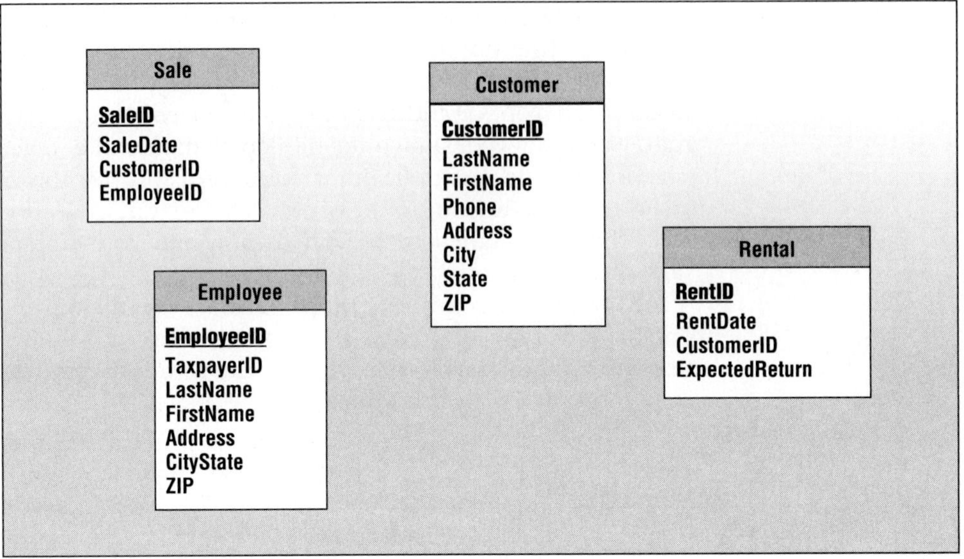

Relationships

Classes or entities are related to other classes. For example, notice that the Sale table contains a CustomerID property. Values in this column match entries in the Customer table, which is keyed by CustomerID. So, if you found a CustomerID value of 112 in the Sale table, you could look up the matching customer data by finding the row in the Customer table that has a primary key value of 112. This association also expresses several business rules. In particular, (1) each sale can be placed by only one customer, (2) a sale must be identified with a customer, (3) any given customer can participate in many sales, but (4) a customer might not have bought anything yet.

Relationships are displayed on the diagram by drawing connecting lines between the two tables involved. The business rules are shown as annotations at the end of each connection. Each side of the connection displays minimum and maximum values. Figure 2.3 shows the association between the Sale and Customer table. Notice that the annotations match the four business rules described in the previous paragraph. The 1 . . . 1 notation on the Customer side represents rules 1 and 2. At a minimum, each sale requires

FIGURE 2.3

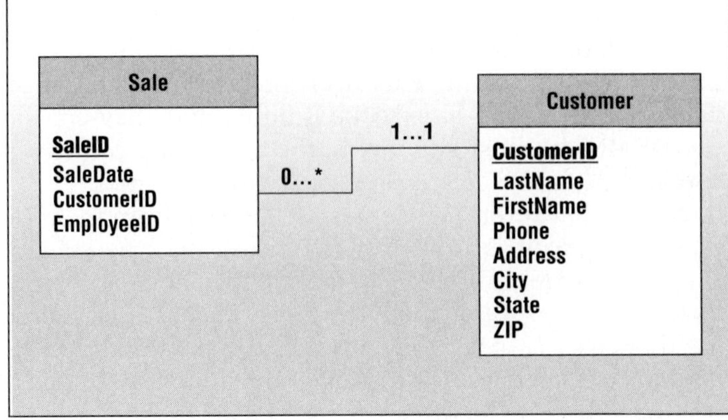

at least one customer, and, at a maximum, a sale can have no more than one customer. Likewise, the 0 . . . * annotation represents rules 3 and 4. A customer can participate in zero to many sales. There is no maximum (*), so a customer can participate in any number of sales, and the zero means that a customer might not have bought anything yet. As a database designer, your job is to identify the entities and relationships needed for this case.

Lab Exercise

Database Design System

The Database Design system is designed as an instructional tool. Your instructor should have already registered to obtain an instructor's account. The instructor will also choose and schedule assignments for the class. You will need a class code to register for a class, so be sure you get the correct admission code from your instructor. You will also need a set of numbers to create a new student account on the system. Check with your instructor to obtain these numbers. With the two sets of numbers and the class admission code, you are ready to create your personal account.

Activity: Getting Started

Use your browser to navigate to the Database Design website and select the link as a new student who has two key numbers. Figure 2.4 shows the

FIGURE 2.4

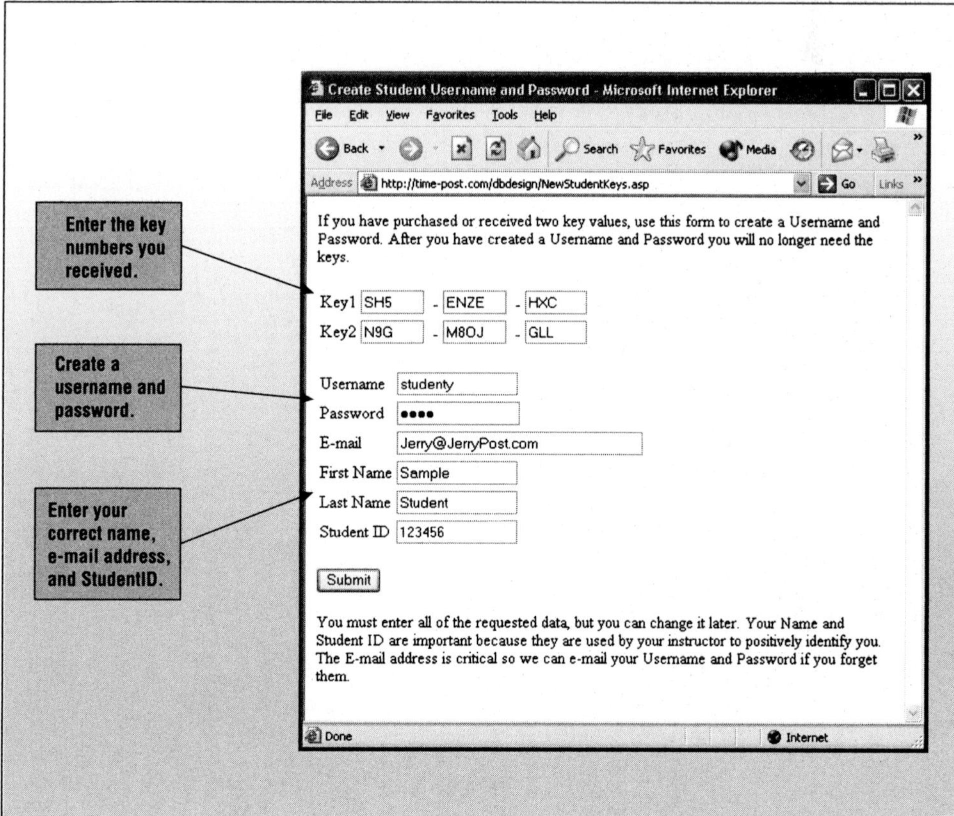

<table>
<tr><td>

Action

Browser: http://JerryPost.com/dbdesign
New student who has two key numbers.

</td></tr>
</table>

form you need to fill out. First, enter the key numbers that you have. Next, create a username and password that you will remember. You must choose a username that is different from all others. Be sure that you enter your name, e-mail address, and Student ID number correctly. The name and ID number will be used by your instructor to correctly identify you so you receive credit for working on assignments. Note that the ID and password are encrypted on the website database to protect them. The e-mail address is important so the system can send you the username and password in case you forget what you selected. When you have entered the data, click the Submit button. If you have an error in the key codes, or if your username has already been selected by someone else, you will receive a message and be asked to correct the items in error. Note that the key codes can be used only one time and can be discarded once the account has been created.

Once you have successfully created the new account, you must register for the specific class. As shown in Figure 2.5, simply choose your university and your correct class. Enter the admission code provided by your instructor and click the button to register for the class. If you do not have the proper code and are unable to register, you can get the code and return later. From the main page, enter your username and password to log in. If necessary, once you are logged in, you can click the link at the bottom of the main Design page to register for a class.

FIGURE 2.5

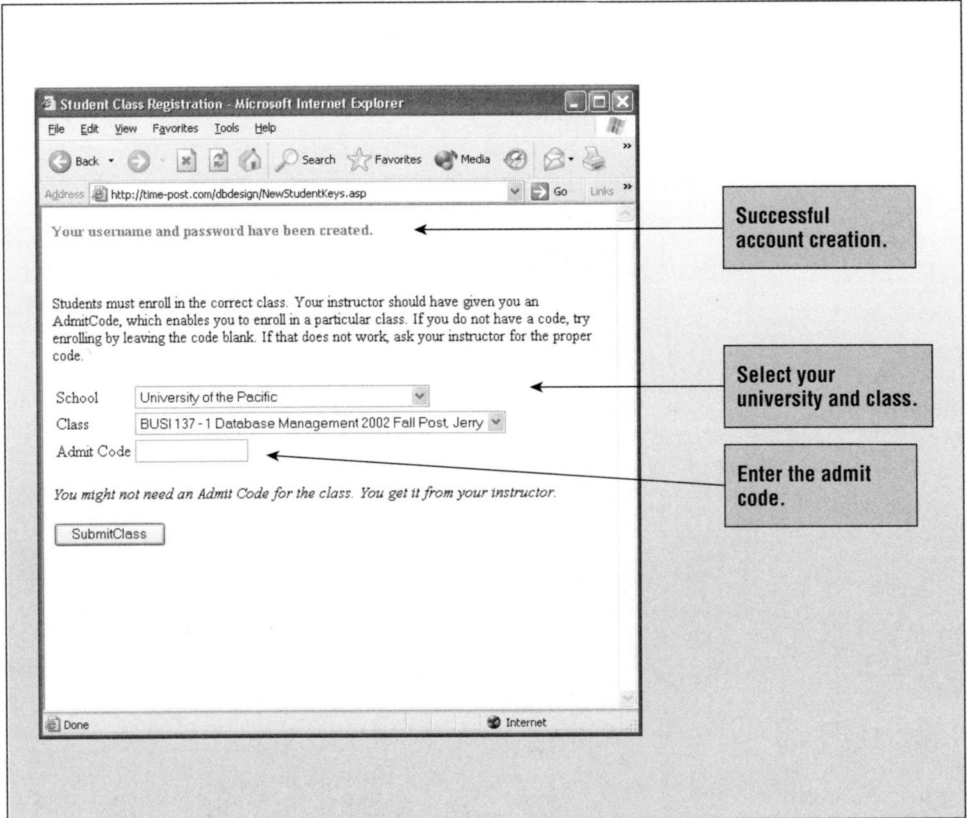

All Powder Design

When you have created an account, registered for a class, and logged into the system, you are ready to begin designing the database.

Activity: Create Tables and Columns

Figure 2.6 shows the main elements of the system with the beginning of the solution. When you begin, the various windows will be empty. You must first open a problem using the File/Open menu choice and select the Workbook case. When the problem loads, the right-hand window will display a list of available columns. Initially, it will probably not include the key columns. You will add those later.

> **Action**
>
> File/Open, choose All Powder case.
> Right-click/Add Table.
> Right-click header/Rename table.
> Drag columns from right onto table.
> Right-click name/set data type.

Create a table (class/entity) by clicking the right mouse button on the main screen where you want the table located. Then select the Add Table option. Rename the table by right-clicking the table heading, typing "Sale" as the new name, and pressing the Enter key.

Now you add columns to the table. All columns are added to a table by dragging them from the right-hand window and dropping them onto the desired table. In the case of the Sale table, you generate a new primary key column (SaleID). To create a generated key column, drag-and-drop the top label for Generate Key. Then rename the newly created column. Rename columns by right-clicking the name either in the table or in the right-hand window. Be careful: Do not give two columns the same name, even if they are in different tables. You will not be able to tell them apart in the main list of the right-hand window. Now you can add some of the other columns needed in the Sale table. Look through the right-hand window to find the SaleDate and SalesTax entries. You can simplify your search if you sort the list by right-clicking on it and selecting Sort. Drag the desired column onto the Sale table. Once a column is in the table, you can change the order by dragging and dropping it higher or lower in the list.

FIGURE 2.6

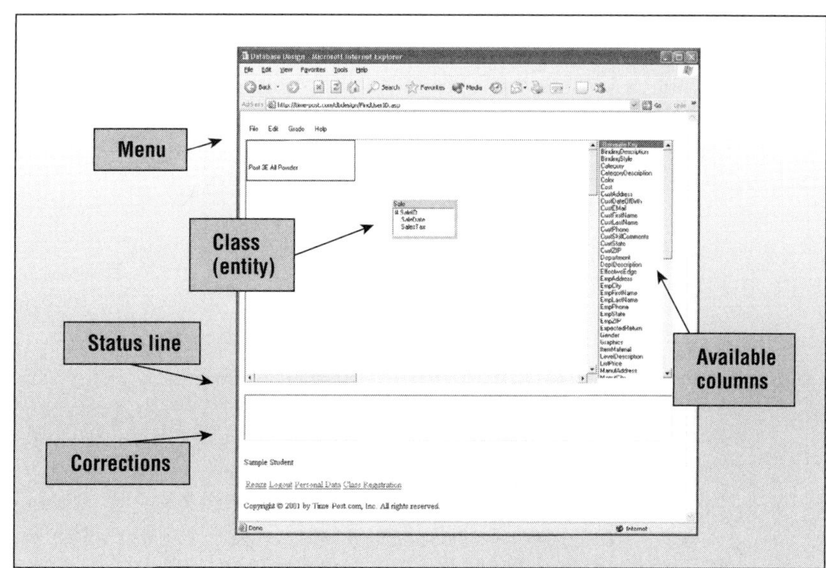

At this point, you should set the data types of the columns in the table. The default type is Text, so in many cases you will not have to change it. However, you should choose Date/Time for the SaleDate, and Currency for the SalesTax column. Right-click on the column name within the table and the current data type is displayed at the bottom of the pop-up menu. When you move the cursor to that item, a complete list of data type choices pops up. Choose the desired data type by highlighting it and clicking the left button. Be sure to save your work every few minutes in case you lose the Internet connection or the server times out.

Activity: Create Relationships

Associations or relationships are a key element of database design. In a relational database, columns in one table are connected to columns in other tables through common data. In this case, the Sale table needs to connect to a Customer table. Eventually, both tables will contain a CustomerID column. First you have to create the Customer table, so right-click on the design screen, add a new table, and rename it. Again, to ensure that each customer is assigned a guaranteed unique identifier, add a Generate Key column to it. Rename this new column the CustomerID. It is critical that you understand that this key value will be generated for each new customer added to the table. This value can only be generated in this table. You would never create another generated key column and call it CustomerID. So, how do you get CustomerID into the Sale table? Scroll the right-hand window to the bottom and note that CustomerID has been added to the list of available columns. You could also sort the list and find it alphabetically. You can now drag this new column into the Sale table. Set its data type to Integer32 (Long). Before attempting to build the relationship, add the other customer properties to the Customer table by dragging them from the right-hand window. You can double-click the table heading to automatically resize the table design box to fit the columns it contains. Set the appropriate data types.

Now that you have both the Sale and Customer table and they both have a CustomerID column, you can build an association or relationship between them. Figure 2.7 shows how to create this relationship in the design system. Click on the CustomerID column in the Customer table and drag it to the Sale table. Release the mouse button to drop the cursor onto the CustomerID column in the Sale table. The relationship window then asks you to specify the minimum and maximum values for each side of the relationship. These values specify the business rules and are often the most difficult items to identify. In the sale case, the typical assumptions are that exactly one customer can place an order, and a customer can place from zero to many orders. So, on the Sale side of the window, select the Optional and Many buttons. On the Customer side, choose the One option for both Min and Max values.

Remember that relationships generally involve at least one side in a primary key, but it is not a requirement. Also, the column names do not have to be identical. However, the data types do have to match, and the relationship has to be logical. For example, it would never make sense to connect an ItemID to a CustomerID, because that relationship would imply that a customer can also be an item and vice versa. Finally, notice that the cascade boxes are selected as the default. You should almost always leave these checked. In the database, cascade on delete

Action
Add Customer and Sale tables.
Add GenerateKey to Customer table.
Rename it to CustomerID.
Drag new CustomerID from right side into Sale table.
Drag CustomerID from Customer and drop it on CustomerID in Sale table.
Fill out relationship box.

FIGURE 2.7

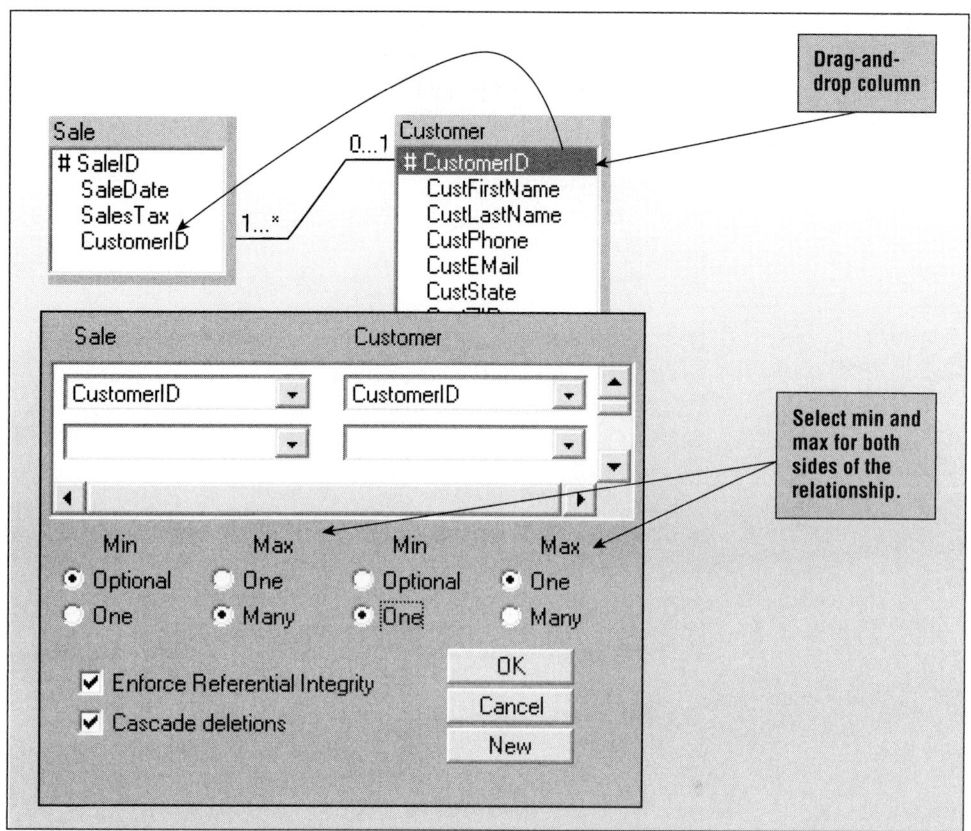

means that if you delete a particular customer, all of the orders placed by that customer will also be deleted. If you do not specify the cascade, you could end up with orders that contain a CustomerID which has no matching customer data. After you close the Relationship window with the OK button, you might have to refresh the display screen by right-clicking the Design window and selecting Refresh.

Activity: Evaluate the Design

One of the most powerful aspects of the Database Design system is that it contains an expert system to help analyze your design for errors. You can quickly obtain comments by selecting the Grade/Grade and Mark option on the menu. At this point, you have only two tables partially created, so the most important comment you should receive is that overall, you are missing several tables. The system might also point out that you are missing columns from the Sales table because you have not yet added the salesperson (employee) and the shipping information.

To illustrate the power of the system, you will add a new table (Item) and then build a new relationship that is incorrect. Add a new table for Inventory, and add the SKU column (a common retail abbreviation for stock-keeping unit) used to identify individual products. Right-click the SKU column in the Inventory table and set it as a key. Add the Size and QOH columns to the Inventory table. Set their data types to Single and Integer16 respectively. Now, add the SKU column to the Sale table as an intentional error. Create a relationship from Inventory to Sale using the SKU columns.

FIGURE 2.8

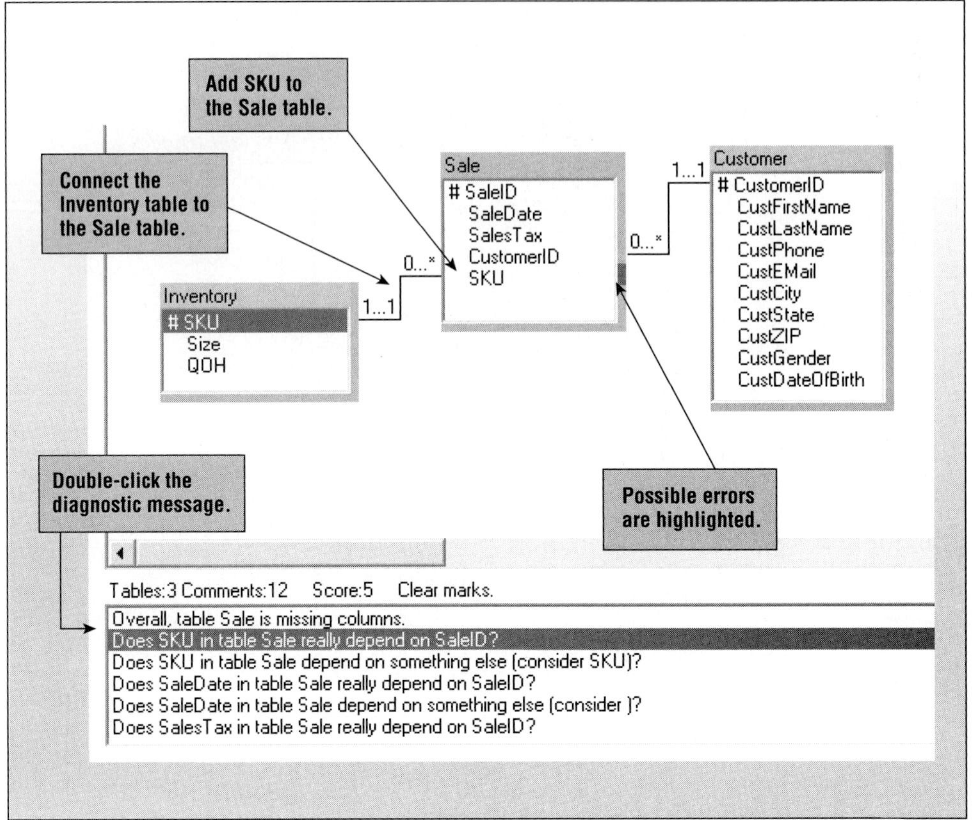

Choose the Grade/Grade and Mark menu option to save the changes and obtain comments on the design. Again, the design is not finished, so focus on the other error messages. In particular, find the message "Does SKU in table Sale really depend on SaleID?" and double-click it. Figure 2.8 shows the resulting diagnostic screen. The SKU column in the Sale table is highlighted as a potential problem. Indeed, it is an issue, because placing SKU into the Sale table as shown would mean that for each Sale, only one item (SKU) can be sold. Notice that SKU is not part of the primary key. You might consider setting the SKU as a key column in the Sale table to solve the problem. But that would cause even more problems. For instance, the SaleDate depends only on the SaleID and not on the SKU. If you leave SaleDate in the table with both SaleID and SKU set as keys, you would be declaring that items within a single sale can be sold on different dates.

If you set SKU as a key and resubmit the problem for grading, it will return several messages. One of them will be the question "Does SaleDate in table Sales really depend on SKU?" Notice that sometimes a table has many errors, so you must carefully review the entire table to make sure you fix the primary problems first. The Grade menu also contains an option to generate a separate HTML file that lists all errors by table. This listing is easier to print.

Primary keys are one of the most difficult things for students to understand when they first start designing databases. In particular, generated keys are

> **Action**
>
> Choose Grade/Grade and Mark.
> Double-click messages in window.
> Fix errors by removing columns and adding new tables.

tricky. In terms of the database design system, primary keys are critical because they are used to identify the tables. If you make major mistakes in the primary keys, the system will give confusing feedback because it cannot correctly identify your tables. For this reason, it is always best to begin with one or two tables, test them, and then slowly add more tables and relationships.

You still need to fix the problem with the Inventory and Sale table association. In a broad sense, it seems that there should be some type of connection between Inventory item and Sale to indicate which items were purchased by the customer. But placing the SKU attribute into the Sale entity appears to be a bad idea. The reason is straightforward. If there is an association between Inventory and Sale, it must be many-to-many; that is, a Sale can include many items (SKUs), and an Inventory item (SKU) can be sold many times. Relational databases do not handle many-to-many relationships directly. Instead, you must create an intermediary or junction table.

Figure 2.9 shows the creation of the intermediary table. It contains the key columns from both the Inventory (SKU) and Sale (SaleID) tables. Both columns are keyed in the new SaleItem table. Examining the keys within the SaleItem tables reveals that each sale can contain many items, and each item can appear on many sales, which is exactly the many-to-many relationship needed. The additional columns of QuantitySold and SalePrice indicate the number of items being purchased and any discounts applied—for an individual item on a specific sale. The dashed many-to-many line is never created; it is used here simply to show the goal of the two relationships.

The new SaleItem table corresponds to the repeating lines of items that you would see listed on a paper sale form. Examining the two new relationships reveals how the table works. Reading from the Sale to the SaleItem table, each sale can contain from one to many items, and, in reverse, each SaleItem line (SaleID and SKU) refers to exactly one sale. Essentially the same association exists from Inventory to SaleItem. But since items might not have been sold, each item can appear on zero to many sales lines, and a given sales line refers to exactly one item. All many-to-many relationships

FIGURE 2.9

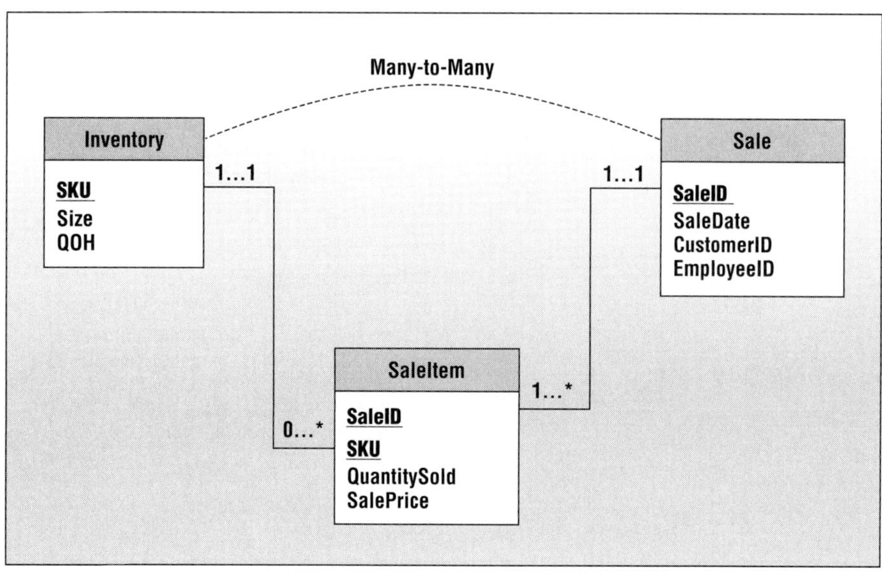

must be split and joined with a junction table that contains the keys from both of the original tables.

Activity: Fix Inventory Design

Return to the Database Design system and delete the association between Inventory and Sale. Then delete the SKU column from the Sale table. Now you can create the SaleItem table. Simply drag the two keys into the table from the right-hand window: Do not attempt to re-create them with the generate key. Finally, build the two new relationships in the Figure 2.9 example.

Action
Create the SaleItem table.
Create the ItemModel table.
Include the proper columns.
Set the keys.
Set the data types.
Grade/Grade and Mark.

If you grade this version, you will see that the detail issues have been corrected. However, some design issues still exist in terms of handling inventory. The inventory for a ski shop is somewhat more complicated than for a typical retail store. In particular, snowboards and skis are sold in varying lengths to match the individual customer. Figure 2.10 shows the two concepts. A manufacturer produces a model line that exhibits certain characteristics such as width, flexibility, and side cut. For a model type, several different lengths are available. From the perspective of the All Powder store, the database has to keep information on each model, but the actual inventory must refer to a specific item or length within the model type. Each item will receive a different SKU. For example, SKU 1173 might refer to a Rossignol Axium ski that is 196 cm in length, while SKU 1174 references a Rossignol Axium ski of 181 cm.

The catch is that it would waste considerable space to repeat all of the model data for every possible size of ski or board. Consequently, it is important to create two entities to handle the details: ItemModel and Inventory. Figure 2.11 shows the basic tables and the resulting relationships. Observe that each model results in many inventory items (multiple sizes of boards or skis), but each item can be only one model type. At this point, you should be able to add more attributes and more tables to the design, but the completion of the design will be left to the next chapter.

FIGURE 2.10

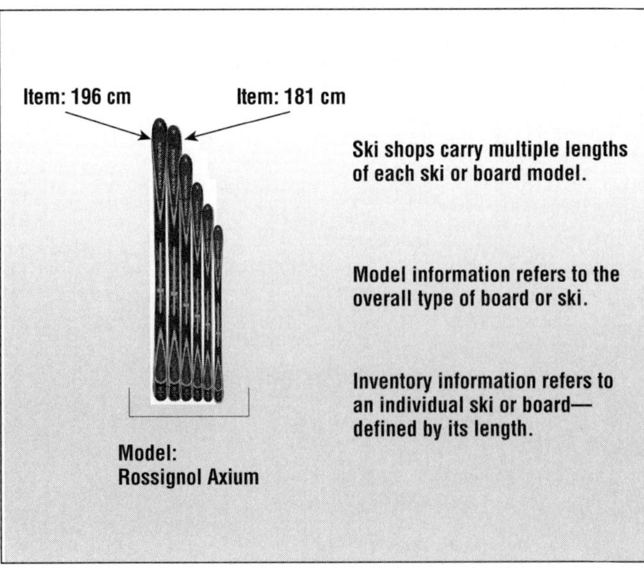

FIGURE 2.11

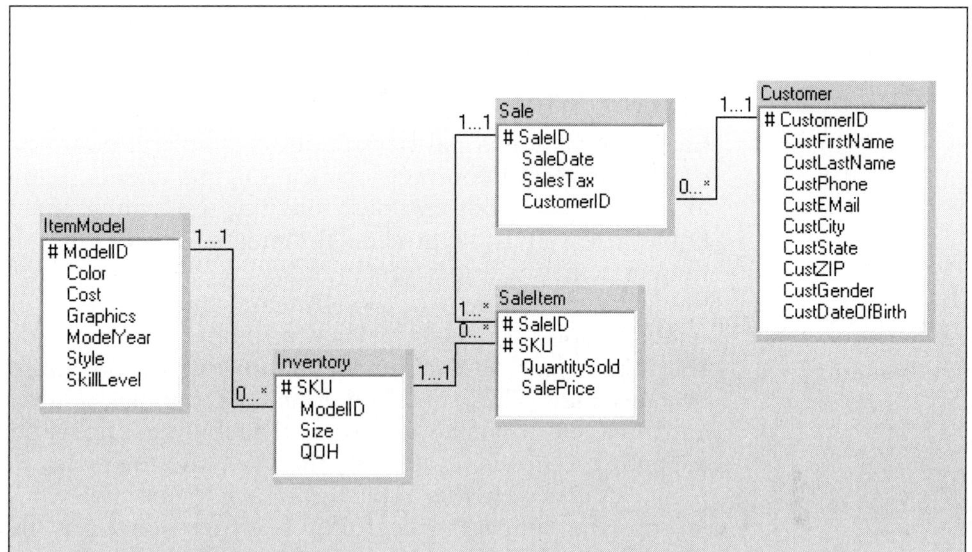

Exercises

Crystal Tigers

Crystal Tigers is a service club with about 150 members. The club primarily sponsors events such as community pancake breakfasts, local concerts, and sporting competitions. The club successfully uses the events to raise money for various charitable organizations. The club needs a database to help track the roles of the various members, both in terms of positions within the organization and their work at the events. The following form represents the basic data that needs to be collected.

<table>
<tr><td>Last name, First name
Phone, Cell phone
Address
City, State ZIPCode</td><td colspan="3">Year Position/Title   Comment</td></tr>
<tr><td>Event title
Start date   End date
Charity
Charity contact
Phone
Amount raised</td><td colspan="3">Member Activities for Event

Date Hours Activity   Comment</td></tr>
</table>

1. Analyze the form and create the main classes and associations needed to maintain the data for this organization.

Capitol Artists

Capitol Artists is a partnership among several commercial artists that work on freelance and contract jobs for various clients. Some jobs are contracted at a fixed price, but complex jobs require billing clients for the number of hours involved in the project. To help the artists track the time spent on each project, the firm wants you to build an easy-to-use database. On a given day, the artist should be able to select the time slot, then choose a category and a job. All jobs are given internal numbers, and each job has only one client. But it is helpful to list the client information on the form once the job has been selected. The artist then enters a short task description, the billing rate, and any out-of-pocket expenses. The billing rate is somewhat flexible and depends on the client, the job, the task, and the artist. For example, the company can charge higher rates for an artist's creative work time but lower rates for copying papers. The following form contains the basic information desired.

Employee
Last name, First name
Date

Time	Category	Client	Job #	Task Description	Hours	Rate	Expenses
8:00 A.M.	Meeting	Name + Phone	1173				
8:30 A.M.							
9:00 A.M.							
9:30 A.M.							
. . .							

1. Analyze the form and create the main classes and associations needed to maintain the data for this organization.

Offshore Speed

The Offshore Speed company sells parts and components for high-performance boats. Some of the customers modify the boats for racing; others simply want faster boats for informal races. The engine parts tend to be highly specialized and new variations are released each year by manufacturers. Compatibility of parts is always a major issue, but most are tested by the manufacturers with data available from their websites. Customers tend to order parts through the store, but sometimes they will buy off-the-shelf components. The store also keeps many spare parts in stock because customers tend to break them often and the profit margins are good. The store also has arrangements with other firms that can help customers redesign and upgrade interiors and cabins, for example, provide new upholstery for seats and complete systems for beds and sinks for cabins. Lately, the store has been successful in selling and installing high-end GPS and communication systems. The form below is used to place custom orders for the clients. Discounts are given to customers based on several subjective factors that will not be entered into the database.

<table>
<tr><td colspan="6">Customer
Last name, First name
Phone, E-mail
Address
City, State ZIP</td><td colspan="2">Employee

Sale date
Estimated receive date</td></tr>
<tr><td colspan="8">Boat: Brand, year, # engines, length
Engine 1: Brand, year, out drive, year
Engine 2: Brand, year, out drive, year</td></tr>
<tr><td>Manuf.</td><td>Mfg Part No.</td><td>Category</td><td>Description</td><td>Quantity</td><td>List Price</td><td colspan="2">Extended</td></tr>
<tr><td></td><td></td><td></td><td></td><td></td><td></td><td></td><td></td></tr>
<tr><td></td><td></td><td></td><td></td><td></td><td></td><td></td><td></td></tr>
<tr><td></td><td></td><td></td><td></td><td></td><td></td><td></td><td></td></tr>
<tr><td></td><td></td><td></td><td></td><td></td><td></td><td></td><td></td></tr>
<tr><td></td><td></td><td></td><td></td><td></td><td></td><td></td><td></td></tr>
<tr><td colspan="6"></td><td colspan="2">Subtotal
Tax
Discount
Total Due</td></tr>
</table>

1. Analyze the form and create the main classes and associations needed to maintain the data for this organization.

Final Project

The main textbook has an appendix with several longer case studies. You should be able to work on one of these cases throughout the term. If you or your instructor picks one, perform the following task.

1. Analyze the forms and create the main classes and associations needed to maintain the data for this organization.

3

Data Normalization

Chapter Outline

Objectives
Database Design
Generated Keys: AutoNumber
Case: All Powder Board and Ski Shop
Lab Exercise
All Powder Board and Ski Database
Creation
Relationships
Exercises
Final Project

Objectives

- Understand how to use generated AutoNumber keys.
- Create tables and specify data types.
- Create relationships and specify cascades.
- Establish column constraints and default values.
- Create lookup lists for columns.
- Estimate the data volume for the database.

FIGURE 3.1

```
OrderIDCustomerID
CustomerOrder(OrderID, CustomerID, ...)
```

Database Design

The main objective of database design is to define the tables, relationships, and constraints that describe the underlying business rules and efficiently store the data. The normalization rules are critical to properly identifying the columns that belong in each table. The first step is to make sure the keys are correct. A key uniquely identifies the rows in the table. If multiple columns are part of the key, it indicates a many-to-many relationship between the key columns. Note that if a base table contains a generated key column, it is the only column that may be keyed.

If you are uncertain about which columns should be keyed, write them down separately and evaluate the business rules between the two objects. Figure 3.1 shows a typical situation with orders and customers. First ask yourself: For a given order, can there ever be more than one customer? If the answer is "yes" based on the business rules, then you would mark the CustomerID column as key. However, most businesses have a rule that each order is placed by only one customer, so CustomerID should not be keyed. Second, reverse the question and ask yourself: For a given customer, can there be more than one order? Obviously, most businesses want customers to place repeat orders, so the answer is "yes." So you mark the OrderID as key. Since only OrderID is keyed, both columns belong in the CustomerOrder table.

Once the keys are correct, you need to check each nonkey column to ensure that it follows the three main normalization rules. First, each column must contain atomic or nonrepeating data, for example, a single phone number, but not multiple values of phone numbers. Second and third, each nonkey column must depend on the whole key and nothing but the key. You need to examine each potential table, determine that the keys are correct, then check each column to ensure that it depends on the whole key and nothing but the key. If there is a problem, you need to split the table. Remember that any time you make a change to the keys in a table, you have to reevaluate all of the columns in that table.

Generated Keys: AutoNumber

Key columns play a critical role in a relational database. The key values are used as a proxy for the rest of the data. For instance, once you know the CustomerID, the database can quickly retrieve the rest of the customer data. That is why you only need to place the CustomerID column in the CustomerOrder table. However, the database requires key values to be unique. Guaranteeing that key values are never repeated can be a challenging business problem. In some cases, businesses have separate methods to create key values. For instance, the marketing department might have a process to assign identifier numbers to customers and products. But the process must ensure that these values are never duplicated. In many situations, it is easier to have the database generate the key values automatically. In particular, orders often require keys that are generated quickly and accurately.

FIGURE 3.2

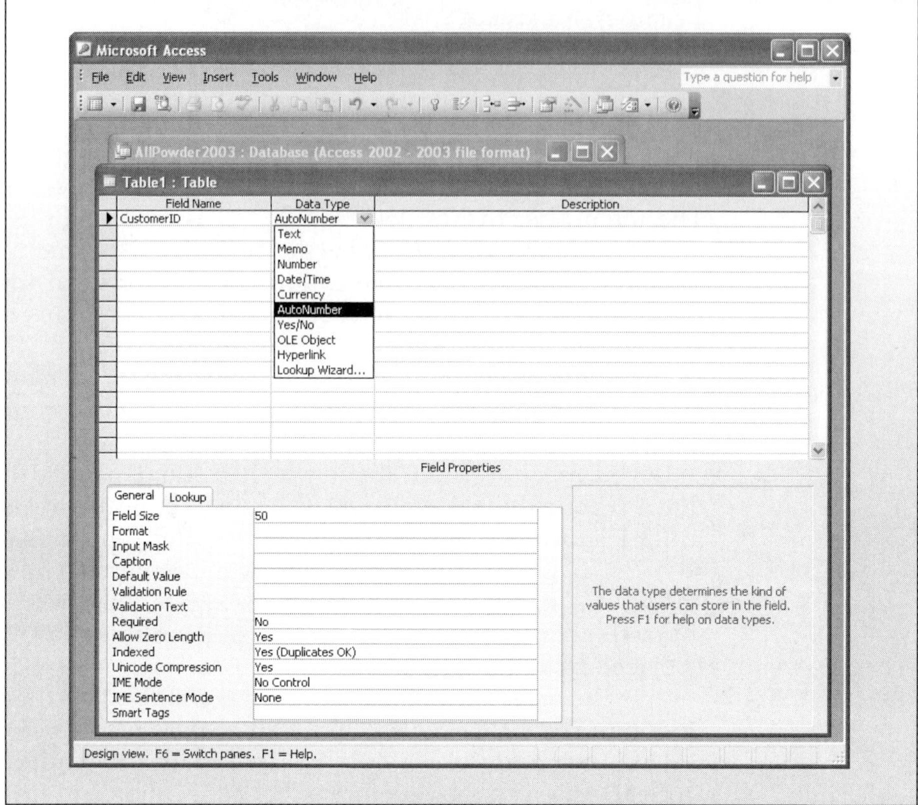

Microsoft Access provides the AutoNumber data type to generate new key values. You assign this type to the primary key in a table where you want the key value created. For instance, the CustomerID column in the Customer table, or the OrderID in the Order table, might be assigned the AutoNumber type. Whenever a row is added to a table with an AutoNumber column, a new key value is generated. The keys are long integers and the value is incremented by one each time a row is inserted. The 32-bit integer supports slightly more than 2 billion positive values and an equal number of negative values.

In general, the AutoNumber approach is relatively easy to use for most simple applications. Figure 3.2 shows how you select the AutoNumber data type when creating a table. No matter how the data is created, whenever a row is inserted a new key value is generated. The rest of the Access system utilizes the AutoNumber column, making it easy to build input forms. In most cases, you do not have to display the key value, so users never need to worry about it or even know that it exists.

The main drawback to the AutoNumber approach is that it is tricky to obtain the newly generated value. If you have an application that creates a new customer, you might have to obtain the newly generated key to use it in a second table. Access does not provide a function to obtain the new key value. There is a way to obtain the key in most cases, but you have to be careful, and it requires programming code.

There is one important step you have to take at this stage when you create tables with the AutoNumber data type. Since the column value can only be created in one table, you need to choose the Number/Long Integer data type if you use that column in a second table. For example, CustomerID can be AutoNumber in the Customer table, so new values are created when a customer is added. But to use CustomerID in the Order table, it will have to be assigned the Number/Long Integer data type in that table.

Case: All Powder Board and Ski Shop

When you first approach a database design problem, you will often experience one of two perspectives: the project seems immensely complicated, or the project seems too easy. Usually, both perspectives are wrong. Even a difficult project can be handled if you divide it into small enough pieces, and few projects are as easy as they first appear. The main issue is to correctly identify the business rules. And there always seem to be complications with some of the rules. For the All Powder case, consider the issue of customer skill level. Whether a customer is renting or buying a board or skis, the salespeople need to match the person to the proper board or ski based on the customer's skill level. In terms of business decisions, managers need to identify the types of customers to plan for the models and inventory decisions for next season.

As shown in Figure 3.3, consider what happens if you try to place the Style (downhill, half pipe, and so on), and SkillLevel directly into the Customer table. The problem is that the business rules state that each customer can have one skill level in many styles, and each style can apply to more than one customer. For example, customer Jones could be an expert downhill skier but only a beginner in half-pipe snowboard. However, customer Sanchez is an expert at half pipe but has never tried any type of skiing. If you place Style and SkillLevel in the Customer table, you might try keying only CustomerID. But that action would state that each customer participates in only one style, with one skill level. On the other hand, if you key just the Style column, you would be indicating that each style can be performed by only one person. The only solution is to key both the CustomerID and the Style columns. Then each customer can participate in many styles (with one skill rating per customer per style), and each style can apply to many people

<table>
<tr><td style="width:22%;vertical-align:top;">FIGURE 3.3</td>
<td style="border:1px solid #000;padding:14px;">

Consider what happens if you (incorrectly) try to place Style and SkillLevel in the Customer table:

<u>CustomerID</u>, LastName, ... Style, SkillLevel
CustomerID, LastName, ... <u>Style</u>, SkillLevel

Business rule: Each customer can have one skill in many styles.
Business rule: Each style can apply to more than one customer.
Need a table with both attributes as keys.

<u>CustomerID</u>, LastName, ... <u>Style</u>, SkillLevel

But you cannot include LastName, FirstName, and so on, because then you would have to reenter that data for each customer skill.

</td></tr>
</table>

FIGURE 3.4

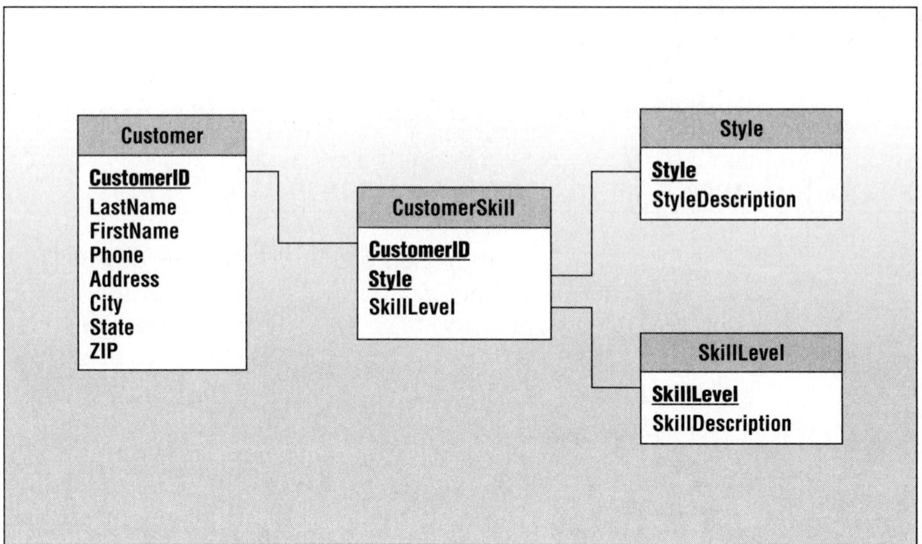

(with possibly different skill ratings). But you cannot leave the Style and SkillLevel columns in the main Customer table along with columns such as LastName. It is clear that a customer's last name does not change for each different style. A customer's last name depends only on the CustomerID, so you need to split the tables.

Figure 3.4 shows the resulting design. The Customer table is keyed only by CustomerID and contains attributes that describe each customer. The Style and SkillLevel tables are used as lookup tables to ensure that clerks select from the defined list of choices. Without them, the database would quickly become a mess because everyone would use different spellings and abbreviations for the entries. The CustomerSkill table contains the CustomerID and Style as key columns to support the business rules.

Lab Exercise

All Powder Board and Ski Database Creation

You should use the Database Design system to refine your table definitions. The system is designed to check the main design rules and ensure that your tables meet the requirements of good database design. However, if you make different assumptions about the underlying business rules, you can create slightly different tables than those recommended by the design system.

Activity: Create Tables

Once you have determined the overall database design, creating tables in Access is straightforward. The Design View visual editor makes it easy to enter column names and select the data types. One of the strengths of Access is that it allows you to change the table design later. So, if you find you made a mistake, you simply go back and edit the table. Of course, if you have already entered data into the table and need to make a major change, it can

Action
Create Customer table in Design view.
Enter column names.
Select data types.
Assign the primary key.
Save the table.

FIGURE 3.5

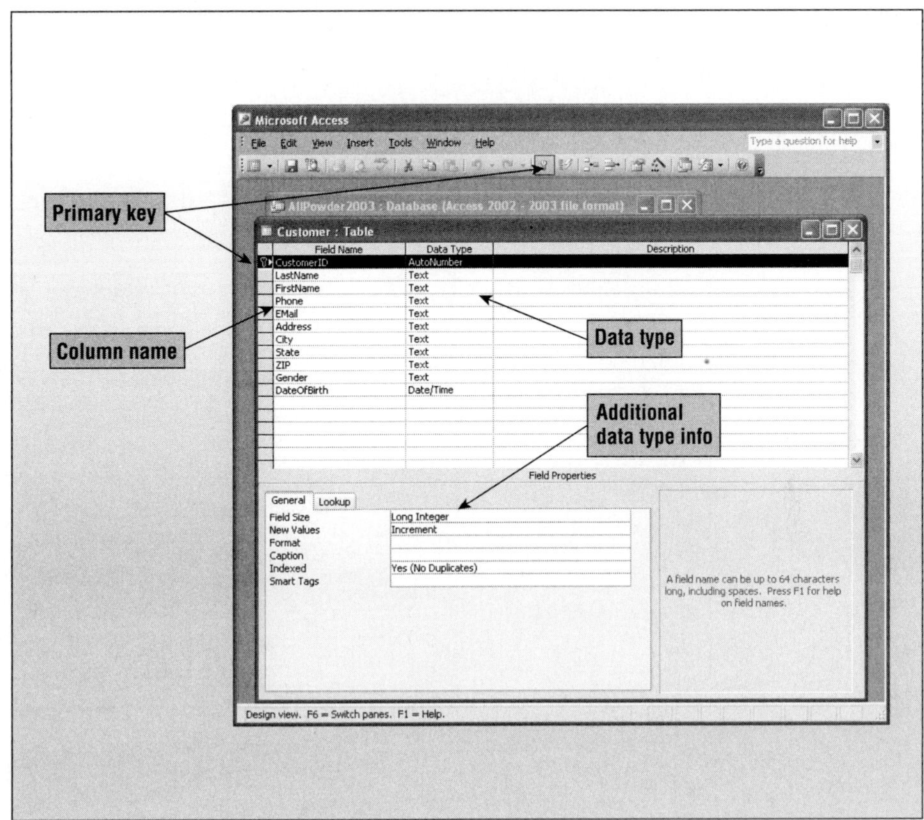

be more complicated because you will want to save the data so you do not have to reenter it.

Figure 3.5 shows the basic elements of the Table Design screen. As you enter the column (field) names, you select the data type from a drop-down list. Additional choices regarding the data type are made in the lower box. These options depend on the initial data type, so the elements in the box change. For example, the text data type is defined with a maximum of 50 characters by default. Access will efficiently store the data even if it takes less than 50 characters, but it will not allow anyone to enter a value with more than 50 characters. You will need to change this limit for some columns. For example, the Email column should probably allow up to 100 or perhaps 150 characters. Access supports a maximum of 255 characters in a text column. If you need more than that, you will have to switch to a Memo type of data. However, there are some limits on searching memo data, so do not use it unless you truly need the space.

You indicate the primary key by clicking the gray box to the left of the column name, and then clicking the Primary Key icon on the top menu bar. A small Key icon is placed in the gray box to indicate the Key column. To set multiple column fields as keys, you first highlight each column field row that needs to be keyed. Then click the Key icon. You can select multiple rows by clicking and dragging the mouse across contiguous rows. Or you can use Shift + click or Ctrl + click to choose multiple rows. You give the table the appropriate name when you save it.

FIGURE 3.6

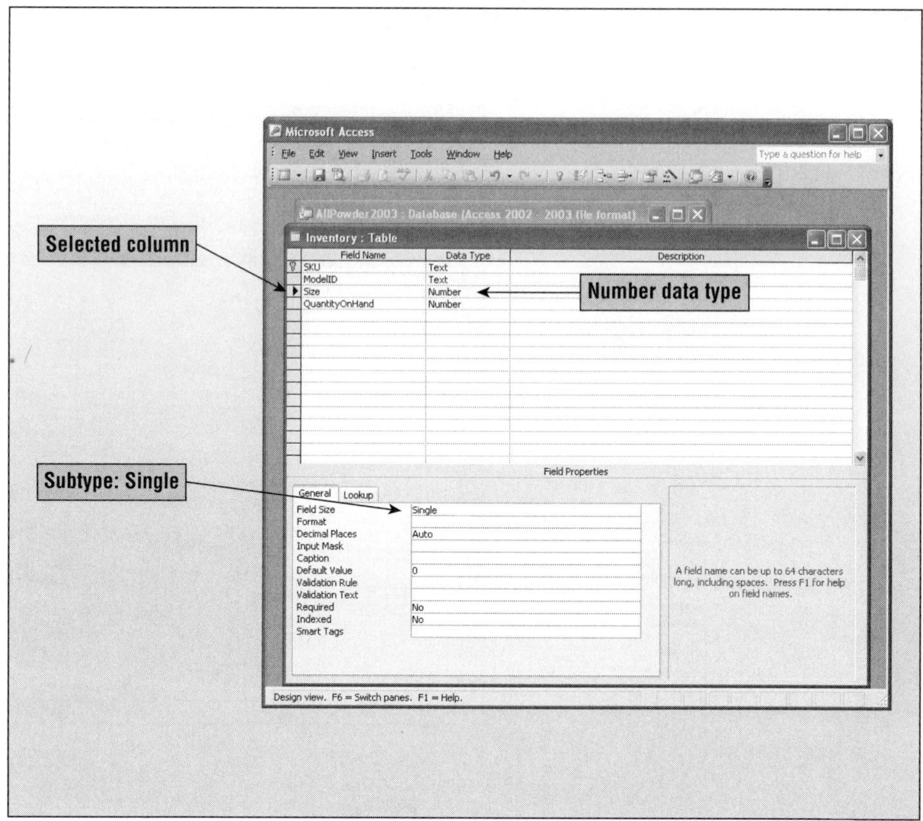

Although the Access Design view is relatively easy to use, you need to be careful when you select numeric data types. In Figure 3.6, the Size column is given the Number data type. Number, however, has several subtypes. You select the appropriate subtype in the lower window. In this case, the data type of Single indicates a relatively small floating point number. Most skis and boards are measured in centimeters, so the numbers are not overly large. However, some manufacturers might choose to use fractional lengths, so the single-precision floating point is appropriate. This step is sometimes difficult for beginners to catch. If you forget to choose the single or double precision subtype, you will not be able to enter fractional values (with decimal points). If you ever encounter that problem, simply return to the Design view and set the proper data type.

Activity: Create Constraints and Default Values

In many cases, you will want the database to enforce the business rules. Placing the rules in the database means that they will be enforced in all situations, without relying on other programs. Figure 3.7 shows the primary elements for setting a condition to ensure gender data is entered consistently. First, select the column that needs to be controlled. Second, enter a validation rule that specifies the acceptable values or range of values. Many times, you will use rules that list acceptable values, such as the list of three items for gender. Other times, you might use a rule which specifies that values must fall within some range. For instance, to indicate that a salary column must be greater than zero, select the Salary column and enter >0 as the validation rule. Finally, enter a

FIGURE 3.7

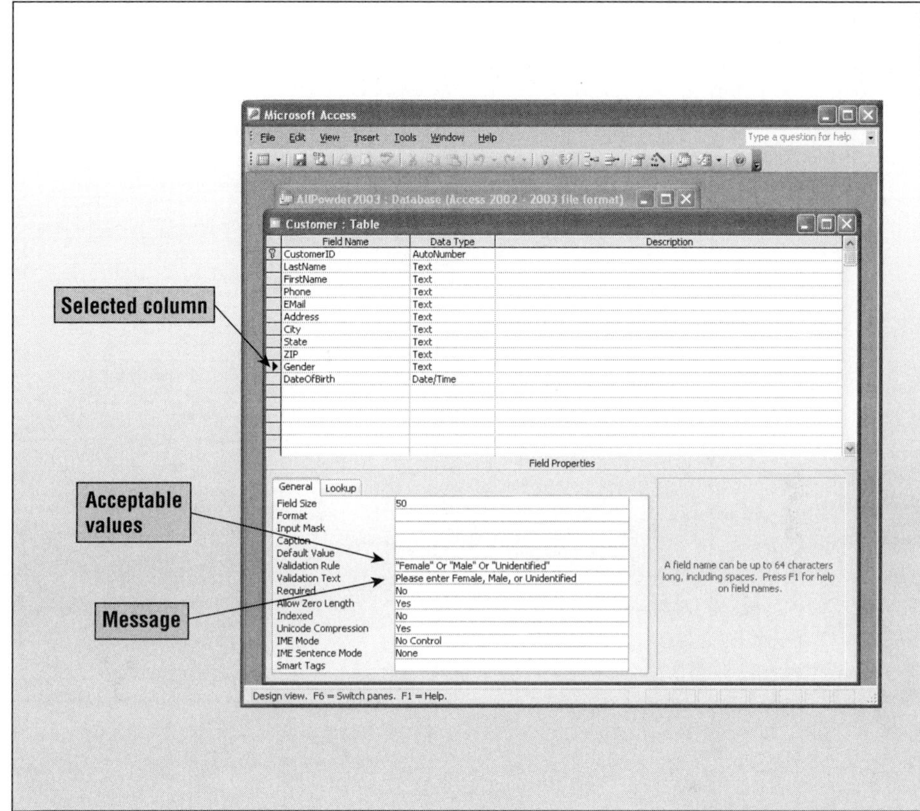

message that will be displayed to anyone who tries to enter an invalid value. This message can be any text message, but keep it precise and friendly.

Notice that it is also easy to specify default values. These are values you want displayed whenever a new row is created. The user can override the default value and enter something else, but it is often convenient to display a commonly used value to save time for users who are entering data. For example, a SaleDate can be set to the Now( ) function so that the current date is automatically entered.

Action
Select the Gender column.
Validation rule: "Female" Or "Male" Or "Unidentified".
Validation text: Please enter Female, Male, or Unidentified.

Activity: Create Simple Lookup Lists

Ultimately, you want to make the data entry process even easier for users. Instead of waiting for users to guess what values they might enter for gender, you can create a simple lookup list that contains the three acceptable values (Female, Male, or Unidentified). Figure 3.8 shows the choices once you select the column and click the Lookup tab. You can choose between a combo box and a list box. The combo box is usually preferred because it uses less screen space; the choices are displayed when the user clicks the familiar drop-down arrow. For the simple list of predefined terms, choose the Value list and enter the values in the next row. Each item is entered in quotes and separated by semicolons.

There is a major drawback to entering a list of values into the table definition: This list is difficult to change later. Consequently, you should use

FIGURE 3.8

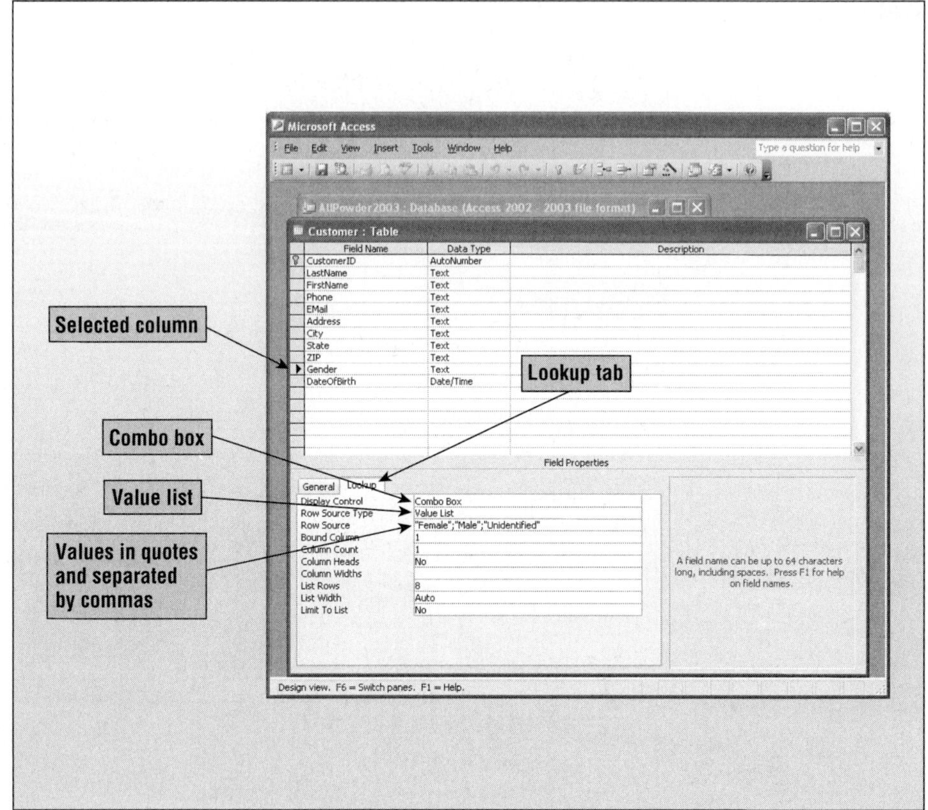

<table>
<tr><th colspan="2">Action</th></tr>
<tr><td colspan="2">Select the Gender column.
Select the Lookup tab.
Display Control: Combo Box.
Row Source Type: Value List.
Row Source: "Female";"Male";"Unidentified".
Switch to datasheet view and test it.</td></tr>
</table>

the predefined list only for items that rarely change. If you suspect the list will need to be updated later, you should create a separate lookup table and store each possible entry as a row within that table. Then you can use this same process to point to that table instead of a fixed list, by selecting Table/Query for the Row Source Type.

Switching to data entry mode, Figure 3.9 shows the effect of this design on the Customer table. In terms of gender, users see a defined list of choices and are not able to enter other values. Even if a programmer attempted to enter a value not in the list, the validation rule would prevent the change. Also, notice the effect of the AutoNumber column for the primary key. Initially, no value is displayed. As data is entered into the row, Access automatically creates a new key value that is one unit higher than the prior value. However, note that if you delete a row, the numbering does not start over. Eventually, some numbers will be missing from the list. Since the actual value does not matter, only the uniqueness, do not worry about any missing values.

Relationships

Activity: Define Relationships

When all of the tables have been created, you need to define the relationships. You can click the Relationships button or choose Relationships

FIGURE 3.9

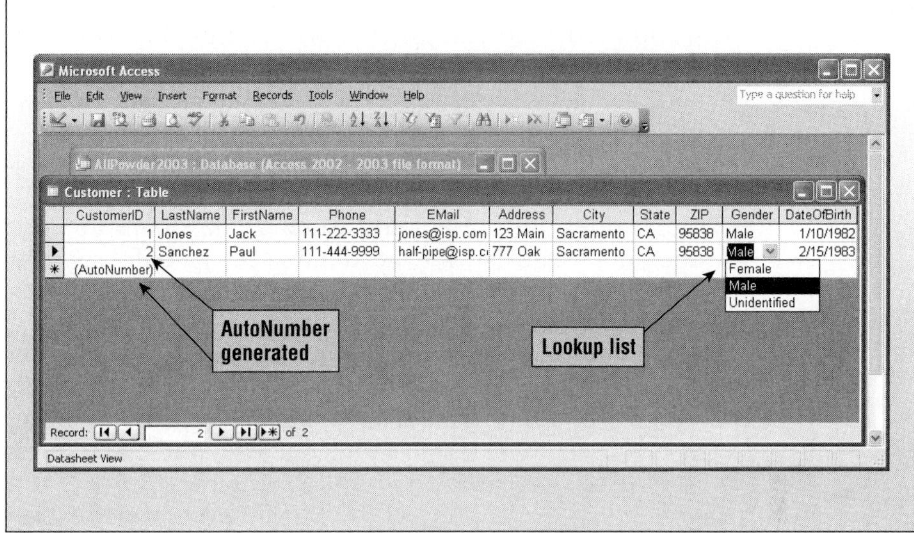

from the Tools menu. Select the tables to be displayed on the screen. Eventually you will need all of the tables, but sometimes it is easier to start with a smaller group and add tables one at a time with the Add Tables button. As shown in Figure 3.10, to build a new relationship, click-and-drag

FIGURE 3.10

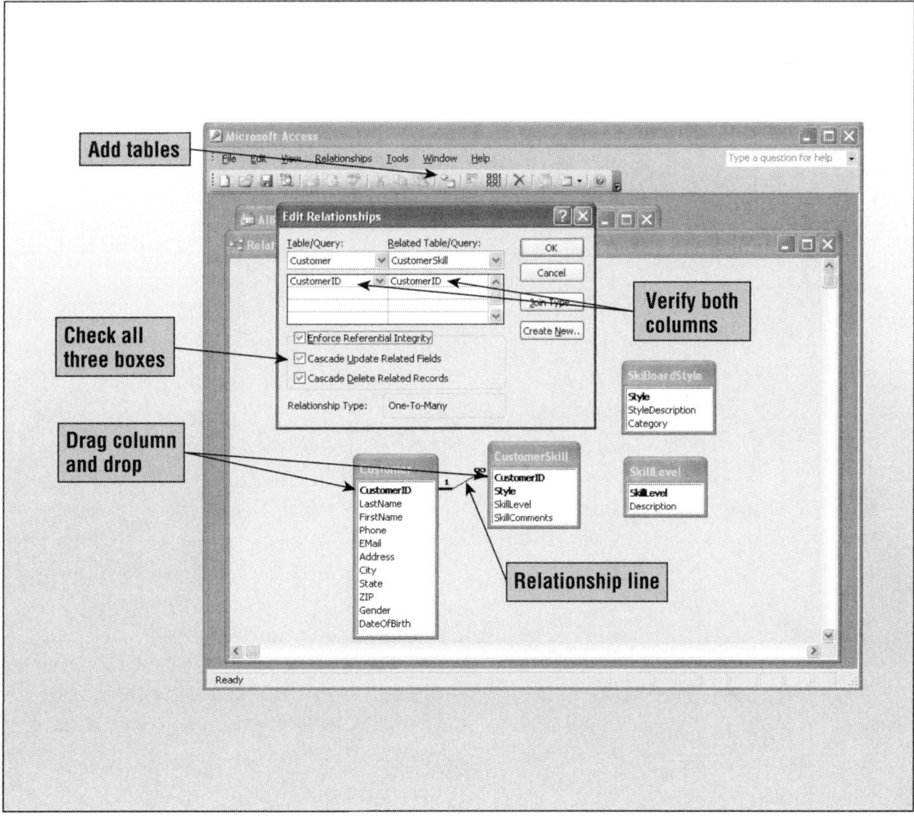

a column from one table and drop it on the corresponding column of the second table. To edit an existing relationship, double-click the relationship line. In the Edit Relationships window, verify that the column names are correct. If a relationship needs to join across multiple columns, you must select the additional columns in the list. When they are correct, check all three of the integrity boxes. These boxes enforce the integrity rules so that users can only enter data that exists in the original base table. For example, it does not make sense to enter skill data for a customer number that does not yet exist, so the database will enforce that rule and display an error message if someone tries to violate it. Click the OK button to establish the new relationship.

Continue adding tables and building the required relationships. Eventually, all of the tables should be tied together. An important consequence of building the relationships is that it forces you to enter data in a specific sequence. In the example, you must first enter data into the Ski-BoardStyle, SkillLevel, and Customer tables before you can create an entry in the CustomerSkill table. In general, you should first enter data into the base lookup tables, like the SkillLevel table. This data is generally relatively static and well-defined. Notice that it could be difficult to explain this process to users. To look ahead a little, users should never enter data directly into tables. Instead, you will create forms that make it easy for users to enter data properly.

As of the XP/2002 version of Access, you can now create tables and relationships using direct SQL statements. However, the syntax does not support all of the SQL standard options. Figure 3.11 shows how you could

<table>
<tr><td>

Action

Tools/Relationships (or button).
Add all tables.
Move and resize them to fit.
Drag-and-drop key columns on foreign keys.
Check integrity and cascade boxes.
Define all relationships.

</td></tr>
</table>

FIGURE 3.11

```
CREATE TABLE Customer (
   CustomerID        Long,
   LastName          Text(50),
   FirstName         Text(50),
   Phone             Text(50),
   Email             Text(150),
   Address           Text(50),
   State             Text(50),
   ZIP               Text(15),
   Gender            Text(15),
   DateOfBirth       Date,
   CONSTRAINT pk_Customer PRIMARY KEY (CustomerID)
)
CREATE TABLE Rental (
   RentID            Long,
   RentDate          Date,
   CustomerID        Long,
   ExpectedReturn    Date,
   PaymentMethod     Text(50)
   CONSTRAINT pk_Rental PRIMARY KEY (RentID)
   CONSTRAINT fk_RentalCustomer FOREIGN KEY (CustomerID)
     REFERENCES Customer(CustomerID)
)
```

use SQL to create two of the tables for the case. Note that you will have to create each table separately, but they are displayed together to highlight the relationship. You can open a new query and switch to SQL view, then enter the CREATE TABLE command and execute the query to create the table.

Why would you want to use this method to create tables—particularly when the Table Design view screen is so easy to use? The answer is that the Design View screen requires someone to create each table and column by hand. That is fine when you are initially creating tables and if you never have to re-create them. However, the text-based approach enables you to save the table definitions so that you can quickly re-create the tables in a new database. It is a useful way to save backup copies of the table definitions. These backup copies are useful when you need to modify the tables at some point, or create a new database, or have someone else re-create the database on a different machine. The method is also useful when a design system generates the CREATE TABLE statements for you.

If you create a file listing all of the tables, be careful about the order in which the tables will be created. Some tables must be created before others. In particular, a table can only establish a foreign key reference to an existing table. In the example, the Customer table has to be created before the Rental table can reference it. Also, keep in mind that the CREATE TABLE command is a recent feature in Microsoft Access, so it does not fully support the SQL standard. In particular, it does not appear to support the ON CASCADE DELETE and ON CASCADE UPDATE options for the foreign key relationship. You will still have to go to the Relationships screen, edit the relationship, and check those boxes separately. Also, Access 2002/2003 does not support the CHECK and DEFAULT options to specify individual column constraints and default values.

Activity: Estimate the Database Size

At some point, you need to estimate the size of the database project. Of course, any estimate at this early stage will be very rough. Your goal is not to be perfect but to be able to categorize the overall project size. The information will help you identify the basic category of database server and perhaps narrow your choice of tools. In particular, it will help you determine whether the project is too large to be handled in Access, or if you should move up to SQL Server or Oracle. You still might want to use Access as a front-end tool, but it would be helpful to know if you need to move the database to a larger server.

To estimate the database size, you begin by estimating the size of each data table. You must already know which columns belong to each table. Figure 3.12 shows the process for the Customer table. Some of the column size estimates are straightforward. Look back to Chapter 2 to see that a long integer uses 4 bytes of storage in Access. The text columns are a little trickier. For instance, although the database will allow up to 50 characters of text for the last name, almost no names will actually be that long. Instead, you need to estimate the average length of customer last names. You could use existing data or perhaps take a sample from a phone book. Perhaps an average last name is 15 characters long. But the DBMS stores text in Unicode format, which requires 2 physical bytes of storage for each character, so the average storage space needed for a last name is 30 bytes. Use a similar

FIGURE 3.12

```
CustomerID          Long                    4
LastName            Text(50)               30
FirstName           Text(50)               20
Phone               Text(50)               24
Email               Text(150)              50
Address             Text(50)               50
State               Text(50)                2
ZIP                 Text(15)               14
Gender              Text(15)               10
DateOfBirth         Date                    8

Average bytes per customer              212
Customers per week (winter)            *200
Weeks (winter)                          *25
Bytes added per year             1,060,000
```

process to estimate the number of bytes needed to store an average row of customer data.

Action

Create a spreadsheet.
Enter table names as rows.
Add columns for Bytes, Rows, Totals.
Calculate the bytes per table row.
Estimate the number of rows.
Compute the table and overall totals.

Next, you need to estimate how many new customers will arrive each year. In a real case, you could look at past records or talk with the expert users. Here, assume it is about 200 per week, but there are only 25 weeks of the ski season; so estimate 5,000 new customers a year. Multiplying the estimated number of customers by the size of an average row yields the initial data size of the customer table of about 1 million bytes.

Follow a similar process for all of the tables in the case. Figure 3.13 lists some of the basic assumptions you can use. You should build a spreadsheet that lists each table, the average number of bytes per row, the estimated number of rows, and the total estimated size for the table. There is still some flexibility in the final number, but your estimate should be around 5 to 6 megabytes. Remember that this is data for only one year. Also, additional space will be required for indexes, overhead, queries, forms, and reports. But even if the final number is closer to 20 megabytes, Microsoft Access should be able to handle the database on a typically configured computer.

FIGURE 3.13

200 customers per week for 25 weeks
2 skills per customer
2 rentals per customer per year
3 items per rental
20 percent of customers buy items
4 items per sale
100 manufacturers
20 models per manufacturer
5 items (sizes) per model

Exercises

Many Charms

Samantha and Madison want you to build the database for their charms sales. They emphasized that the system has to be easy to use. They also pointed out that a key element of their business is tracking all of the products and the various suppliers, then monitoring the costs so they can set their prices accurately. They are also concerned about monitoring how quickly their charms sell. They figure they will need to start with at least 200 basic charms, but most charms come in two sizes, along with the different metals and finishes. When asked, the women indicate they are uncertain how many customers they will have but would like to get at least 50 sales a week. Although some of the sales might be small, they hope to build a solid list of clients who return for new purchases on a monthly basis. To encourage return customers, they are thinking about offering some type of frequent-buyer program, where customers receive discounts, or maybe a free charm, after purchasing a specified number of charms.

1. Define the final tables needed for this case.
2. Create the database.
3. Estimate the size of the database for one year of operation.

Standup Foods

Laura's business has been established for several years. Many of her clients are old customers, and she has a couple of thousand in her files—although some have gone out of business. Her business has grown considerably based on referrals from existing clients. She gets so many good comments and referrals, she is thinking that she needs to track which customers pass her name on to others so she can call them or send thank-you gifts. But her more immediate concern is tracking employees. Over the course of a year, she has a relatively high turnover in some positions. Other employees have been with her for years. In total, she probably deals with 400 to 500 employees a year. Employees are rated after each job, and typically employees work 15 to 20 jobs a year for her. On average, employees tend to have three tasks per event. For instance, a driver will also be a server, and possibly also a busboy or dishwasher. They are evaluated on 10 items for each task they perform, as well as given an overall rating. Client food preferences are somewhat more complex, so Laura wants the capability to add free-form comments to cover extreme cases. For common elements, such as allergies to nuts, she wants to keep itemized lists—both for desired items and forbidden items. Some clients are easygoing, but this is Hollywood, so many have long lists of items—often ranging to 50 or even up to 100 items.

1. Define the final tables needed for this case.
2. Create the database.
3. Estimate the size of the database for one year of operation.

EnviroSpeed

For good or bad, Tyler and Brennan have been busy. Their firm has been averaging four to five cleanups a week. Although there are not many permanent employees (fewer than 100), they have close associations with about

200 experts in various areas. All of these people need access to the environmental documents and other information. Additionally, about 400 crews around the world are called in to work on various problems. The crews consist of 10 to 20 people. Initially, experts used to contribute the most information. Sometimes an expert will contribute hundreds of pages of documents and comments. Once an incident is opened, most of the new data and the searches come from the emergency crews. Time schedules, environmental factors, and comments can arrive quickly from all of the crew members. Some of the notes are on paper and saved until the emergency is over, when clerks enter the basic data to the database. A typical incident can generate dozens of pages of notes and schedules from each crew member. Although there are hundreds of possible chemicals, the firm has found that only about 50 major chemicals are typically involved in critical incidents. One important aspect of this case is the need for experts and crew members to search through documentation based on keywords. For example, crews will need to search for certain chemicals, possibly in combination with other chemicals, and often include the type of problem, such as water or road spill. Brennan estimates a typical document needs to include at least 20 keywords to identify the exact purpose of the document.

1. Define the final tables needed for this case.
2. Create the database.
3. Estimate the size of the database for one year of operation.

Final Project

The main textbook has an appendix with several longer case studies. You should be able to work on one of these cases throughout the term. If you or your instructor picks one, perform the following instructions.

1. Finalize your database design.
2. Create the tables in the DBMS.
3. Estimate the amount of data that might be generated for one year.

Chapter 4

Data Queries

Chapter Outline

Objectives
Database Queries
Case: All Powder Board and Ski Shop
Lab Exercise
  *All Powder Board and Ski Data
  Computations and Subtotals*
Exercises
Final Project

Objectives

- Create or import sample data into a database.
- Create basic queries to answer common business questions.
- Use joins to create multitable queries.
- Use queries to perform simple calculations.
- Answer business questions involving totals and subtotals.

Database Queries

Relational databases are designed to store data efficiently. Efficiency results in splitting the data into many tables, interconnected by the data. Consequently, you need a good query system to retrieve data. SQL is a powerful standard designed to perform several tasks in retrieving and manipulating data in relational database systems. Most modern systems implement some version of SQL. The catch is that the standard continues to evolve, and it takes time for the DBMS vendors to catch up. Also, vendors tend to include proprietary extensions to provide additional features. Because the SQL syntax can be difficult for managers, most vendors also include some type of query-by-example (QBE) system to make it easier to construct common queries. The visually oriented QBE also saves some typing effort and provides lists of tables and columns so you do not have to memorize them. But, ultimately, you need to learn SQL because it is a standard and because some queries are easier to understand in SQL. With Access, the query designer makes it easy to switch from QBE to SQL, so you should get in the habit of checking the SQL to see that the query is being built correctly.

This chapter focuses on the data retrieval aspects of queries. SQL can also be used for data definition (e.g., CREATE TABLE), and for data manipulation (e.g., UPDATE and DELETE). These features and more complex queries are covered in Chapter 5. Once you learn the foundations of queries presented in this chapter, the other topics are easier to understand.

In any database, it helps to have a copy of the class (relationship) diagram handy when you are writing queries. One of the more difficult aspects to creating a query is to find which tables hold the data you need. This problem is one of the reasons it is so important to label your tables and columns carefully when you create the database. Managers need to be able to identify the tables and columns that match the business questions. With dozens or even hundreds of tables with confusing or abbreviated names, it can be difficult to find the correct data.

Case: All Powder Board and Ski Shop

Before you can build queries, you need data in the tables. Even with a small number of tables, it is time-consuming to create reasonable data. You have to match the foreign keys across the relationships. For instance, it is straightforward to create basic customer data, although it would take a while to type in data for a thousand customers. But then, when you want sales data, you have to select CustomerID values from the existing list. You also have to create ski and board models and then generate data for items with appropriate attributes, then choose the proper ID values for the sales and rentals. In a typical business project, you can test the database with a few dozen examples, and then wait for the business to generate real data to analyze. In a class setting, it is better to use sample data. For that reason, sample data is available for the tables in the All Powder case. The one catch is that your tables might not contain exactly the same columns. So you might have to edit the data slightly in Excel before you import it into your database. This data was randomly generated with specially built generators. The business interpretations might not be useful, but the dataset is consistent.

Lab Exercise

All Powder Board and Ski Data

At this point, the main tables of your database should be similar to those in Figure 4.1, although several supporting tables have been removed from the figure. The Manufacturer, Customer, Sale, and SaleItem tables are common to most business databases. The Rental and RentItem tables simply mirror the sale aspects. The Inventory and ItemModel tables arose because of the characteristics of the board and ski products.

To save time and effort, sample data files are provided on the main textbook CD for each of these tables, plus the common supporting tables. Access can easily import the data files into your tables.

Activity: Import Data

To import data you will first have to extract the files from the compressed archive. Also, if your table definitions are different from these, you will have to edit the data files. For example, your ItemModel table might not have all of the columns. In this case, you can open the data file in a spreadsheet program, delete the unneeded columns, and save the file in comma-delimited format.

One other possible issue is that you might already have sample data in your tables. It is possible that your data might conflict with the generated

FIGURE 4.1

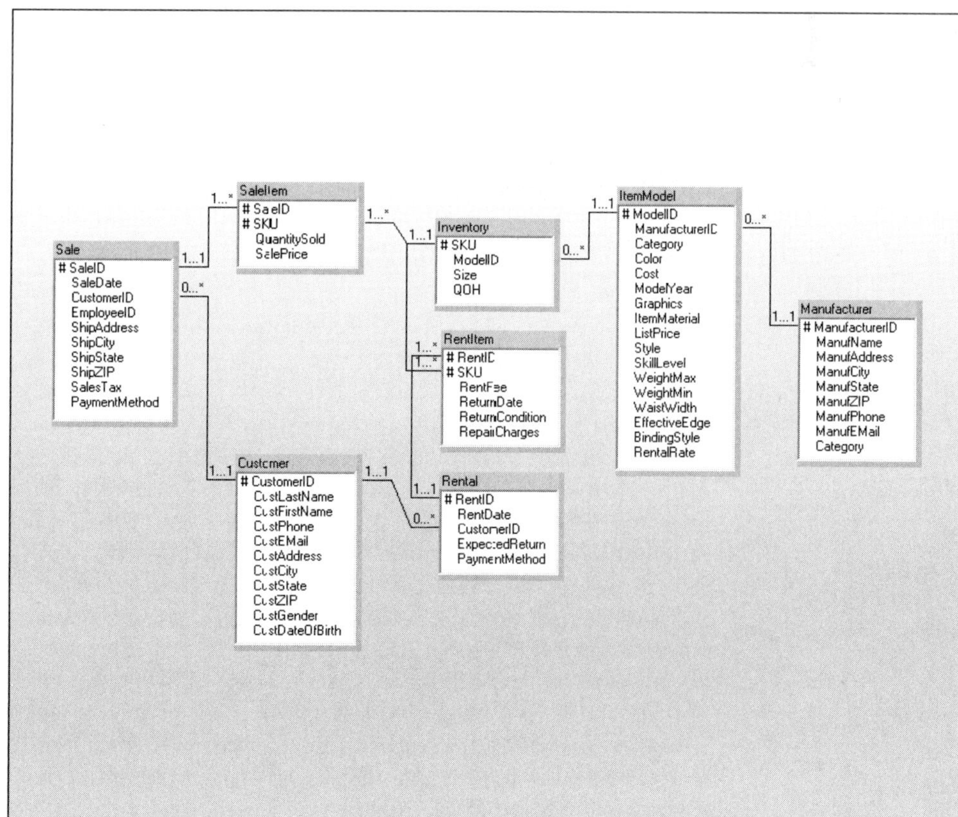

FIGURE 4.2

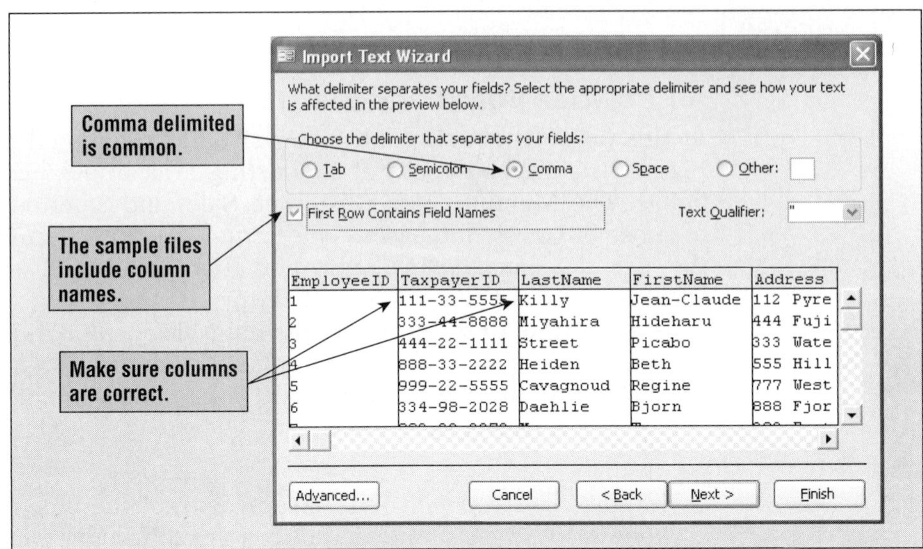

<table>
<tr><td>

Action

Choose File/Get External Data/Import.
Browse to the appropriate csv file.
Set comma delimited.
Check the box to include column names.
If your table matches the file, check the box to read into an existing table.

</td></tr>
</table>

values—particularly some of the keys. You might want to delete your existing data before attempting to import the sample data files.

Access makes it relatively easy to import data into tables. In this case, the sample data is stored in plain text files in a comma-delimited format. This format can generally be read by most database systems and other software packages. Use the File/Get External Data/Import option to read the data from the files. Figure 4.2 shows the options that you need to set to read the files correctly. By default, Access sets comma delimited and the correct quotes. However, you have to check the box to indicate that the file contains the list of column names as the first row. If necessary, this option enables you to read the data into an entirely new table with the proper column names. If you do create new tables with the import method, you will have to rebuild the relationships for them.

Activity: Create Basic Queries

Creating a query requires that you translate a business question into a form that the query system can process. Sometimes this step is straightforward; other times it is difficult. It helps if you format your query in terms of the four main questions: (1) What do you want to see? (2) What do you know or what are the constraints? (3) What tables hold the data? (4) How are the tables connected? You can use the query grid in Access to reduce the typing, or you can switch to SQL. Either way, you have to answer the four questions. Figure 4.3 shows the basic elements of the query grid. Tables that have been selected are displayed in the top half of the grid screen. Connections among them will be displayed as lines. Columns or computed fields that you want to see are displayed in the top row of the grid. Conditions that apply to individual columns are displayed in the Criteria row. You can also sort the results by selecting the appropriate sort order in any column.

FIGURE 4.3

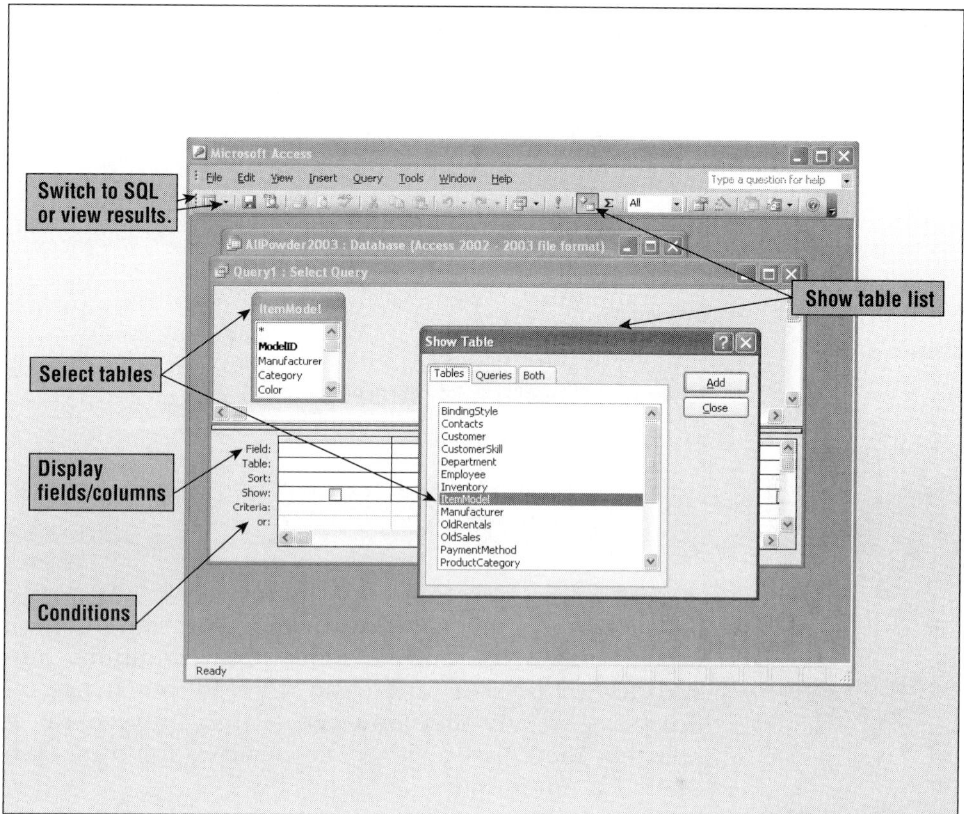

<table>
<tr><td>

Action

Create a new query in Design view.
Add the ItemModel table.
Select columns for Category, ListPrice,
WeightMax, Color, and Graphics.
Enter conditions for Board, ListPrice,
and Weight.
Run the query.

</td></tr>
</table>

Begin with a straightforward query: Display the snowboards with a list price under $300 for riders over 150 pounds. The potential buyer wants to know what color and graphics are available for boards that meet those conditions. The most difficult step in this query is to identify the table and columns that match the conditions. For example, snowboards are identified by the Category column in the ItemModel table. If you examine the data, you will see a Board entry for each item that is a snowboard. The list price, maximum weight, color, and graphics columns are also in the ItemModel table.

Figure 4.4 shows the basic query, both using the query grid and switching to the SQL. In the grid, once you have selected the ItemModel table, you can double-click or drag the desired columns down to the display grid. In SQL, you would type the names of the columns you want to see immediately after the SELECT command. Notice that Access automatically includes the name of the table (ItemModel.Category). With only one table, this step is not required, but Access plans ahead in case you add more tables that might have similar column names. The conditions you are given (snowboard, list price, and weight) are entered on the Criteria row of the grid, or typed immediately after the WHERE clause of the SQL statement. The grid conditions can be tricky at first. Notice that you enter < 300 in the ListPrice column. Since it is in the ListPrice column, this line is read as ListPrice < 300.

FIGURE 4.4

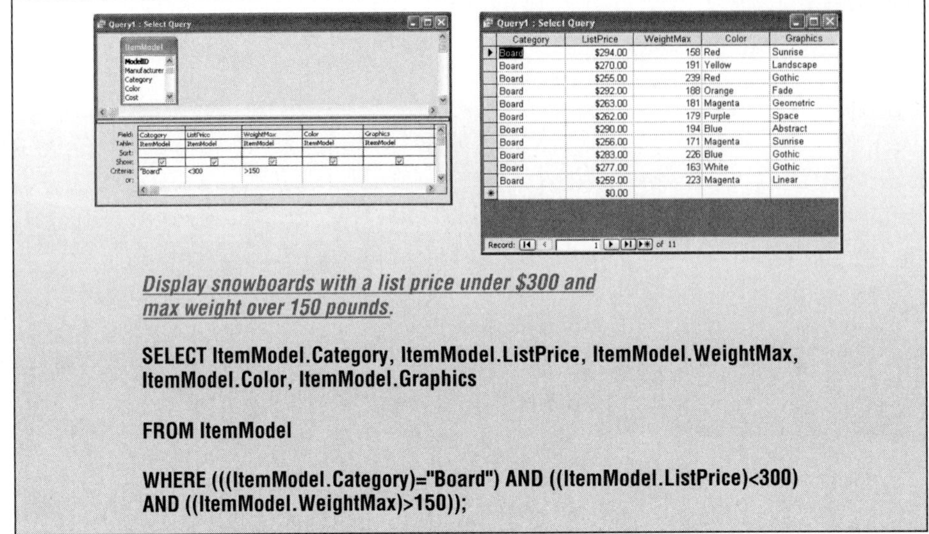

Because the three conditions are on the same Criteria row, they are connected with ANDs, meaning all three conditions must be true. The SQL WHERE clause is a little easier to read, but it has more parentheses than necessary. At any time you can switch between the grid and the SQL by selecting the desired view. The results show the 11 boards that meet the desired conditions.

Activity: Create and Test Multiple Boolean Conditions

Interpreting business questions can sometimes be difficult because of the ambiguity of natural languages. It is one of the reasons SQL remains so important. SQL requires you to specify exactly what you want to see and to write the conditions mathematically. Of course, these conditions can become relatively long when the business question is complex. Consider a customer who wants skis for jumping. She wants them made from composite materials, and the main color can be red or yellow. She does not want to spend more than $300, but if they are red, she is willing to pay up to $400.

> **Action**
>
> Create a new query in Design view.
> Add the ItemModel table.
> Add columns: Category, Color, ItemMaterial, Style, and ListPrice.
> Set requested conditions.
> Check the SQL.
> Run the query.

Begin with a new query, and again recognize that all of the attributes are in the ItemModel table. Looking through the data, the first three conditions are straightforward: the Category is Ski, the ItemMaterial is Composite, and the Style is Jump. The colors appear to be straightforward, except that the choice is connected with Or. Whenever a query contains both And and Or conditions, you must be careful; so start with basic conditions and check the results as you go. Figure 4.5 shows the initial query with the three main conditions that must always hold (ski, jump, and composite).

Now you can think about how to add the other two aspects of the question. If yellow skis must cost less than $300, what happens if you add both conditions to the query? Figure 4.6 shows the query and the results. Since all of the conditions are on the same Criteria row, all five must be true at the same time. The query therefore returns only yellow skis.

FIGURE 4.5

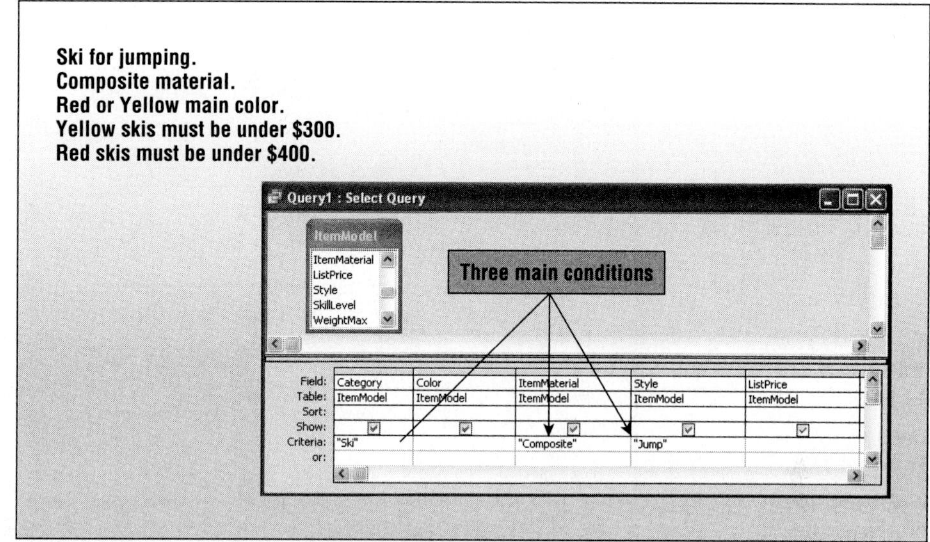

To see the red skis, you somehow have to add the option of Red as a color, but you also have to establish the higher acceptable price for red skis. The solution is to add a new criteria row. Again, the Category, ItemMaterial, and Style are set to Ski, Composite, and Jump. As shown in Figure 4.7, the Color this time is set to Red and the ListPrice must be under $400. Conditions on

FIGURE 4.6

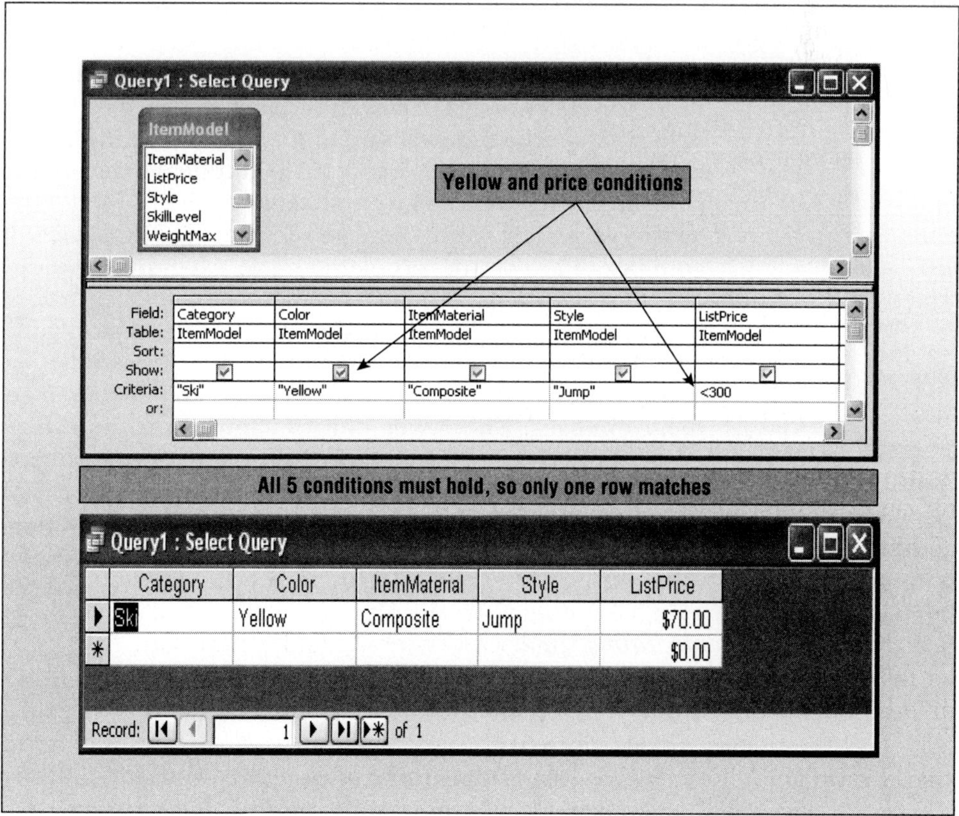

FIGURE 4.7

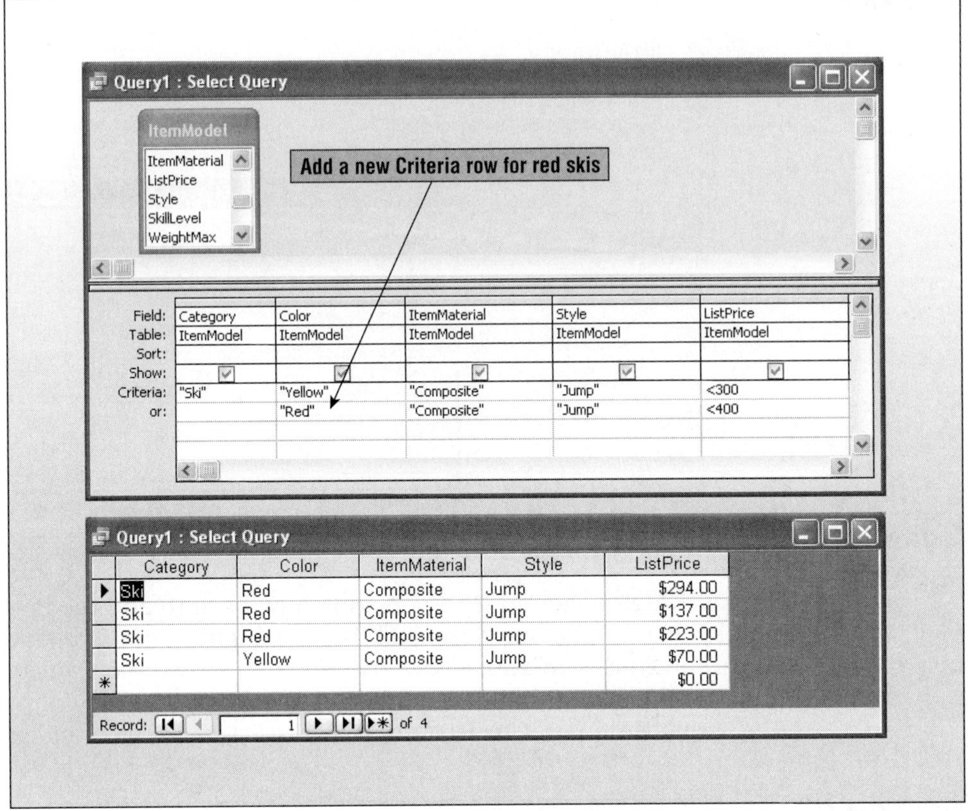

multiple rows are connected with Or clauses, so the final query displays skis that are yellow or red. The yellow skis must be composite jumping skis priced below $300. The red skis must be composite jumping skis priced below $400. Note that the grid requires you to duplicate the main conditions that hold true across the yellow and red skis.

If you switch from the grid view to the SQL view, the SQL query looks complex. Part of the problem is the excessive use of parentheses, but the query is also longer than it needs to be because Access duplicates the three main conditions. Figure 4.8 shows the SQL version generated from the query grid. However, you would never type the query in that way. Instead, the query can be simplified by removing the excess parentheses and the unneeded table name prefixes. The lower half of Figure 4.8 shows the simpler SQL query. You should enter this query into the SQL editor in Access and verify that it produces the same answers as the grid query. The SELECT statement lists the columns that you want to see. The FROM clause lists the single table. The WHERE clause begins with the three items that must be true. It also includes the two choices of colors with their associated price limits.

Activity: Use Multiple Tables in a Query

Relational databases require the tables to be carefully designed so that the DBMS can efficiently store large amounts of data. This process entails placing data into multiple tables. Consequently, a key feature of SQL is its ability to join the tables to make it easy to retrieve data from many tables with one query. The Access query grid makes it easy to join tables. Once the

FIGURE 4.8

```
SELECT ItemModel.Category, ItemModel.Color, ItemModel.ItemMaterial,
ItemModel.Style, ItemModel.ListPrice
FROM ItemModel
WHERE (((ItemModel.Category)="Ski") AND ((ItemModel.Color)="Yellow")
AND ((ItemModel.ItemMaterial)="Composite") AND
((ItemModel.Style)="Jump") AND ((ItemModel.ListPrice)<300)) OR
(((ItemModel.Category)="Ski") AND ((ItemModel.Color)="Red") AND
((ItemModel.ItemMaterial)="Composite") AND ((ItemModel.Style)="Jump")
AND ((ItemModel.ListPrice)<400));
```

```
SELECT Category, Color, ItemMaterial, Style, ListPrice
FROM ItemModel
WHERE (Category="Ski" AND ItemMaterial="Composite" AND Style="Jump")
AND ((Color="Yellow" AND ListPrice<300)
OR (Color="Red" AND ListPrice<400));
```

tables are joined, you can generally treat the columns as if they came from a single table.

To understand the joining process, create a new query and add just the Sale table. The objective is to find all of the sales in May that were made with a cash payment. Figure 4.9 shows the initial query. Note the use of the Between clause to specify the month of May. Also observe that Access automatically places pound signs (#) around the dates. These marks enable you to enter dates in any common date format. Notice that the query returns the

FIGURE 4.9

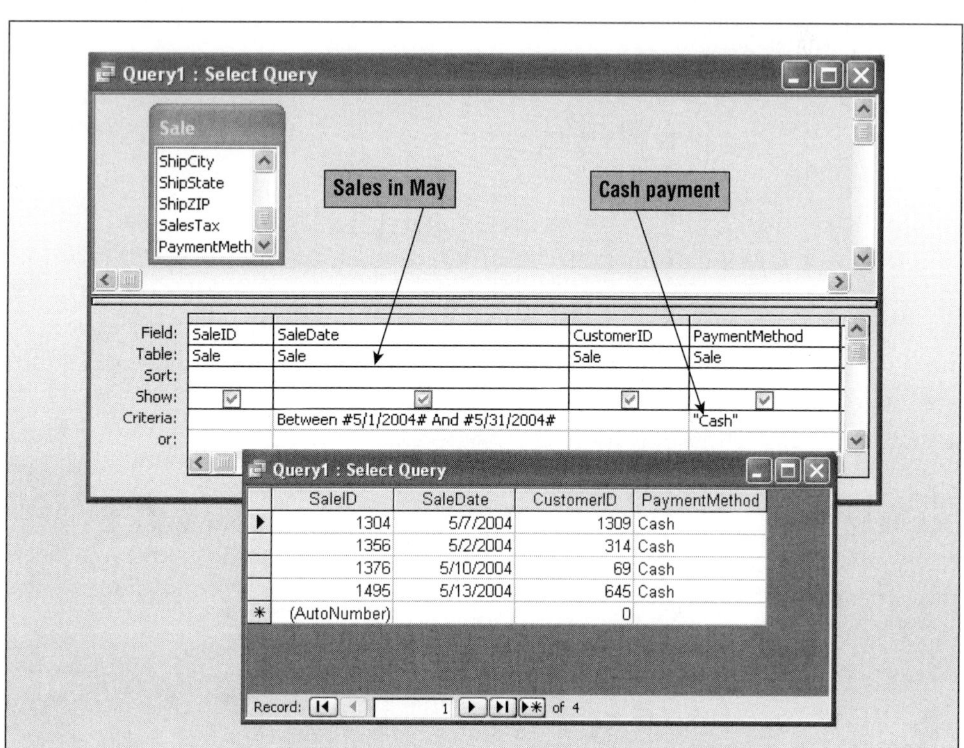

CustomerID, but no one is going to memorize CustomerID numbers. Instead, you need to look up matching customer names. If you look at the relationship diagram (part of it is shown in Figure 4.1), you find that the CustomerID and matching names are stored in the Customer table. You could take each of the ID values returned by the Sale query and create a new query on the Customer table to find the names; however, the table JOIN command is much easier and more powerful.

<table>
<tr><td>

Action

Create a new query in Design view.
Choose the Sale table.
Select columns: SaleID, SaleDate,
CustomerID, and PaymentMethod.
Set conditions for Cash sales in May.
Choose Query/Show Table (or button).
Add the Customer table.
Add columns: LastName, FirstName.
View the SQL.
Run the query.

</td></tr>
</table>

With the Sale query in Design view, click the Show Table button on the menu. Then add the Customer table to the query. The Customer table is added to the top half of the query screen, and the join to the Sale table is shown with a connecting line between the CustomerID columns. This connection exists because the relationship was created when the tables were designed. Most of the time, these automatically created joins will be correct. But sometimes you will have to delete or add connections. You can remove a join by right-clicking on the line and selecting the delete option. You can create a new join by dragging a column name from one table and dropping it onto the matching column in the second table.

Figure 4.10 shows the basic query design. Once the tables are joined correctly, you can move any column down to the query grid. In this case, place the Customer LastName and FirstName columns in the grid. Run the query

FIGURE 4.10

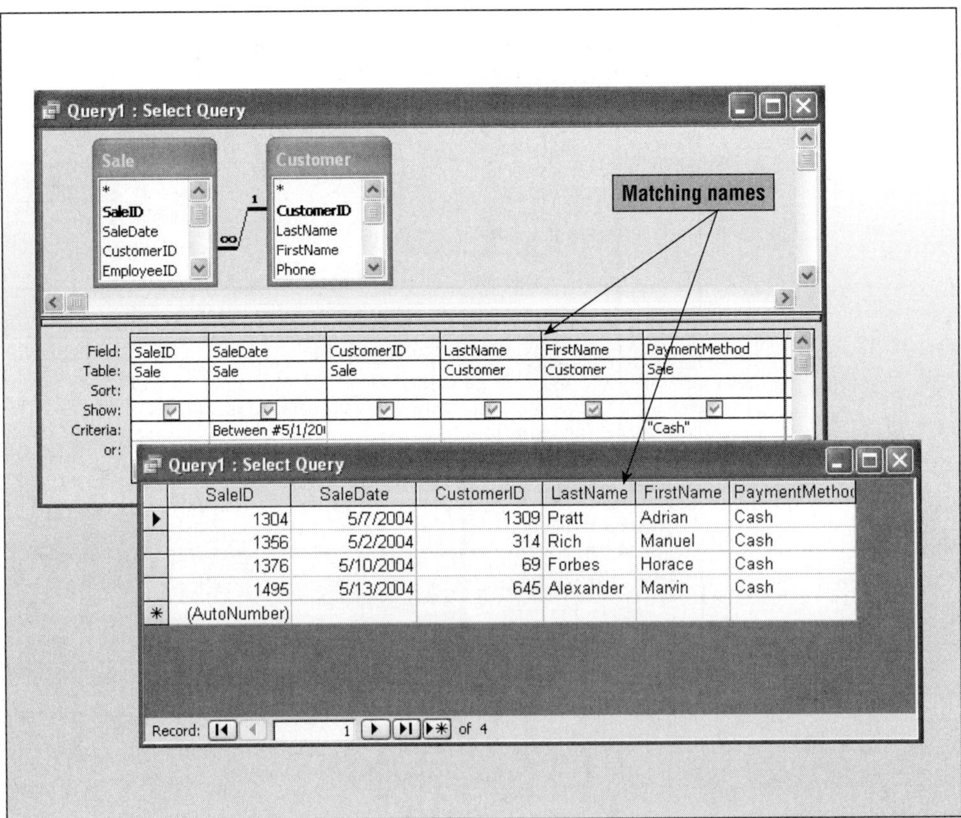

FIGURE 4.11

```
SELECT Sale.SaleID, Sale.SaleDate, Sale.CustomerID,
Customer.LastName, Customer.FirstName,
Sale.PaymentMethod

FROM Customer INNER JOIN Sale ON
Customer.CustomerID = Sale.CustomerID

WHERE (Sale.SaleDate Between #5/1/2004# And
#5/31/2004# AND Sale.PaymentMethod="Cash");
```

to see that the DBMS automatically looks up the names that match the ID values. If you want to double-check the lookup, you can add the CustomerID column from the Customer table and see that it matches the CustomerID values from the Sale table.

Figure 4.11 shows the SQL for the same query. The FROM and INNER JOIN statements specify the tables and how they are joined. If you read the FROM statement carefully, you can see that it provides the same information as the query grid join. It lists the two tables and specifies that they are connected by the CustomerID column. Because the column has the same name in both tables, you are required to specify the full name of the column in the ON statement. For two tables, the FROM and INNER JOIN syntax is relatively easy to follow. With more tables, the join begins to look a little messier. Consequently, it is often easiest to join tables using the visual connections in the query grid, and then switch to SQL view to ensure that the query is correct.

To see the power of the SQL joins, consider a slightly more challenging business question: Which customers bought Atomic skis in January or February? Note that Atomic is the name of a ski manufacturer. Before leaping into the Access query screen, it is best to think about the query and look at the relationship screen for a minute. As shown in Figure 4.12, you can begin with what you want to see: the names of the customers. These are in the

FIGURE 4.12

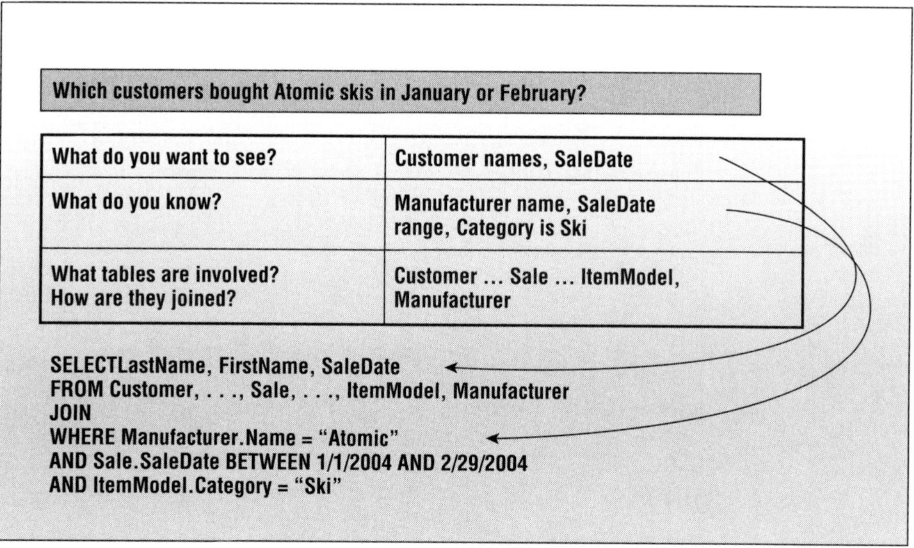

FIGURE 4.13

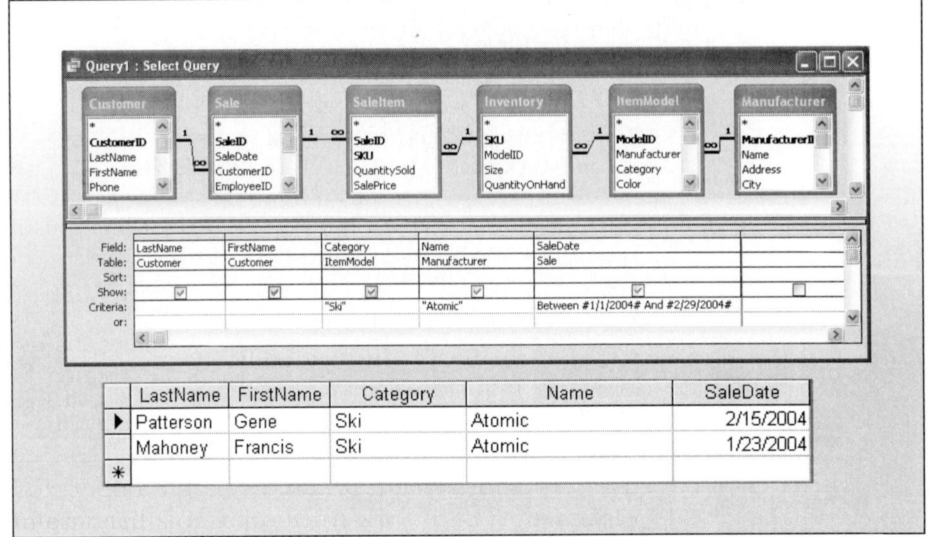

Customer table. Now, what facts do you know? In this case, you are given the name of the manufacturer, the ItemModel.Category, and the range for the SaleDate. You should also begin writing down the tables you need to provide these facts: Customer, Sale, ItemModel, and Manufacturer so far. When you examine the relationships for the database, you will see that these four tables are not enough—they do not connect together. You will also need the SaleItem and Inventory tables.

Figure 4.13 shows the final query in Design view. Notice the large number of tables involved. But you need to verify that each connection is correct for the specific problem. Once the tables have been selected and joined, you can quickly place the columns you need on the query grid, and then enter the desired conditions. Running the query reveals the two people who meet the desired conditions.

Figure 4.14 shows the matching SQL for the same query. The INNER JOIN and ON statements seem complex, but you do not need to worry about the order of the statements, so it is more flexible than it first appears. The

FIGURE 4.14

```
SELECT Customer.LastName, Customer.FirstName,
ItemModel.Category, Manufacturer.Name, Sale.SaleDate

FROM Manufacturer INNER JOIN (ItemModel INNER JOIN
(Inventory INNER JOIN (SaleItem INNER JOIN (Sale INNER
JOIN Customer ON Customer.CustomerID =
Sale.CustomerID) ON Sale.SaleID = SaleItem.SaleID) ON
Inventory.SKU = SaleItem.SKU) ON ItemModel.ModelID =
Inventory.ModelID) ON Manufacturer.ManufacturerID =
ItemModel.ManufacturerID

WHERE (((ItemModel.Category)="Ski") AND
((Manufacturer.Name)="Atomic") AND ((Sale.SaleDate)
Between #1/1/2004# And #2/29/2004#));
```

main thing is to make sure you list all of the tables and include the correct connections within the ON statements. Nonetheless, it is easier to join tables with the visual design and let it enter the matching SQL statements. You can always switch to the SQL view to examine the statements or make minor changes.

Computations and Subtotals

Activity: Compute Values with Queries

In general, it does not make sense to store some columns in the database. In particular, the DBMS query system has the ability to perform common calculations. Figure 4.15 shows how the query system can easily calculate the profit margin for each item. In this case, the table holds the item's list price and the acquistion cost. The profit is simply the difference between the list price and the cost. In the grid, you enter the name of the new column (Profit), followed by a colon (:) and the calculation (ListPrice − Cost). Observe that Access will place square brackets around the column names. It does this to be cautious. Anytime a column name is a reserved word or contains special characters (such as a space or the # sign), you must place the brackets around the column name. Notice that the query is sorted by Category and ListPrice. You make these selections on the Sort row. The

> ### Action
> Create a new query in Design view.
> Add the ItemModel table.
> Select columns: Category, ItemMaterial, and ListPrice.
> Create new column as Profit: [ListPrice] − [Cost].
> Run the query.

FIGURE 4.15

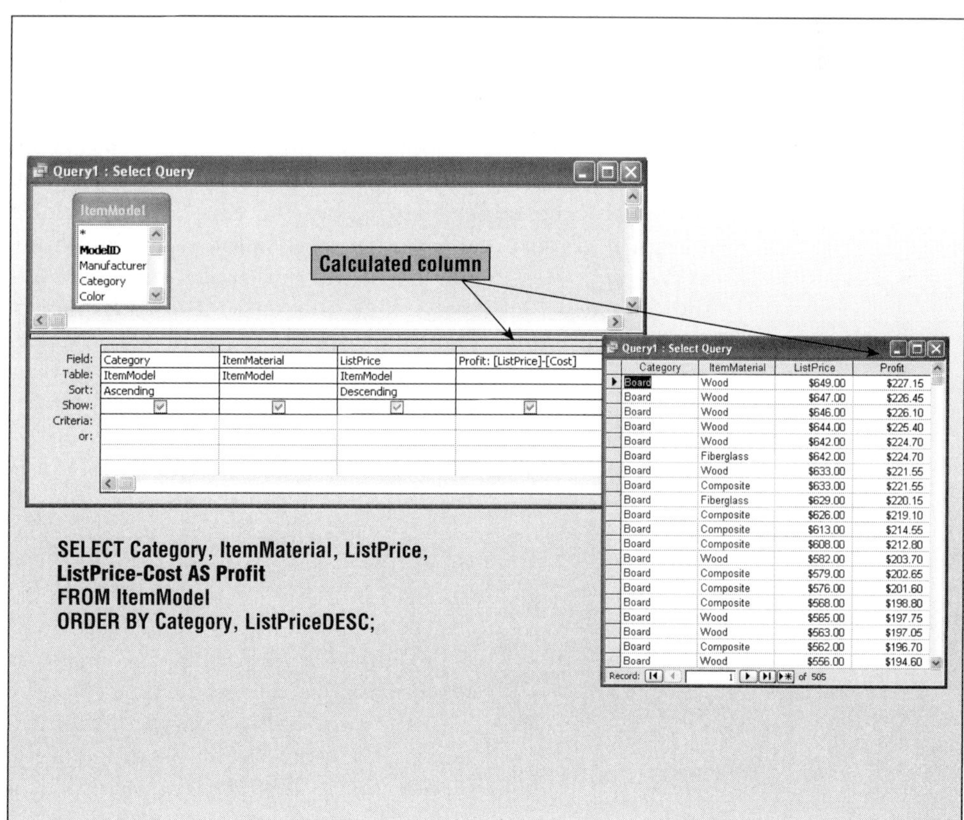


```
SELECT Category, ItemMaterial, ListPrice,
ListPrice-Cost AS Profit
FROM ItemModel
ORDER BY Category, ListPriceDESC;
```

FIGURE 4.16

Lcase	To lowercase
Len	Length/number of characters
Mid	Get substring
Trim	Remove leading and trailing spaces
Ucase	To uppercase
Date	Current date
DateAdd	Add days, months, years to a date
DateDiff	Subtract two dates
Format	Highly detailed formatting
Now	Current date and time
Abs	Absolute value
Cos	Cosine, all common trig functions
Int	Integer, drop decimal values
Sgn	Signum
Round	Round-off

SQL is also straightforward. To add the computed column to the display, enter the calculation in the SELECT line, followed by AS and the name of the new column.

Calculations written in this form are always performed on data on the same row. It does not calculate across rows. You can use the standard mathematical operators (add, subtract, divide, and multiply). You can also use several standard functions built into Access. Figure 4.16 shows some of the commonly used functions. Most are straightforward, but the date functions require a little explanation and practice. The Format function enables you to specify detailed formats for date and numeric columns.

To illustrate the power of some of the date functions, create a new query using the Sale table and display the SaleID and SaleDate columns. Now, as shown in Figure 4.17, add a new column as SaleMonth: Format(SaleDate," yyyy-mm"). Be sure to enter the quoted format correctly—it controls the way the date will be displayed. In this case, it will display the four-digit year, followed by a two-digit number for the month. You may want to format months this way to ensure that they sort correctly. The Format function has many options, and you will have to consult the Access Help documentation for details.

The DateAdd and DateDiff functions are even more versatile. Create a new query, again using the Sale table. Display the SaleID and the SaleDate. Then, as shown in Figure 4.18, add the column LateDate: SaleDate + 30. This calculation generates the new date that is 30 days in the future. Now add the column LateMonth: DateAdd("m", 1, SaleDate). Run the query to compare the two calculations. The first one adds 30 days to the SaleDate. The second adds one month to the SaleDate. Of course, you could specify any number of days or months and the system would correctly compute the date across month or year boundaries.

For many business questions, you will only need the standard SQL date arithmetic. But occasionally, you will

Action
Create a new query in Design view.
Add the Sale table.
Select columns: SaleID and SaleDate.
Create new column as LateDate: [SaleDate] + 30.
Create another new column as LateMonth: DateAdd("m",1,[SaleDate]).
Run the query.

FIGURE 4.17

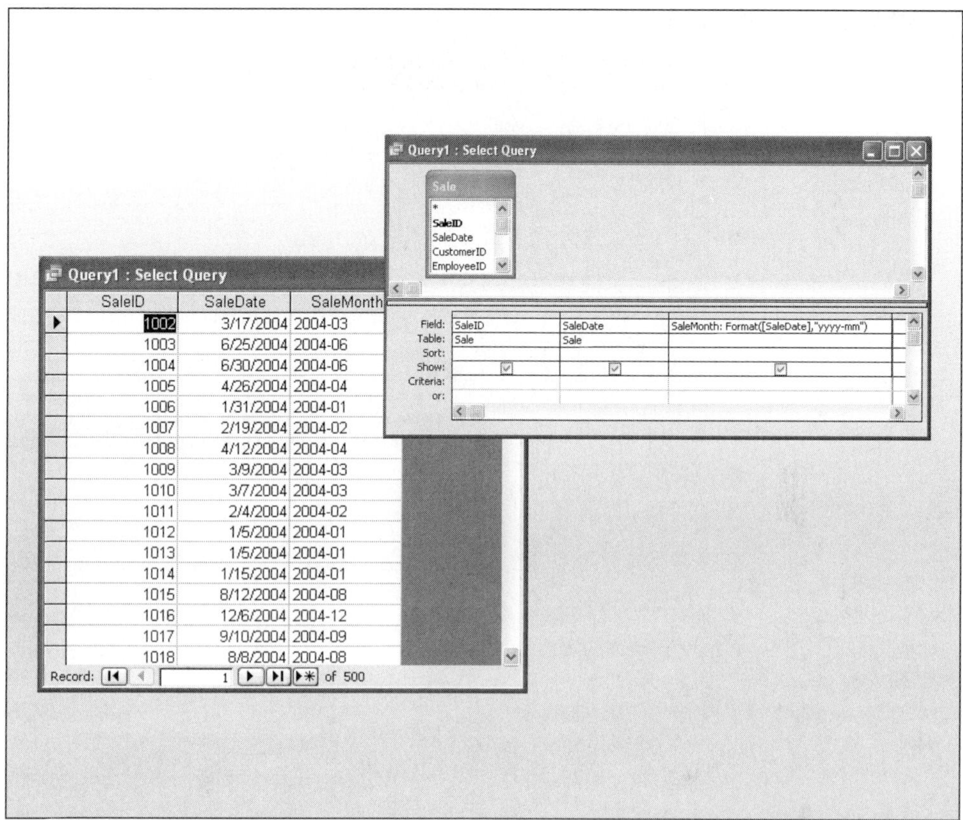

find it useful to apply the power of DateAdd or DateDiff. DateDiff is similar to DateAdd, but it subtracts two dates. In both the addition and subtraction, you can specify how you want the date arithmetic performed—by dates ("d"), months ("m"), years ("yyyy"), or other options. Check the Access documentation to see how to count the number of workdays or even the number of Fridays between two dates. *Note:* You might have to open the Visual Basic Editor before the Help system can find the documentation for some of these specialized functions. To open the VB Editor, open a form in Design view and then select View/Code.

Activity: Calculate Totals and Subtotals

Business managers often need to compute totals across rows of data. SQL provides several aggregation functions to perform these tasks. The most commonly used functions are Sum, Average, and Count. Of the three, the Count function can be the most confusing to use. Just remember that it simply counts the number of rows, while Sum adds up the numbers within a row. The challenge is to identify when you need to use Count instead of Sum.

The Sum function is straightforward. For example, how much sales tax does the company owe to the State of California? Begin by creating a new query based on the Sale table, because it has the ShipState and

Action

Create a new query in Design view.
Add the Sale table.
Select columns: ShipState and SalesTax.
View/Totals (or Totals button).
Select "Where" for Total row in State.
Enter "CA" as a criteria.
Select "Sum" for SalesTax Total row.
Run the query.

FIGURE 4.18

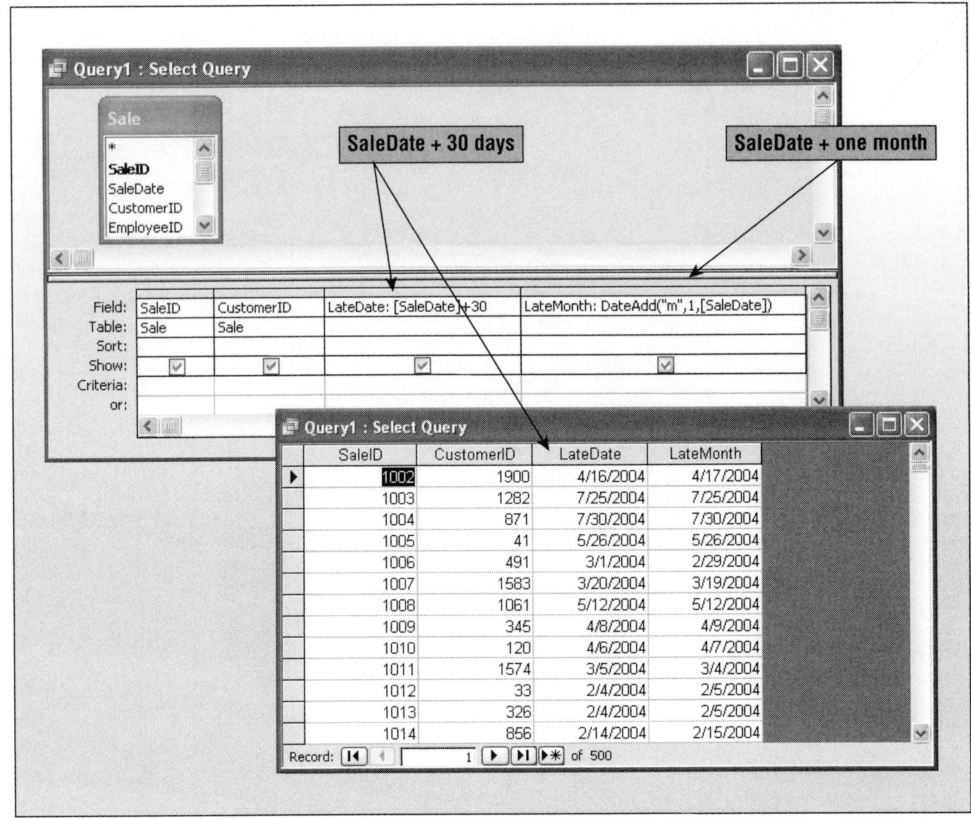

SaleID	CustomerID	LateDate	LateMonth
1002	1900	4/16/2004	4/17/2004
1003	1282	7/25/2004	7/25/2004
1004	871	7/30/2004	7/30/2004
1005	41	5/26/2004	5/26/2004
1006	491	3/1/2004	2/29/2004
1007	1583	3/20/2004	3/19/2004
1008	1061	5/12/2004	5/12/2004
1009	345	4/8/2004	4/9/2004
1010	120	4/6/2004	4/7/2004
1011	1574	3/5/2004	3/4/2004
1012	33	2/4/2004	2/5/2004
1013	326	2/4/2004	2/5/2004
1014	856	2/14/2004	2/15/2004

SalesTax columns. As a criterion for ShipState, enter the CA abbreviation for California. Run the query, and you should see two columns: Each row will have CA in the state and a value for the SalesTax. To compute the total, return to Design view. You now need to indicate that you want to compute totals by clicking the Totals button on the menu bar. As shown in Figure 4.19, this button adds the Total row to the grid. Select the Sum option under the SalesTax column and the Where option for the ShipState column. The Sum option makes sense since you want the total of the sales tax. When you run the query, you will see a single value—the total amount of sales tax collected for the State of California.

Figure 4.20 shows the SQL syntax for the query. Note that setting the Where option for the SaleState was not strictly necessary, but it makes the SQL clearer. Note the use of the column alias SumOfSalesTax to provide a name for the output column. You can set this name to almost anything, but it should indicate the business interpretation of the column. Of course, you can use multiple tables with the FROM and INNER JOIN syntax.

To understand some of the power of SQL, what if you want to see the total tax owed to each state? Of course, it would be possible to edit the CA condition and replace it with each state, but there is an easier way. Close this query and begin a new query the same way. Add the Sales table and use the ShipState and

---

Action

Create a new query in Design view.
Add the Sale table.
Select columns: ShipState and SalesTax.
View/Totals (or Totals button).
Select "Sum" for SalesTax Total row.
Run the query.

FIGURE 4.19

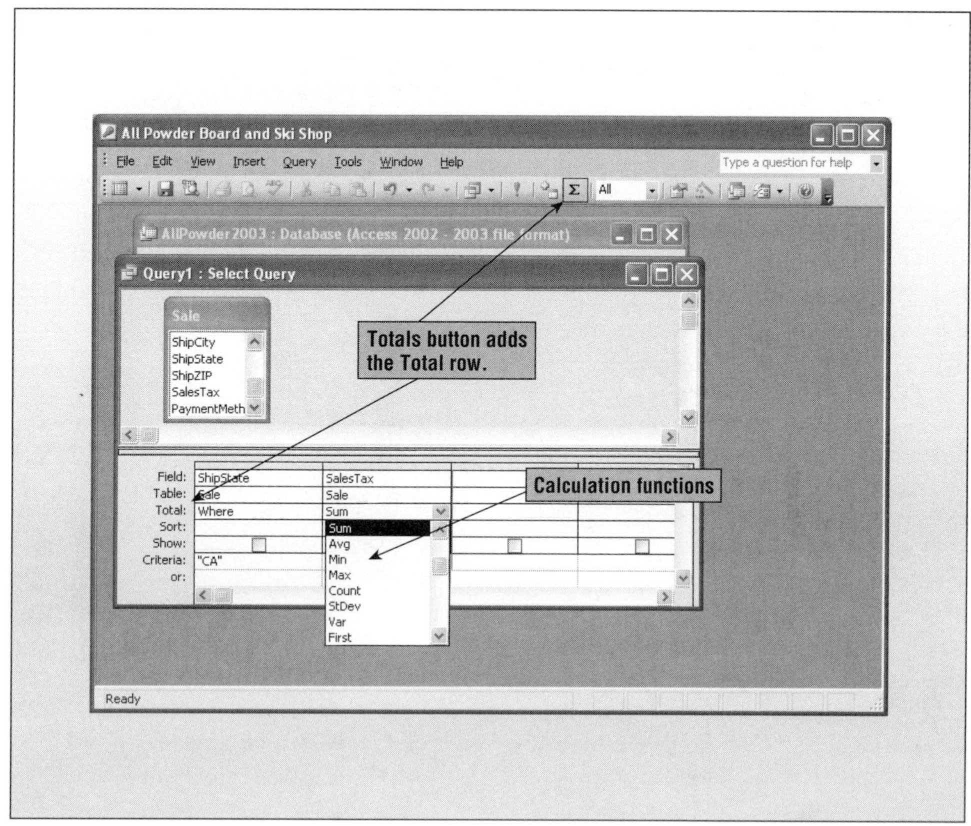

SalesTax columns, but do not specify any limiting conditions. Click the Totals button to see the totals row. Select the Sum option under the SalesTax column, but do not change the setting for the ShipState. The default option for the Totals row is Group By. This choice instructs the DBMS to identify each unique entry in that column and compute the selected subtotal for each element. Figure 4.21 shows the query and the result. The result lists each state, followed by the total sales tax collected for that state.

Figure 4.22 shows the corresponding SQL statement. The main addition is the actual GROUP BY clause. Note that any column listed in the GROUP BY clause must be included in the SELECT clause. It would not make sense to compute subtotals and then not display the values you are grouping. Of course, you could compute the average or count the number of items in a group just as easily. In fact, you can compute multiple functions at the same time, just by including multiple copies of the desired column and selecting a different aggregation function.

FIGURE 4.20

```
SELECT  Sum(Sale.SalesTax)  AS  SumOfSalesTax
FROM  Sale
WHERE  Sale.ShipState="CA"
```

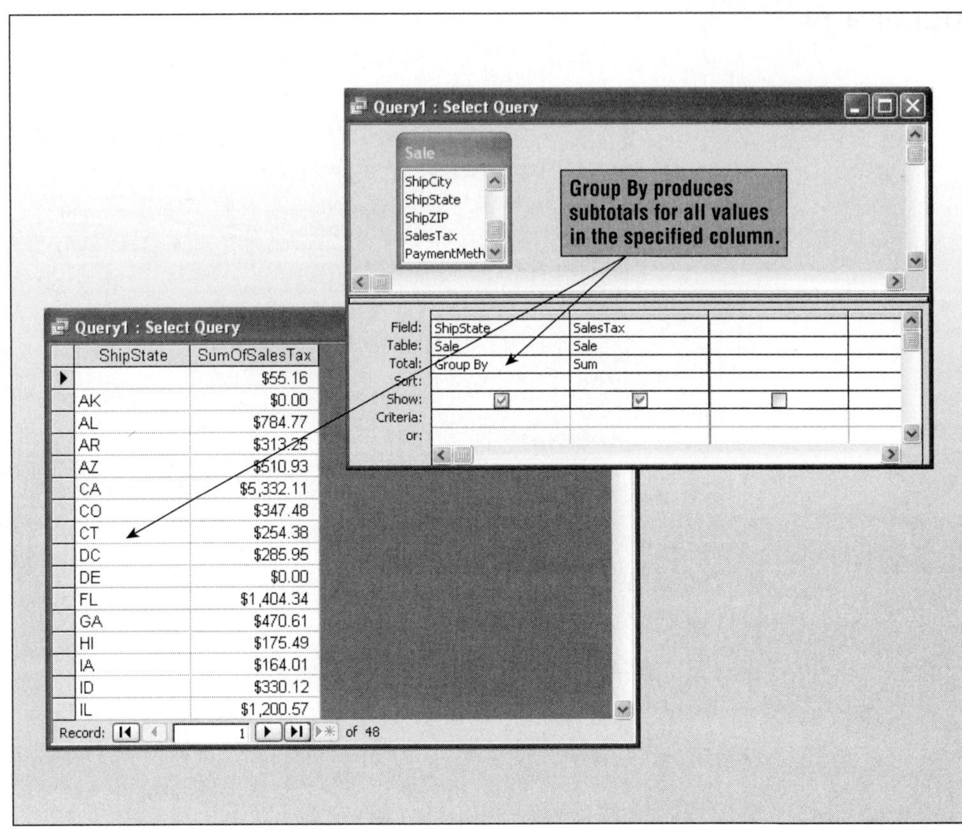

For practice, you should compute the total value of sales to customers in Colorado (the state code is CO). Create a new query and add the Sale and SaleItem tables. Use the ShipState column from the Sale table. To compute the total value of the actual sale is slightly trickier. You need to multiply the QuantitySold by the SalePrice from the SaleItem table, then compute its sum. To be safe, first do the multiplication and check your progress. In a new field, enter the name SaleTotal, followed by a colon, and the formula: QuantitySold * SalePrice. Enter CO as the criteria to select the state, then run the query and check the results to see if they make sense. You might want to list the QuantitySold and SalePrice separately, and then use a calculator or spreadsheet to verify some of the calculations. Returning to Design view, you need to compute the total. Click the Totals button and select Sum for the SaleTotal column, and Where for the ShipState column. Technically, the query will work if you leave the ShipState as Group By, but the SQL is clearer and potentially faster if you use Where. Figure 4.23 shows the query.


```
SELECT  Sale.ShipState,  Sum(Sale.SalesTax)  AS  SumOfSalesTax
FROM  Sale
GROUP  BY  Sale.ShipState;
```

FIGURE 4.23

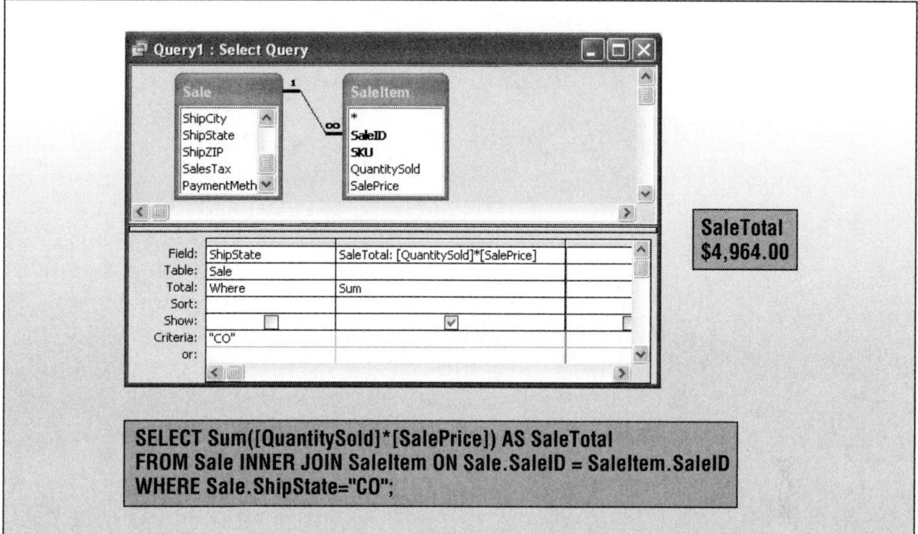

Exercises

Crystal Tigers

Enter sample data for the Crystal Tigers service club database. You can make up data, but remember that it has to be consistent. You might want to share data with other students so that everyone has a larger database to work with. Then create queries to provide the following business information.

1. List all of the members who have been president of the organization.
2. List the charities for which the club has raised more than $1,000.
3. Pick an event and list all of the members who worked at that event.
4. Count the number of events and the amount of money raised for each charity.
5. List the total number of service hours provided in the latest year.
6. List the number of service hours provided by each member.
7. List the members who have held the most number of officer positions.

Capitol Artists

Enter sample data for the Capitol Artists business. You can create random data, but remember that it has to be consistent. You might want to share data with other students so that everyone has a larger database to work with. Then create queries to provide the following business information.

1. Pick a date and an employee and list all of the tasks by that person on that date.
2. List all of the tasks performed for a specific job (e.g., Job #1173).
3. List all of the client jobs that had active tasks on a specific date.
4. Count the number of meetings held regarding one client (pick any client).
5. List the employees who have attended the most number of meetings.

6. Pick a job and compute the amount of money billed (hours * rate).
7. List the clients in order of the ones that have provided the greatest revenue (billing + expenses).

Offshore Speed

Enter sample data for the Offshore Speed company. You can create random data, but remember that it has to be consistent. You might want to share data with other students so that everyone has a larger database to work with. Then create queries to provide the following business information. If you have not created data that matches these questions, either add more data, or change the query to match your data. For instance, if you do not have any sales of propellers, pick a category of item that you have sold several times.

1. Pick a month and list all of the customers who purchased propellers (Category).
2. List all of the parts sold on a particular day.
3. What is the most expensive steering wheel we have sold?
4. List the manufacturers sorted by the number of parts we sell from each one.
5. List the employees to identify the best salespeople in terms of value.
6. List the brands of boat for which we sell the most oil pumps (Description).
7. For a given order, compute the total value of the order and the sales tax, assuming a 6 percent tax rate.

Final Project

The main textbook has an appendix with several longer case studies. You should be able to work on one of these cases throughout the term. If you or your instructor picks one, perform the following tasks.

1. Create a few rows of sample data for all of the tables.
2. Identify at least five business questions that a manager would commonly ask and provide the queries to answer those questions. At least two of the questions should involve subtotals or averages.
3. Exchange three business questions with other students in your class and write the queries for the questions you receive.

Chapter 5

Advanced Queries and Subqueries

Chapter Outline

Objectives
Advanced Database Queries
Case: All Powder Board and Ski Shop
Lab Exercise
  *All Powder Board and Ski Data
  SQL Data Definition and Data
  Manipulation*
Exercises
Final Project

Objectives

- Create more complex SELECT queries using subqueries.
- Understand the role of INNER and LEFT joins.
- Create theta joins using inequalities to match categories.
- Use a UNION statement to merge rows of data.
- Use DDL to CREATE and DROP tables.
- Use DML to INSERT, UPDATE, and DELETE data.

Advanced Database Queries

SQL is a powerful language. For many queries, you will not need the full power of SQL, but some seemingly innocent business questions can be tricky to answer. In these cases, you need some additional capabilities. Some of these capabilities can be challenging to understand, but if you follow the examples carefully, you should be able to use the ideas to create similar queries in the future.

Subqueries are one of the more interesting features of SQL. A subquery is a query that calls a second query to obtain additional data. Instead of looking up a second set of numbers yourself, you can add a second query to do the work automatically.

Joins offer other powerful options. Joins are commonly used as a lookup link between tables, making it easy for you to build a query that uses data from multiple tables. However, joins have several options to help you answer even more complex questions. It is especially important that you understand the difference between inner and outer joins.

One of the strengths of SQL is that it operates on sets of data. Instead of thinking in terms of individual rows, you can concentrate on collections of rows that meet specified conditions. SQL offers some interesting set-operation commands that provide detailed control over rows of data. For example, the UNION statement combines rows of data from multiple SELECT statements.

Chapters 2 and 3 hinted at the ability of SQL to define tables. In fact, you can use a DBMS without the fancy visual screens. Generally, everything you need to do can be handled with SQL commands. For example, the data definition command CREATE TABLE is a powerful method to create new tables. Storing these SQL statements in a text file makes it easy to quickly rebuild or transfer a database. Similarly, the data manipulation commands (INSERT, DELETE, and UPDATE) are powerful tools for copying and deleting rows, and quickly changing thousands or millions of pieces of data.

Case: All Powder Board and Ski Shop

As the queries become more complex, it is better to work from a common set of data. Figure 5.1 shows the primary tables for the All Powder Board and Ski Shop. Your tables and sample data should be very close to these tables. Note that several supporting tables are not displayed in this diagram, but you will also need those in your database. As explained in Chapter 4, you can import the sample data to these tables. If you add more data, your query results may be slightly different from the ones shown in this chapter. Although the query is more important than the actual results, the results are useful to help you decide if you have constructed the query properly.

One of the greatest challenges with any database query is that most queries return values, but they might not be answers to the question you thought you were asking. You must learn to build the queries and test each intermediate step carefully so that you can be sure the final result is an accurate answer to the question being asked.

FIGURE 5.1

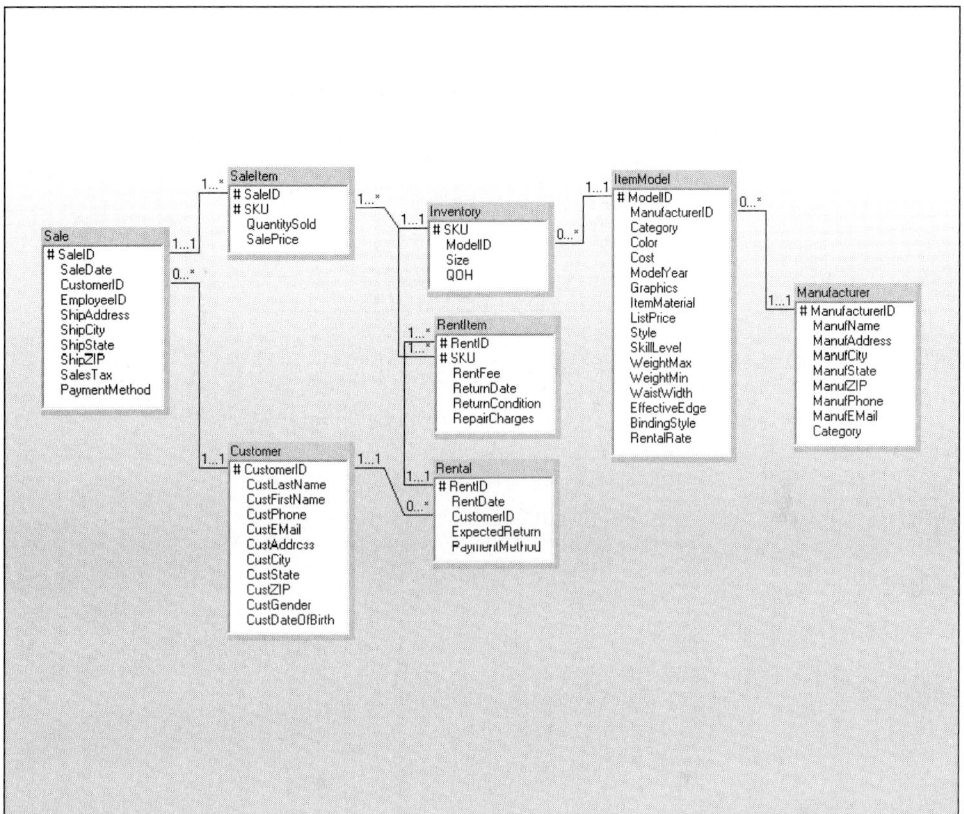

Lab Exercise

All Powder Board and Ski Data

Subqueries are used to create a second (or more) query to look up additional data that can be used in the primary query. The value is often used within a WHERE clause to make comparisons in more depth. For example, Katy the manager wants to identify the best customers of the shop. In particular, she would like to know which customers have placed the most sales. You could just give her the complete list of customers and the sales made by each person. Eventually, however, this list would be too long. Instead, she wants a list that displays the customers whose total purchases are larger than the average purchase per customer.

Although the business question is reasonable, this question is slightly tricky because you have to build the query in pieces.

Activity: Create a Subquery

The first step in the query is to recognize that you need to compute total sales by customer. The phrase "by customer" is an indication that you need to compute subtotals using the GROUP BY clause. Figure 5.2 shows the

Action
Create a new query in Design view.
Tables: Customer, Sale, SaleItem.
Columns: CustomerID, LastName, FirstName, SalesValue: [QuantitySold] * [SalePrice].
Sum the SalesValue, Group By the rest.
Save query as CustomerSales.
Create new query in Design view.
Table: CustomerSales query.
Columns: SalesValue.
Set Totals and select Avg.
Run the query.

FIGURE 5.2

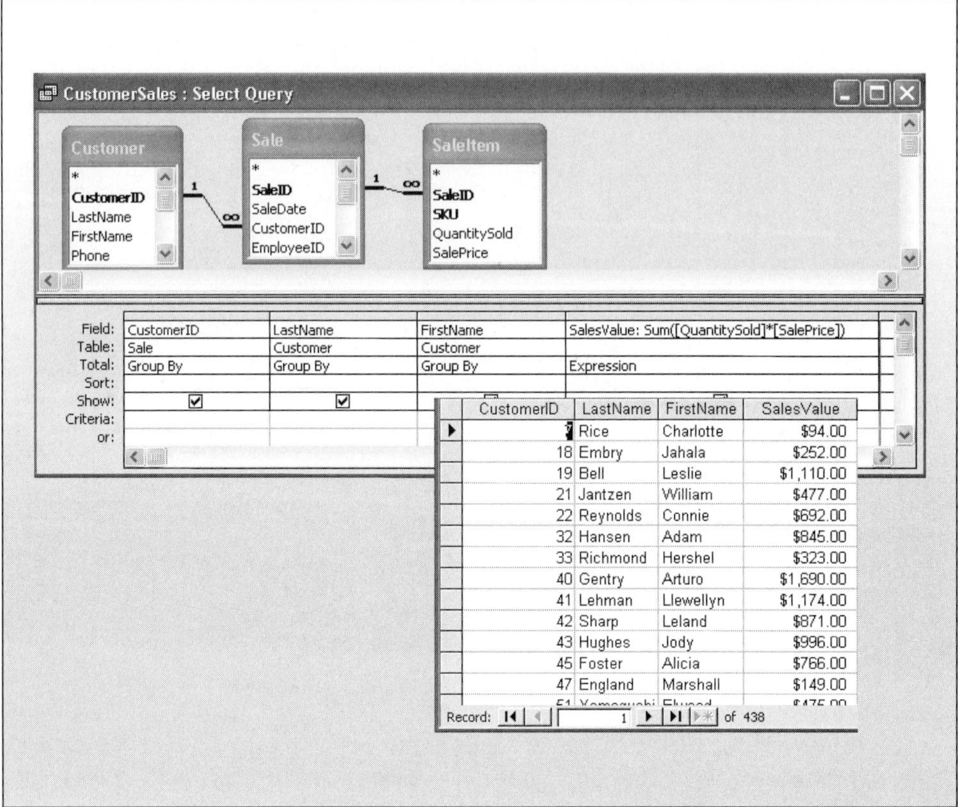

initial query that computes these subtotals. Of course, it lists the sales for every customer, and Katy wants only the ones with greater-than-average sales. But this query is an important step and needs to be saved as "CustomerSales."

The next step is to use this first query to compute the average amount of sales for customers. This computation is straightforward. Simply build a new query using CustomerSales as the only table, and calculate the average of the sales column. Figure 5.3 shows the basic query and the result based on the current data. Notice that the SQL is straightforward. In this case, the

FIGURE 5.3

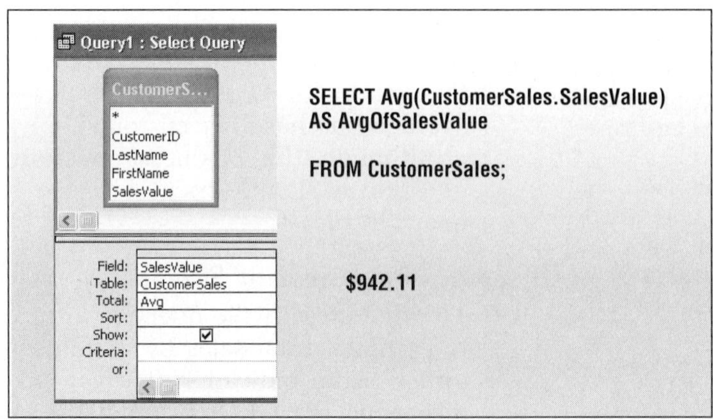

SQL is critical for the next step. It is not necessary to save this query, but you might want to leave the SQL window open for the final step.

The last step is to create a new query that answers the overall question to determine which customers spend more than average. The new query will also be based on the CustomerSales query created in the first step, so just add that query. This time, select the LastName, FirstName, and SalesValue columns. If you ran the query at this point, you would get the same results as in the first query. Instead, you want to add a criterion to only display the customers with a SalesValue greater than the average. The simple approach is to enter the value 942.11 as a condition in the query.

Although this approach works this time, it does not work very well over time. It would require the owner to run the average query first, then copy the value into the Design view of the main query. It makes more sense to automate the entire process. So instead of entering the actual number as the condition, you need to enter the subquery calculation. You can write the complete SQL statement, but it must be contained within parentheses. Figure 5.4 shows the final query that you can give to Katy. Notice that it is sorted in descending order by SalesValue so that the customers with the largest total purchases are listed at the top. Also, always remember to put the subquery inside parentheses; otherwise the query will not run at all. If you want to save some typing and reduce errors, you should create the subquery first in a separate query to test it. When it is correct, you can copy the SQL statement and paste it into the WHERE clause for the final query. Again, remember to add the parentheses around the subquery.

> **Action**
>
> Create a new query in Design view.
> Table: CustomerSales query.
> Columns: LastName, FirstName, SalesValue.
> Criteria for SalesValue (enter in SQL)
> >(SELECT Avg(SalesValue) FROM CustomerSales).

Activity: Build Outer Joins

Joining tables is one of the more complex issues in SQL. Up to this point, the joins have been simple equality joins designed to show how a column in one table links to data stored in a related table. It is important that you understand the effect of this join. Jim the sales manager and David the rental

FIGURE 5.4

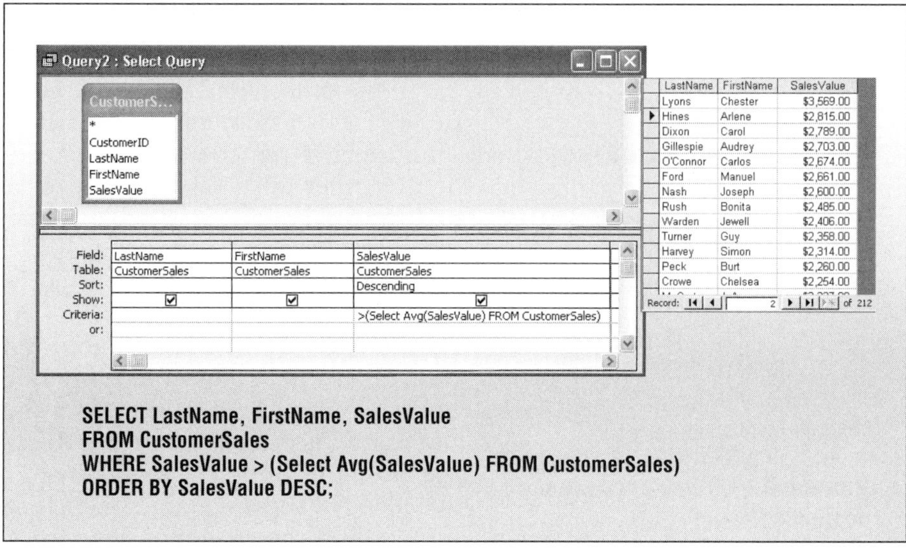

```
SELECT LastName, FirstName, SalesValue
FROM CustomerSales
WHERE SalesValue > (Select Avg(SalesValue) FROM CustomerSales)
ORDER BY SalesValue DESC;
```

FIGURE 5.5

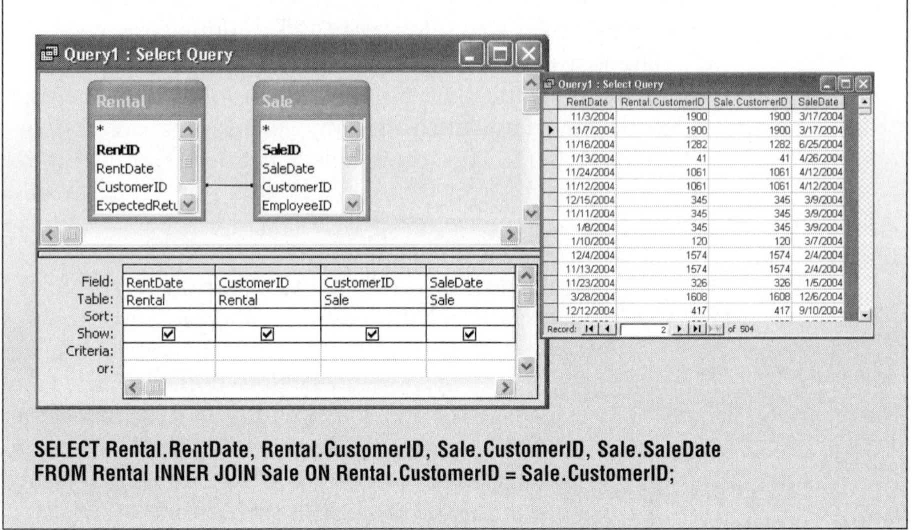

manager want to know if customers who rent equipment also purchase items for sale. As with many questions, there are several different ways to build this query. Figure 5.5 shows the effect of an inner join. Build a new query and add the Rental and Sale tables. Join these tables through CustomerID by dragging and dropping the CustomerID from one table onto the column in the other table. When you display both CustomerID values in the query and run it, you can see that they are the same. The effect of this join is that the results show the customers (ID only) who participated in a sale and a rental—at any time.

If you want to know which customers made a purchase and a rental on the same day, you could add a condition that RentDate equals SaleDate. Or you could add a second join that connects RentDate and SaleDate. Figure 5.6 shows the query with the second join condition. Notice the use of the AND in the join statement. This query demonstrates the effect of the inner join. In many respects, it is equivalent to a WHERE clause. The inner join restricts the rows that you will see by forcing values to be equal.

On the other hand, perhaps Jim would like to see a list of all of the customers who participated in sales, and then check to see which of those have rented items. You need to build a new query. This time include the Customer table so their names can be displayed. Then add the Sale and Rental tables. Delete the join from Customer to Rental. That join would force all of the CustomerIDs to be equal, which is not what Jim wants. Then connect Rental to Sale by CustomerID, but this time, double-click the resulting line to modify the join properties. Figure 5.7 shows the basic query. Select the option to display all of the values from the Sale table and only the matching values from the Rental table. As shown in the SQL, this option sets up a LEFT JOIN, which displays all values in the Sale table (the left table in the SQL query list), even if the customer never rented items. If you have

---

Action

Create a new query in Design view.
Tables: Rental and Sale.
Columns: RentDate, SaleDate, and CustomerID from both tables.
Join the tables on CustomerID.
Run the query.
Join the tables on RentDate=SaleDate.
Run the query.

Action

Create a new query in Design view.
Tables: Customer, Sale, Rental.
Columns: LastName, FirstName, and CustomerID from Sale and Rental.
Delete join from Rental to Customer.
Add join from Sale to Rental.
Double-click this new join.
Select option to include all from Sale.
Run the query.

FIGURE 5.6

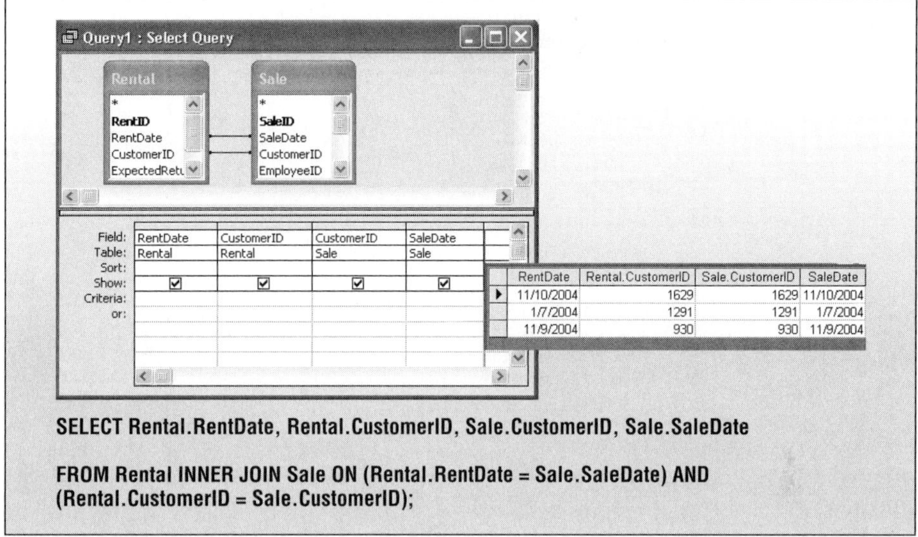

SELECT Rental.RentDate, Rental.CustomerID, Sale.CustomerID, Sale.SaleDate

FROM Rental INNER JOIN Sale ON (Rental.RentDate = Sale.SaleDate) AND
(Rental.CustomerID = Sale.CustomerID);

problems running the query, you might have to remove the Customer table from the query. Sometimes Access cannot figure out how to establish left joins when more than two tables are in the query. In these cases, you build the left join with only two tables, save the query, then create a second query based on the saved query and any other tables needed.

Figure 5.8 shows some of the results from running the query. Notice that several of the rows show missing values for the Rental.CustomerID. These are the customers who purchased items but have never rented an item. If you want to see only this list, you can add the condition that Rental.CustomerID Is Null. Observe that the full list from the main query might not include all of the customers. To review your knowledge of joins, you should be able to identify the customers that might not be in this list. Looking at the design, notice that there is still an inner join between the Customer and

FIGURE 5.7

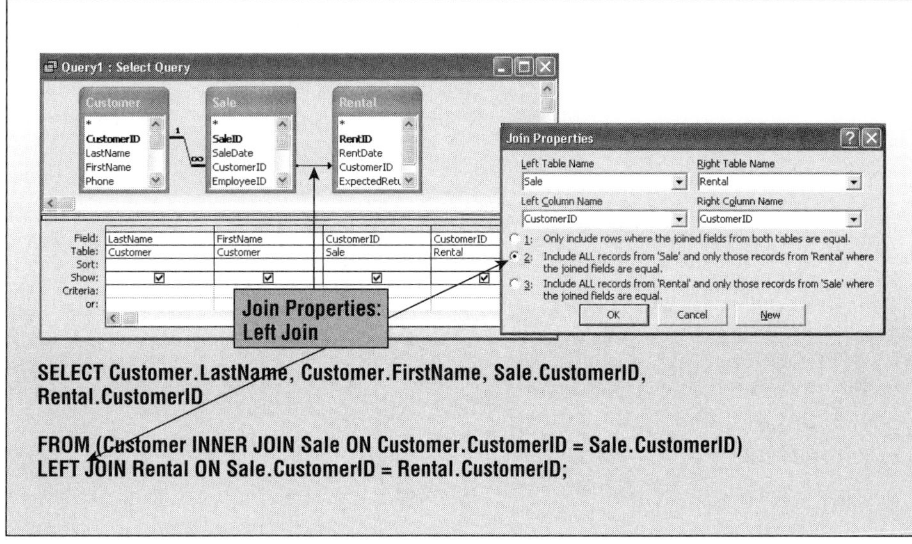

SELECT Customer.LastName, Customer.FirstName, Sale.CustomerID,
Rental.CustomerID

FROM (Customer INNER JOIN Sale ON Customer.CustomerID = Sale.CustomerID)
LEFT JOIN Rental ON Sale.CustomerID = Rental.CustomerID;

FIGURE 5.8

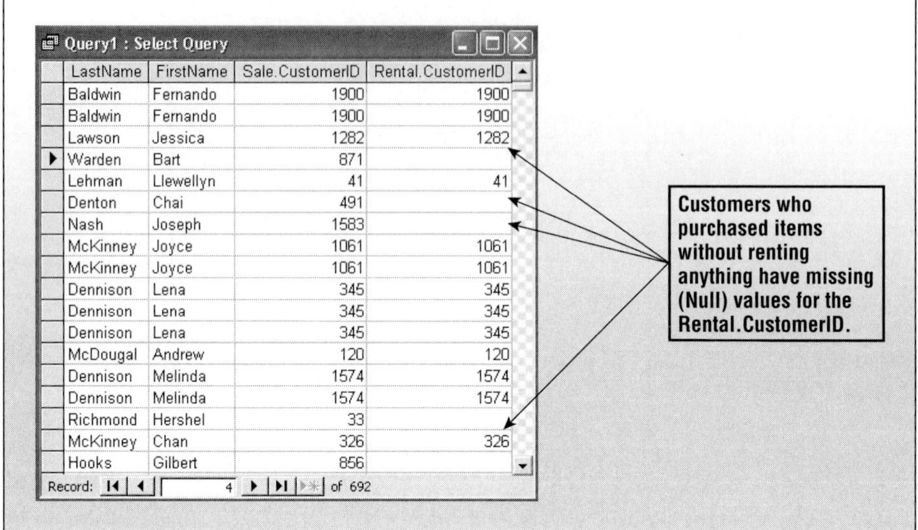

Sale tables. Consequently, customers who have not participated in sales at all will not be displayed in this list. If you truly wanted a list of all customers, you would have to use a left join from the Customer to the Sale table. However, you will probably have to do one of the joins at a time, save the query, and then do the second join.

Recall the question of listing the customers who have purchased items but have not rented anything. With the left join, it is straightforward to get this list by adding the Is Null condition. But you must be very careful when creating this query. If you forget to specify the left join and stick with the standard inner join, the query will indicate that no customers match that condition. The reason for this result is that an inner join automatically leaves out the customers you are searching for. This question can also be answered with a subquery. Figure 5.9 shows the subquery approach. Start a new query and add the Customer and Sale tables. Sort the columns by LastName and

FIGURE 5.9

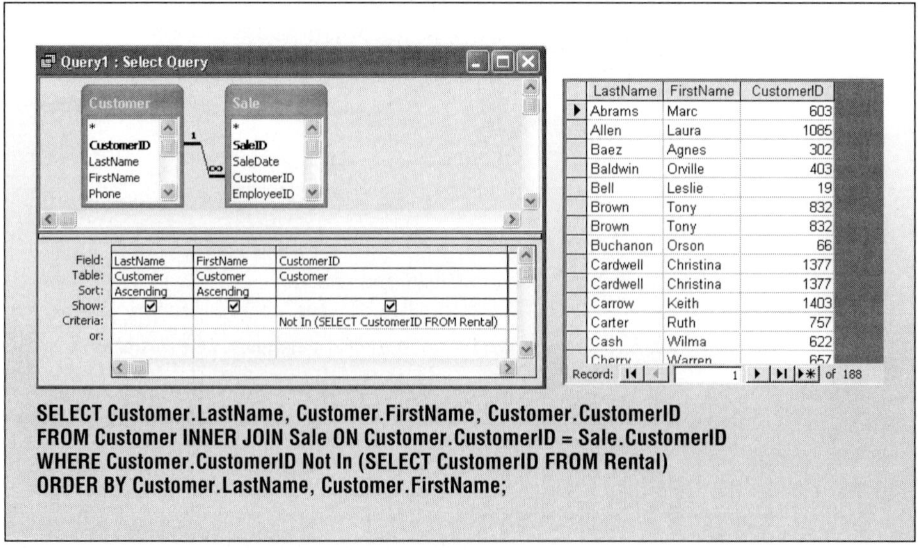

```
SELECT Customer.LastName, Customer.FirstName, Customer.CustomerID
FROM Customer INNER JOIN Sale ON Customer.CustomerID = Sale.CustomerID
WHERE Customer.CustomerID Not In (SELECT CustomerID FROM Rental)
ORDER BY Customer.LastName, Customer.FirstName;
```

> **Action**
>
> Create a new query in Design view.
> Tables: Customer and Sale.
> Columns: LastName, FirstName, and CustomerID.
> Criteria for CustomerID (use SQL): Not In (SELECT CustomerID FROM Rental).
> Check the SQL.
> Run the query.

FirstName. Then add the condition CustomerID Not In (SELECT CustomerID FROM Rental). As always, remember to put the subquery in parentheses. This query will retrieve all Customers who have participated in sales but have not rented any items. You should compare the results from this version to the left join version to ensure that both queries return the same results. Most systems support either method to answer the question, but there can sometimes be performance differences between the two approaches. Access seems to be faster using left join, but you would have to time large sets of data to measure the difference.

Activity: Create Complex Joins

Jim the sales manager is concerned about excess inventory. He wants to be able to monitor the status of quantity on hand (QOH) for all inventory items. He is particularly concerned about identifying which models are selling quickly versus models that have large numbers of items sitting around. Remember that models are product lines from the manufacturers, while individual items are specific sizes within a model group. He wants the totals for the model. To see if there is a problem, construct a new query that totals the quantity on hand and sorts it in descending order by ModelID. Figure 5.10 shows the total QOH for the various models. Save the query as "ModelsOnHand."

> **Action**
>
> Create a new query in Design view.
> Table: Inventory.
> Columns: ModelID and QuantityOnHand.
> Sum the QuantityOnHand and sort it in descending order.
> Run the query.
> Save it as ModelsOnHand.
> Create a new table in Design view.
> Columns: CategoryID, CategoryName, LowLimit, HighLimit.
> Save it as SalesCategory.
> Enter data.

But Jim does not want to wade through the entire query every day. Instead, he is proposing a categorical system, where items with more than a certain QOH will be called slow sellers, and items with minimal QOH will be hot sellers. He also wants a few categories in-between. While you have the tools to build this query, there is one catch: he wants the ability to fine-tune the numbers on the ranges for each category. The solution is to create a new table that defines the category and the upper and lower limits for each category: SalesCategory(<u>CategoryID</u>, CategoryName, LowLimit, HighLimit). If the QOH

FIGURE 5.10

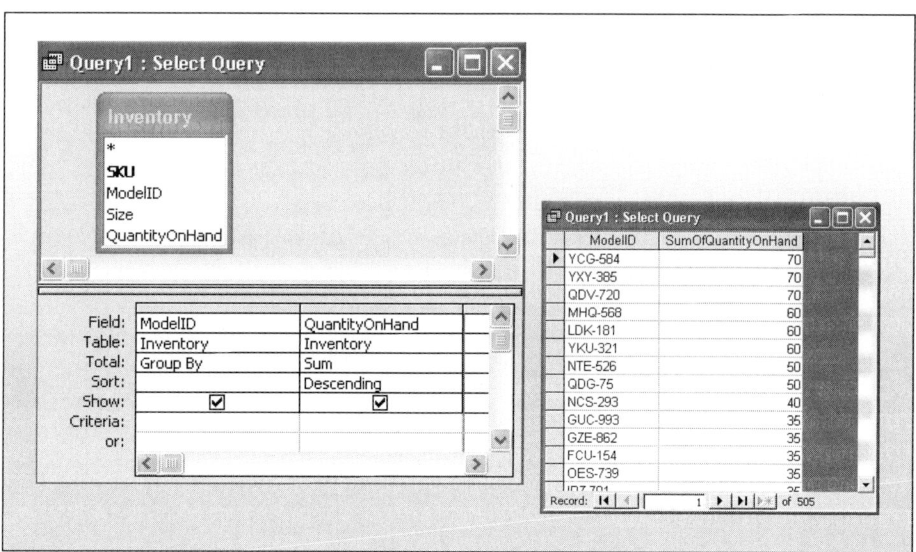

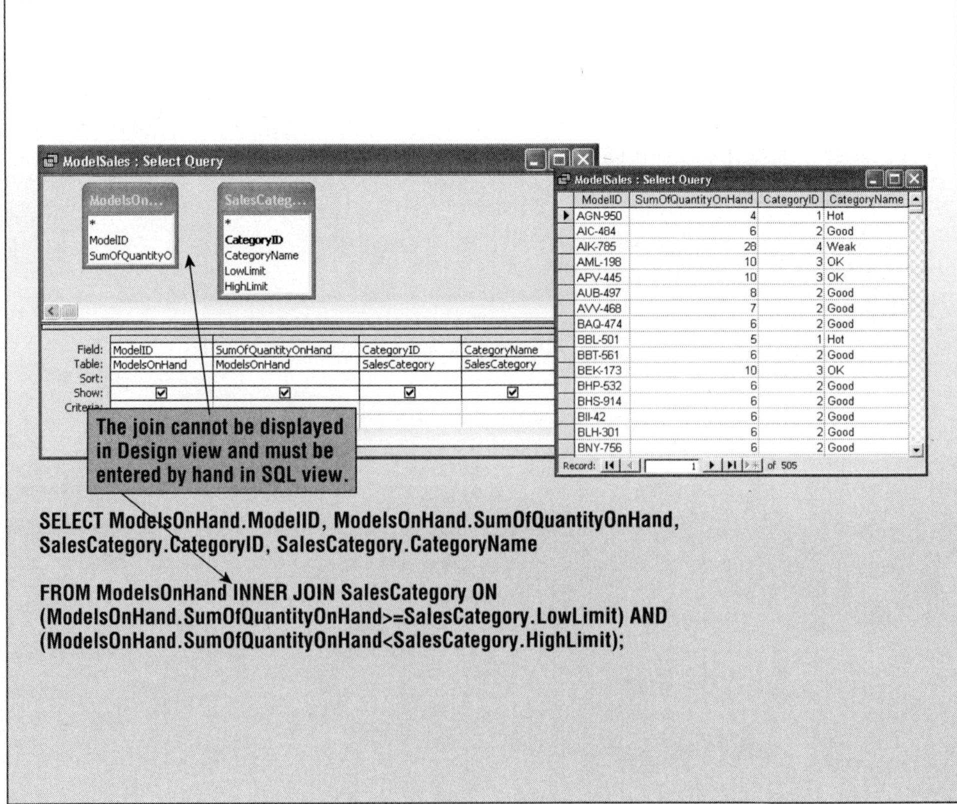

for a model is greater than or equal to the LowLimit and less than the High-Limit, it falls into the specified category. The CategoryID ensures a unique key and could be used to sort the rows if necessary. Figure 5.11 shows the initial categories.

Using the categories in a query requires slightly tricky join conditions. You need to use inequality (theta) joins. Begin with a new query based on the ModelsOnHand query and the SalesCategory table. Display the ModelID and SumOfQuantityOnHand along with the CategoryName. But do not attempt to join the tables in Design view. Instead, switch to **SQL** view and modify the FROM clause to match the Figure 5.12 inequality join statement. Access

FIGURE 5.12

FIGURE 5.13

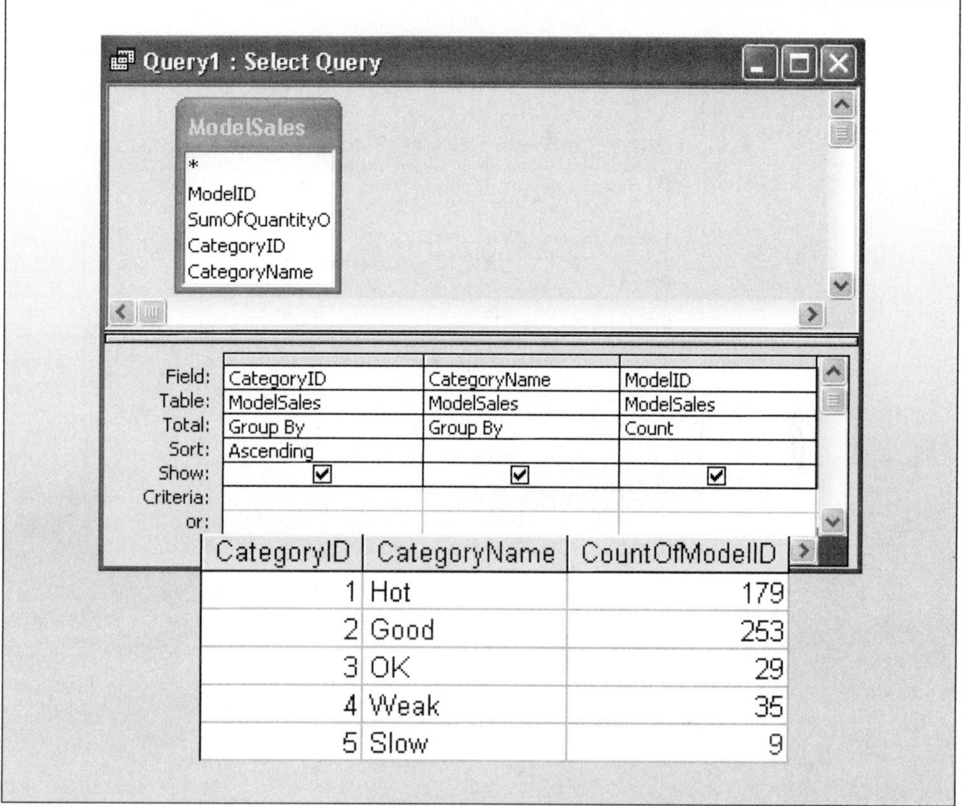

Field:	CategoryID	CategoryName	ModelID
Table:	ModelSales	ModelSales	ModelSales
Total:	Group By	Group By	Count
Sort:	Ascending		
Show:	☑	☑	☑
Criteria:			
or:			

CategoryID	CategoryName	CountOfModelID
1	Hot	179
2	Good	253
3	OK	29
4	Weak	35
5	Slow	9

Action
Create a new query in Design view. Tables: ModelsOnHand and SalesCategory. Columns: ModelID, SumOfQuantityOnHand, CategoryID, and CategoryName. In SQL view add the inequality join. Run the query.

can handle inequality joins but cannot display or edit them in Design view. Figure 5.12 also shows the sample result from the query. Save the query as ModelSales so Jim can perform some additional analysis on the data.

Jim might create a new simpler query that counts the number of models that fall within each of the categories. Figure 5.13 shows the basic query. It is built simply using the results of the previous query. This query hides the complicated details as Jim needs to see only the simple data results. The final aggregation query uses the CategoryID to sort the results logically; otherwise, they would be sorted alphabetically by the category name. Fortunately, most of the models appear to be in the categories indicating that they sell relatively quickly. Although the category definitions might not be accurate, Jim can quickly alter the range numbers and rerun the query to see the results.

Activity: Combine Data Rows with UNION

You need to understand the role of the UNION command. It is designed to combine rows from multiple queries. Read that line carefully. It says combine *rows* not *columns*. If you have two queries that retrieve similar columns of data, the UNION statement will combine the results into one set of data. To illustrate the process, consider a request that Katy made to see a single list of customers who purchased items in January or in March. You could build this query using simple WHERE conditions, but if you want to list

FIGURE 5.14

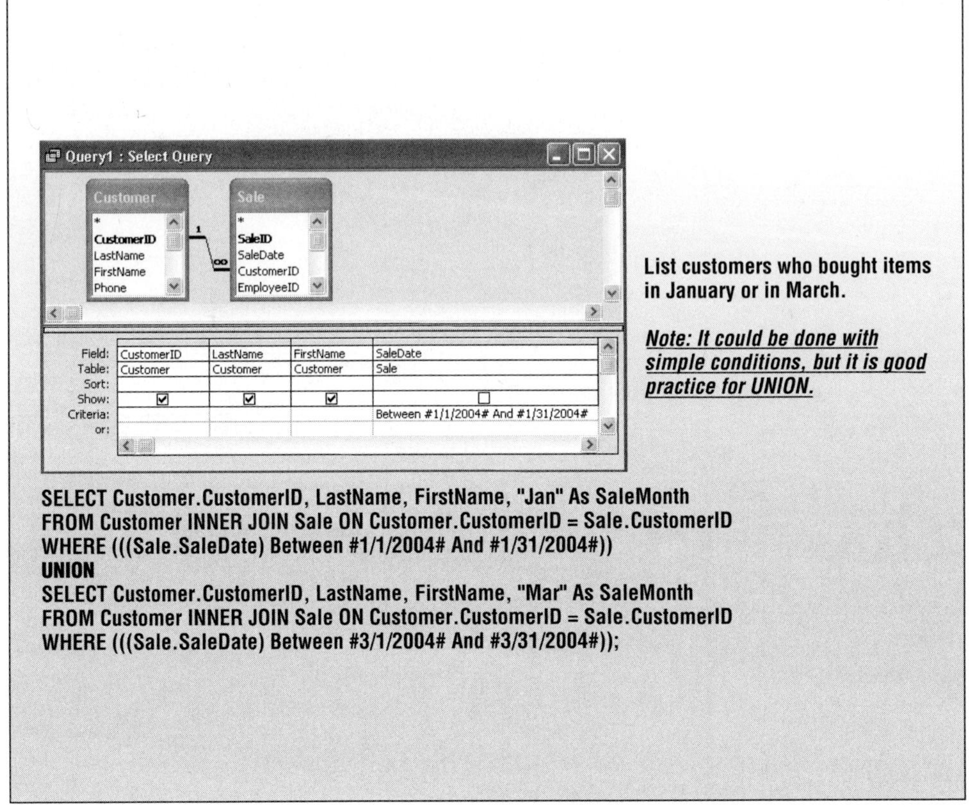

Action

Create a new query in Design view.
Tables: Customer and Sale.
Columns: CustomerID, LastName, FirstName, and SaleDate.
Set January sale date in criteria row.
Switch to SQL.
Copy the entire statement.
Add the word *Union*.
Paste the SELECT statement and change the date condition to March.
Run the query.

people twice if they bought items both in January and in March, the UNION query is easier.

As shown in Figure 5.14, create a new query using the Customer and Sale tables. Display the CustomerID, Last-Name, and FirstName columns. Add the SaleDate column, but uncheck the box to display the date. Add the condition to select sales only in January. If you run the query at this point, you will see a list of customers who bought items in January. To get the March customers, switch to SQL view. Mark the entire SQL statement and copy it. Delete the semicolon at the end, add the word *UNION* after the existing query, then below that, paste a copy of the query. Now modify the dates in this copy to indicate March instead of January. Finally, in the first SELECT statement (January), add a computed column to display "Jan" As SaleMonth. Do the same thing for the second SELECT statement, but display "Mar" for March. This column will identify each row to indicate the month for the sale. Run the query, and you will see a combination of rows from both queries. If you want to sort the data by Customer or by date, first you will have to save the query, then you can build a second query based on the first and sort the columns as needed.

Activity: Create Parameter Queries

Parameter queries are useful when you need to create a query that a manager runs on a regular basis but needs to change some of the constraints.

FIGURE 5.15

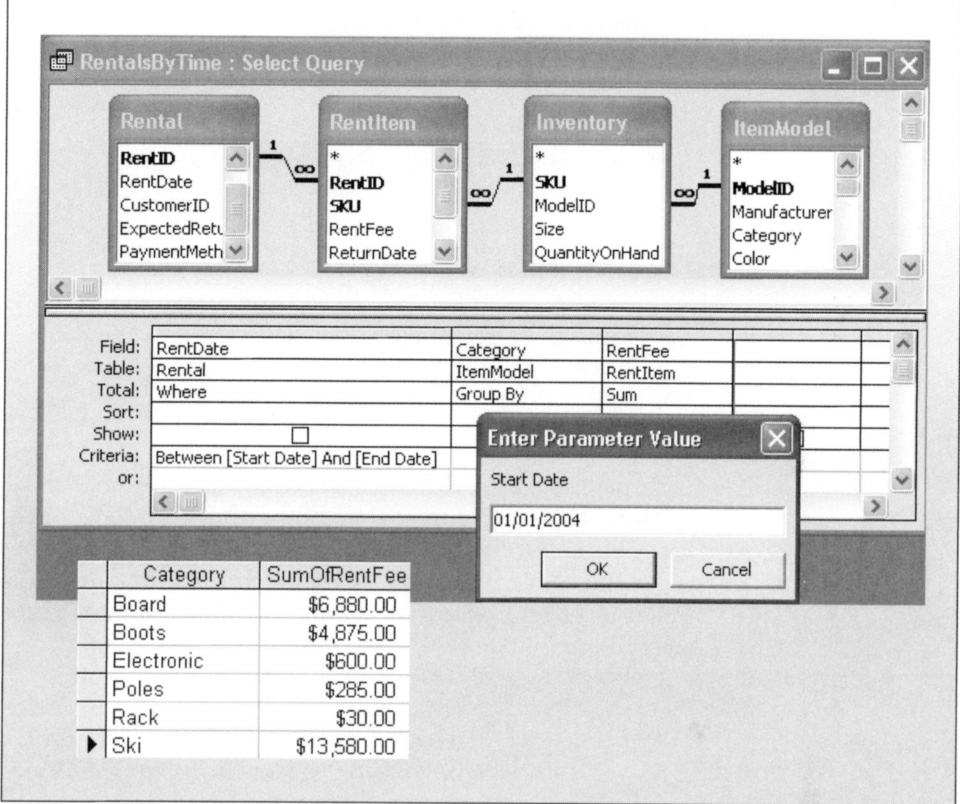

For instance, you often use parameters to set starting and ending dates so the manager can easily select a range of data without having to know anything about building queries. The example in Figure 5.15 shows a query that displays the total rental income by Category for a specified range of dates. Save the query as RentalsByTime, so David the rental manager can run the query whenever he needs. When the query is run, two boxes pop up to request the starting date and ending date.

> **Action**
>
> Create a new query in Design view.
> Tables: Rental, RentItem, Inventory, and ItemModel.
> Columns: RentDate, Category, RentFee.
> Set totals to sum RentFee.
> Set "Where" and criteria for RentDate to Between [Start Date] And [End Date].
> Run the query.

You can build complex queries and insert parameters to request specific data from the person running the query. In your query, simply enter a brief description in brackets, and treat that parameter as any other number or date. When the query runs, the user will enter a value and it will be applied to the query. It is a useful method to quickly build queries that users can control without having to alter the query.

SQL Data Definition and Data Manipulation

Activity: Create Tables

Although Access makes it easy to create and delete tables using the visual designer, sometimes you will need to know how to create a table using the data definition language (DDL) CREATE TABLE command. After working with the database for a while, you realize that it would be nice to have a separate table that lists salespeople and other contacts at the manufacturers.

FIGURE 5.16

```
CREATE TABLE Contacts
(
    ContactID          Long,
    ManufacturerID     Long,
    LastName           Text(25),
    FirstName          Text(25),
    Phone              Text(15),
    Email              Text(120),
      CONSTRAINT pk_Contacts PRIMARY KEY (ContactID),
      CONSTRAINT fk_ContactsManufacturer FOREIGN KEY
      (ManufacturerID)
        REFERENCES Manufacturer(ManufacturerID)
)
;
```

Each person has a direct phone number and an e-mail address. To practice building tables, Figure 5.16 shows the CREATE TABLE command for the new Contacts table. Essentially, you list each desired column along with its data type. Note that you have to choose the basic data type, and not the higher-level type you might select in the designer. For instance, you have to enter "Long" instead of just "Number."

Action
Create a new query in Design view.
Do not select any tables.
Switch to SQL view.
Enter the **CREATE TABLE** command.
Run the query.

To enter the code, you must open the SQL Query window. Create a new query and close the Table Selection window without choosing any tables. Then click the SQL button or select it from the View option. Delete any statements in the window and type the CREATE TABLE query as shown.

You should also create the primary key constraint to indicate the ContactID is the sole primary key column. If you need multiple columns, simply create a comma-separated list. The foreign key constraint is similar, but you must also specify the table and column that is referenced by the foreign key. The Access 2002 version does not support the ON DELETE CASCADE or ON UPDATE CASCADE options for the foreign key, so you should add them by hand in the relationships screen. If you have a more recent version of Access, you should try adding these two lines immediately after the foreign key constraint to see if support has been added. To run the query, you must use the exclamation point Run button. You can only run this query one time; otherwise it will try to create duplicate copies of the same table with the same name—which is not allowed.

Generally with Access, it is easier to create tables with the design screen. However, sometimes you will want to create temporary tables—eventually within a section of program code. For the next section, you will need a temporary table to transfer data. Figure 5.17 shows the table that you need to create.

FIGURE 5.17

```
CREATE TABLE MyTemp
(
    ID        Long,
    LName     Text(25),
    FName     Text(25),
);
```

FIGURE 5.18

```
INSERT INTO Customer (LastName, FirstName, City, Gender)
VALUES ('Jones', 'Jack', 'Nowhere', 'Male');
```

The **SQL ALTER TABLE** command can also be used to add new columns to an existing table. However, you rarely need this command, since it is easier to use the table design view in Access to add a new column to a table.

Activity: Insert, Update, and Delete Data

SQL also provides data manipulation language (DML) commands to insert, update, and delete rows of data. Consider the INSERT command first. The simple version of the command shown in Figure 5.18 inserts a single row into one table. Notice that you specify the table columns in the first list and the corresponding values in the second list. By listing the column names, you choose to enter the data in any order and to skip columns. Of course, you will rarely enter data this way, but occasionally it comes in handy. More importantly, the SQL statement can be generated using programming code with complex routines to extract data from one source, clean it up, and transfer it to the desired table.

On the other hand, a second version of the INSERT command is more useful because of its power. You use it to transfer large blocks of data from one table into a second table. Note that the second table must already exist. The example in Figure 5.19 copies some data from the Customer table and transfers it to the temporary MyTemp table you created in the previous section. Again, you list the columns for the new table that will hold the data, then write a SELECT statement that retrieves matching data for those columns.

You should keep in mind that the SELECT statement can be as complex as you wish. It can include calculations, multiple tables, complex WHERE conditions, and subqueries. For complex queries you should first build the SELECT statement on its own and test it to ensure that it retrieves exactly the data you want. Then switch to the SQL view and add the INSERT INTO line at the top. The ability to perform calculations has another benefit. You can add a constant to the SELECT statement that will be inserted as data into the second table. For example, you might write SELECT ID, Name, "West" to insert a region name into a new table. The INSERT INTO command is useful when you need to expand a database or add new tables. You can quickly copy selected rows and columns of data into a new table.

> **Action**
>
> Create a new query in Design view.
> Do not select any tables.
> Switch to SQL view.
> Type the INSERT command: INSERT INTO Customer (LastName, FirstName, City, Gender) VALUES ('Jones', 'Jack', 'Nowhere', 'Male');.
> Run the query.

FIGURE 5.19

```
INSERT INTO MyTemp (ID, LName, FName)
   SELECT CustomerID, LastName, FirstName
   FROM Customer
   WHERE City='Sacramento'
;
```

<table>
<tr><td>

Action

Create a new query in Design view.
Table: ItemModel.
Columns: Category, ModelYear, and Cost.
Criteria: Category:="Board" And ModelYear=2004.
Run the query.
Choose Query/Update Query.
Under Cost set Update To: Round([Cost]*1.04,2).
Run the query.

</td></tr>
</table>

The UPDATE command is used to change individual values for specified rows. It is a powerful command that affects many rows. You must always be cautious when using this command because it can quickly change thousands of rows of data. To illustrate the power of the command, consider that the manufacturers have announced that costs will increase by 4 percent for the 2004 boards. The ItemModel table contains an estimate of the Cost for each model, so you need to increase this number by 4 percent, but only for the boards.

To be safe, begin by creating a query that displays the Cost for the 2004 boards. You should run the query to ensure that it returns exactly the data that you want to update. Next, as shown in Figure 5.20, select the Query/Update Query option on the main menu to display the Update To row on the grid. In the Cost field, enter the new calculation as Round([Cost] * 1.04, 2) to indicate the 4 percent cost increase. Note that you will have to type the brackets around the Cost column name. If you do not, Access might place the entire formula in quotes, which would result in an attempt to write the formula text into the column instead of the actual values. The Round function is used to ensure that the final Cost value is rounded off to cents instead of extended fractions. You can run the query by clicking the Run button on the main toolbar.

FIGURE 5.20

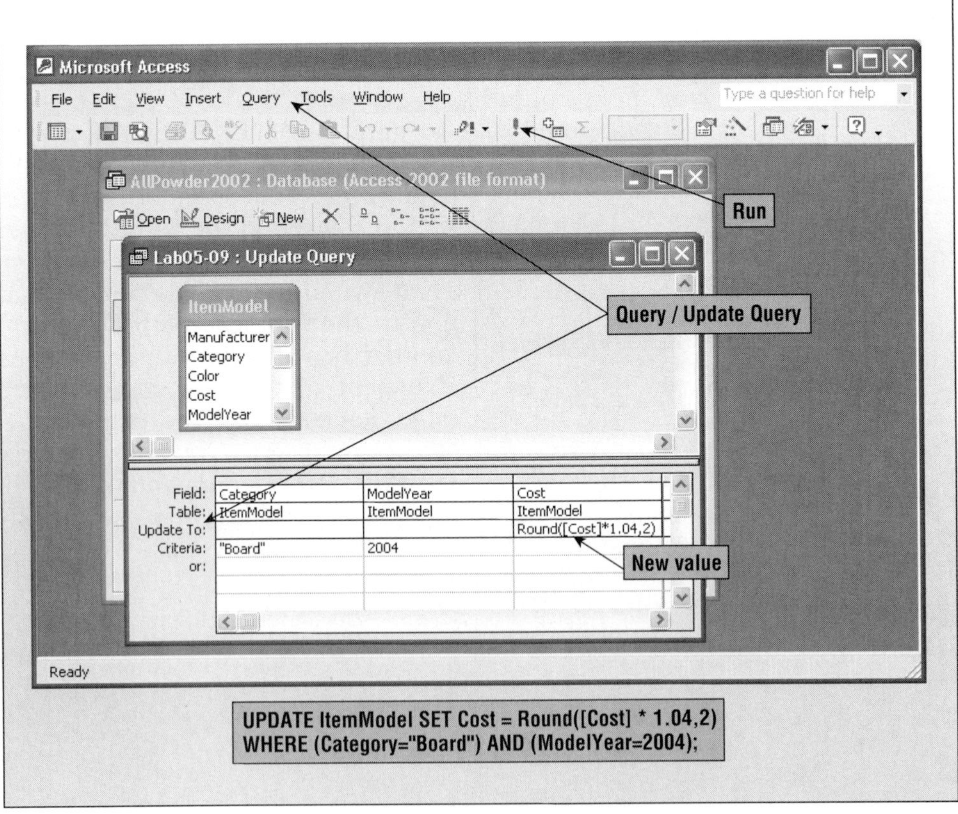

Notice that the SQL statement is straightforward. It is also easy to change multiple columns at one time. On the grid, just add the new column and the new formula. In SQL, add a comma after the first calculation and enter a new one in the SET clause. Of course, you can use multiple tables. In SQL, they are added with the standard join statement, but it is generally easier to add the tables in the Design view grid and let Access build the join statement. If necessary, you can then switch to SQL to modify the lines.

The DELETE command is similar to the INSERT and UPDATE commands, but it is more dangerous. It is designed to delete many rows of data at a time. Keep in mind that because of the relationships, when you delete a row from one table, it can trigger cascade deletes on additional tables. For the most part, these deletes are permanent. If you are not careful, you could wipe out a large chunk of your data with one delete command. To minimize the impact of these problems, you should always make backup copies of your database—particularly before you attempt major delete operations. You should probably take a break and do that now. Use Windows to copy the main database file.

<table>
<tr><td>

Action

Create a new query in Design view.
Table: MyTemp.
Columns: ID, LastName, FirstName.
Criteria: ID > 100.
Test the query.
Choose Query/Delete Query.
Run the query.

</td></tr>
</table>

To be extra safe, this example is just going to delete data from the temporary table that was created in the previous section. Create a new query in Design view using the MyTemp table. To see the rows you are going to delete, add all three columns to the display and set a condition to show only rows with an ID > 100. You can then use the Query/Delete Query option to set up the delete query. If you switch to the SQL view, you will see that the individual columns are listed. These columns are not necessary because the query will always delete the entire row. Figure 5.21 shows both the Design view and the basic SQL needed to delete the specified rows. In practice, it is best to stick with simple WHERE clauses when possible. However, it can be complex and include

FIGURE 5.21

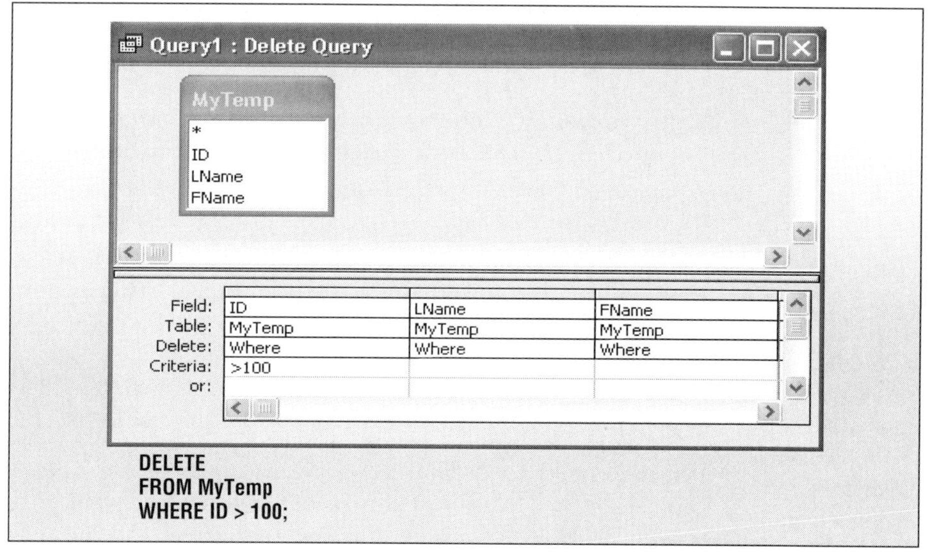

FIGURE 5.22

```
DROP TABLE MyTemp;
```

subqueries. Particularly in the complex cases, you should first build a SELECT statement using the same WHERE clause to ensure that you are deleting exactly the rows you want to delete. Then convert the query into a Delete Query, or delete the SELECT statement and replace it with the DELETE command.

The DROP TABLE command is even more dangerous. It removes the entire table and all of its data. Generally, you should only use it for temporary tables. As shown in Figure 5.22, the syntax is straightforward; just make sure you enter the correct table name. Again, it would be wise to make a backup copy of your database before removing tables.

The main aspect to remember about these commands is that they operate on sets of rows that you control with the WHERE clause. The WHERE clause can be complex and can include subqueries with detailed SELECT commands. All of the power of the SELECT command is available to you to control inserting, updating, and deleting rows of data.

Exercises

Many Charms

You will need to create some additional sample data for each table. Madison and Samantha know that they will want certain information on a weekly basis, but they will not be able to build complex queries to retrieve the data. You will have to build a few queries for them that they can run when they want to see the results or need to change prices. Some of the queries should be parameter queries so they can easily select the values they need to control the results. *Note:* You will have to modify the queries slightly to match the data that you have entered.

1. Which customers who ordered bracelets have not ordered necklaces?
2. Which customers bought more gold charms than silver ones?
3. Which categories generated the most profit over a parameterized time period?
4. Are expensive charms more profitable than mid-priced or low-priced charms? *Hint:* Create categories based on the prices.
5. Create a parameterized query to enable Samantha to increase the prices of a certain category of charms by a given percentage.
6. Create a new table with SQL and copy into it all of the customers who have not purchased items within the last three months.
7. Delete customers from the new table in the prior exercise who have spent more than $100 in the past year.

Standup Foods

You will need to create some additional sample data for each table. Laura knows she will want certain information on a weekly basis, but she will not be able to build complex queries to retrieve the data. You will have to build a few queries for her that can be run to display results or change prices. Some of the queries should be parameter queries so Laura can easily select the values she needs to control the results. *Note:* You will have to modify the queries slightly to match the data that you have entered.

1. Identify the employees who have below-average overall job evaluations.
2. Identify the main menu items that have not been served to a particular director or other celebrity. (Pick one from your list who wants something different.)
3. Which customers have not yet referred her business to other clients?
4. Create a category table to segment the employee ratings (excellent, good, average, poor). Use the table to identify the employees with excellent evaluations as both server and dishwasher.
5. Create a temporary table and copy into it information about employees who have worked as drivers but have not driven within the last month.
6. Delete from the temporary table in the previous question the drivers whose average evaluations are less than 6 (on the 10-point scale).
7. Write a parameterized query that enables Laura to increase the base wage rate of employees by specifying a category, a minimum overall average evaluation, and the percentage increase.

EnviroSpeed

You will need to create some additional sample data for each table. Brennan and Tyler know that they will want certain information on a weekly basis, but they will not be able to build complex queries to retrieve the data. You will have to build a few queries for them that they can run when they want to see the results or need to change prices. Some of the queries should be parameter queries so they can easily select the values they need to control the results. *Note:* You will have to modify the queries slightly to match the data that you have entered.

1. List the experts who have worked with two or more crews in the same month.
2. Which experts have not contributed any documents within the last three months?
3. List the crews that are more than 25 percent larger than the average crew.
4. Create a table to categorize the expense of cleanups. For example, spills costing more than $1 million to clean up are expensive; cleanups costing $500,000 to $1 million are merely costly; and so on. Create a query to apply these categories to the actual spills.
5. Write a query that retrieves documents based on a list of keywords entered by a user. The keywords might appear anywhere in the document, and the final query should sort the list based on the number of matches.
6. Write a parameterized query to update a severity value for an incident by allowing the user to enter a chemical name and a point increase in severity.
7. Write a query to copy the data on experts to a new table who have participated in a total of at least three incidents in the last year.

Final Project

The main textbook has an appendix with several longer case studies. You should be able to work on one of these cases throughout the term. If you or your instructor picks one, answer the questions below. You will have to create sample data for each of the tables.

1. Identify and create at least two parameter queries that would be useful to managers. Share the business question (not the query) with other students and solve their queries.
2. Identify a business question to list items greater (or less) than average. Write the query to return the results.
3. Create a temporary table and write a query to copy some rows of data from one table into the new table.
4. Write a delete query to remove a few rows of data from the temporary table.
5. Write an update query using parameters to change the value of one of the numeric columns in a table based on a percentage and conditions entered by the user.

Chapter 6

Forms, Reports, and Applications

Chapter Outline

Objectives

Applications

Case: All Powder Board and Ski Shop

Lab Exercise

All Powder Board and Ski Shop Forms
All Powder Basic Reports
Building the All Powder Application

Exercises

Final Project

Objectives

- Create forms (main, grid, and subforms) that make it easy for users to enter data.
- Create reports to display and summarize data.
- Build applications that connect forms and reports.
- Add toolbars and menus to forms.
- Add Help files to the database application.

Applications

The main purpose of the DBMS is to store data efficiently and provide queries to retrieve data to answer business questions. But from the perspective of businesses, the true value of the DBMS lies in the applications that can be built on top of the database. One of the strengths of Access is the tools provided to build forms, reports, and applications. Once the database is designed, you can use the wizards to quickly build common business applications.

Forms are used to make it easier for users to enter data. You would never want users to enter data directly into the tables. For example, look again at the Sales table (see page 67). It contains mostly ID numbers, and you cannot expect workers to memorize thousands of ID numbers. Instead, you build forms to match the processes and styles of the business. Likewise, you rarely ask managers to build queries themselves; rather, you create reports that display details and subtotals within a layout that is easy to read. You can even include charts to make it easy to compare values or examine trends over time.

A finished application contains all of the forms and reports needed to solve a particular problem. It also needs finishing touches such as menus and other navigation links between forms. Additionally, you usually have to create Help files to provide assistance to users when they first learn the system.

Case: All Powder Board and Ski Shop

The primary application at All Powder Board and Ski Shop is the need to track sales and rentals. Of course, these applications also require you to build forms and reports for inventory items and customers as well. Eventually you will have forms that store data into each of the tables in the relationship diagram. However, before you leap to the Forms wizard, make sure you understand the three major form types shown in Figure 6.1: main

FIGURE 6.1

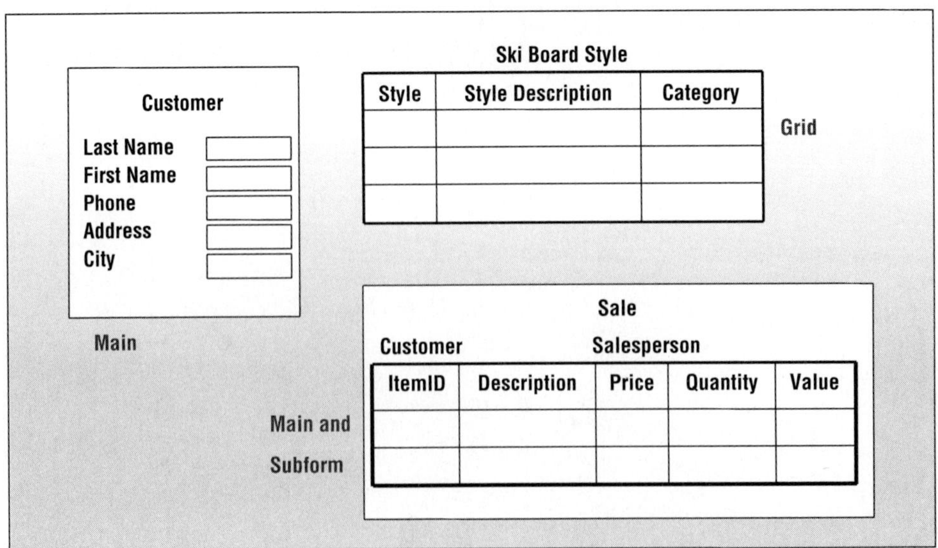

form, grid form, and main with subform. A main form shows one row of data at a time, such as a form to edit basic information about one customer. A grid form appears similar to the Table view in that it shows several rows at one time. Main and subforms combine the two: The main form shows one row of data from one table and the grid subform shows matching rows from a related table. The classic business example is the Sale form and SaleItem grid, where the main form shows data from one sale and the grid shows the repeating items purchased and stored in the SaleItem table. At this point, your responsibility is to examine the business operations and determine the best type of form to handle each operation.

Lab Exercise

All Powder Board and Ski Shop Forms

Many of the forms in an application are straightforward main forms. Users want to see data for one row—such as one customer or one employee. You generally create main forms when you need more control over the layout.

Activity: Create Basic Main Forms

Figure 6.2 shows a simple version of the form to edit customer data. In its simplest layout, the main form contains labels and text boxes for each column in the table. You can enter any text into the label to help tell the user what data is to be entered into each text box. The data on the form is bound to the database table. Changes made to the data in the text boxes are automatically written to the database table. However, these changes are written only at certain times—such as when the user moves to a new row. The importance of the main form is that you have considerable control over the layout and presentation of the items. You can change the image of the form by setting the properties for the form or the controls to control things such as

FIGURE 6.2

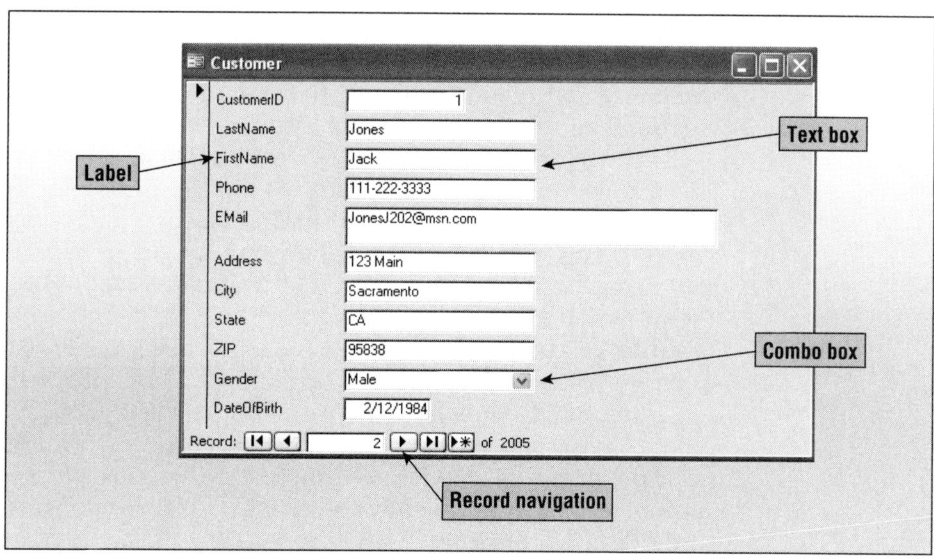

FIGURE 6.3

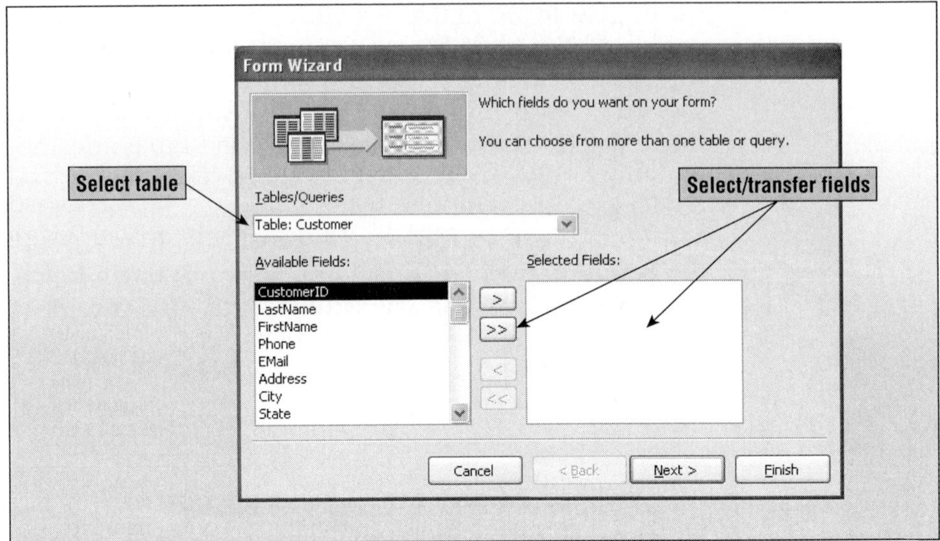

size, position, and color. You can add new controls to display images or include buttons to delete or find records.

Creating a main form is straightforward using the wizard. To build the Customer form, create a new form using the Form wizard. Figure 6.3 shows the most important step of the wizard: choosing the tables and fields. For this form, select the Customer table and choose all of its columns by transferring them to the box on the right. In the next step, select the Columnar form, which is how Access describes the main form type. Then you can select the overall style. If you are ambitious, you can create your own template styles for other developers in your company to use. The style simply applies some basic design elements to the form, such as font size and background colors. For the most part, you want to pick a style that is easy to read.

Action
Start the Form wizard.
Select the Customer table.
Transfer all columns to the right window.
Use the Columnar layout.
Select a style.
Enter a name for the form.

Also, be sure that you remain consistent. All of the forms in an application should have the same style. Figure 6.2 shows a Customer form that should be similar to yours. If you finish the wizard and realize that you made a mistake or simply want to change the design, the easiest way to make the change is to delete the form and start over.

The wizard does a decent job of displaying the data for the form, but invariably you will want to modify the design of the form. Sometimes you simply need to change the layout, formatting, and colors. At other times you want to add buttons to open additional forms or reports, or to add or delete data rows. As shown in Figure 6.4, you can switch to Design view to edit the details of the form and its controls. Right-click a control, the form background, or the small square in the top-left corner of the form to set the various properties. The property box shows you which properties can be set for each item and helps you select the appropriate values. The toolbox contains additional controls that you can place on the form. The field list box is a quick way to add a standard data field to the form. For example, if you delete one of the existing fields and its label, you can open the field list box and drag the field back onto the form.

FIGURE 6.4

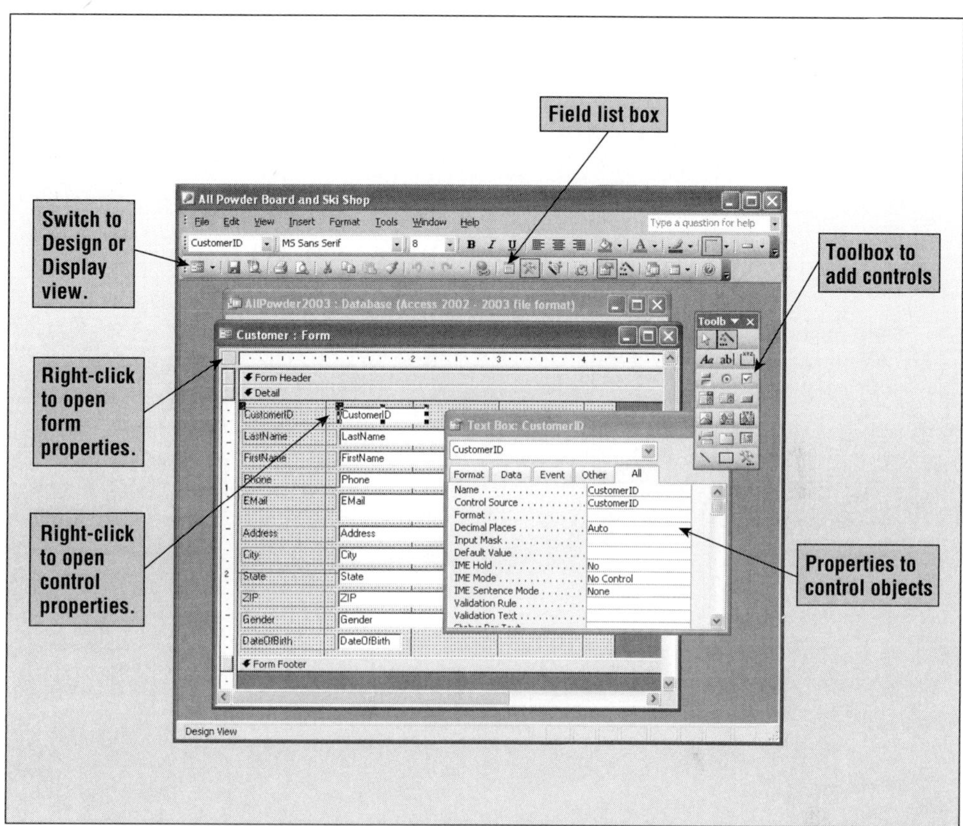

To understand how the form works, you should look at two main properties: the Record Source for the form and the Control Source for a text box. As shown in Figure 6.5, in this example, the Record Source is the Customer table and the Control Source is the CustomerID. The Record Source is a table or query that retrieves all of the columns that can be displayed and edited on the form. The field list box uses this query to show you the fields available to be placed on the form. In this example, remember that only the Customer table was selected when the form was created. You could have added columns from additional tables, in which case the Record Source would be a query. You can still make changes—simply click the Ellipses button (. . .) and you will be shown a query edit screen in which you can add more tables and columns. However, you must be careful to make sure the query is updatable. The main trick is to use the primary key from only one table. You can pull in other columns from additional tables, but use the primary key from only one table. This condition is critical to understanding the role of forms: Each form is designed to edit only one table at a time. You can stretch that statement a little and actually change some data values in several tables, but the main form should only be used to add data rows to a single table. Once you have the table or query chosen, you can set the Control Source for each individual control. Of course, it is much easier to let the wizard or the field list box do the work, but once in a while you might have to edit a Control Source—particularly if you go back and change the name of a column in a table.

FIGURE 6.5

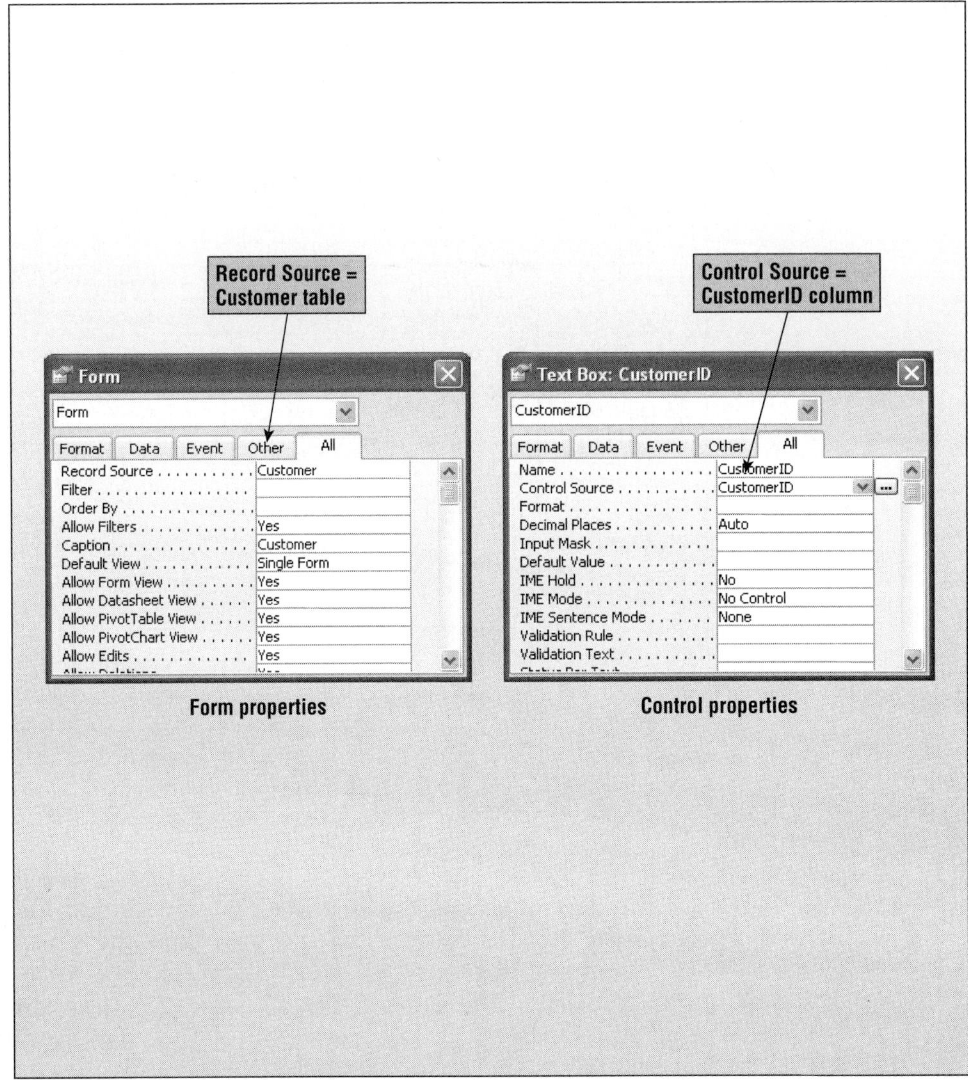

Adding labels and command buttons to the form is a common step. For instance, you probably want to add a label to the top of the form, enter a title, and set its properties to select a larger, more colorful font. These properties can also be set using the buttons on the design toolbar. If you run the form, you will see that the menu provides options to delete and add rows, but users sometimes forget to check the menu. It is often useful to place buttons on the form to delete and add new rows of data. To begin the process in Design view, select the command button in the toolbox and click a desired location on the form. Figure 6.6 shows the main command button wizard screen. It provides many common options that you might want to use on a form. In this case, select the Record Operations and then Delete Record options. You can use one of the default icons or enter a word that will be placed on the button.

Action
Switch Customer form to Design view.
Add a label as a form title.
Add a Command button.
Select Record Operation/Delete Record.
Add a Command button to insert records.
Run the form and test the buttons.
View/Tab Order and verify the sequence.
Save the form.

FIGURE 6.6

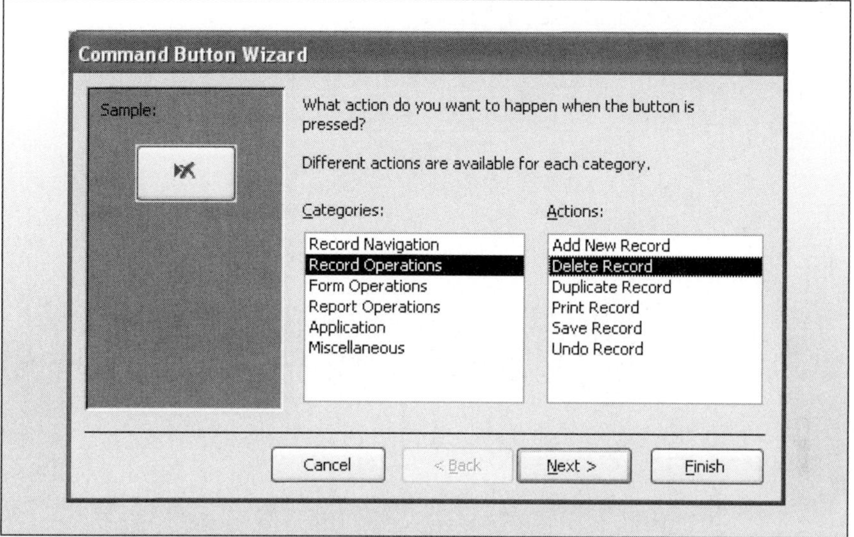

The wizard writes the code necessary to carry out the desired command. This code is stored in a subroutine on the form, and you should give it a descriptive name so you can find it later if needed. In this case, cmdDelete is a useful name, where the cmd prefix indicates that the routine is tied to a command button. The wizard then creates the button and the necessary code. If you selected an icon for the button, set the button's tooltip property to add a short description of the button's role. In this case, "Delete this customer" is a good start. It will be displayed when the user rolls the cursor over the button. Follow the same procedure to create a button to add a new customer. To see the code that was created, you can use the menu option View/Code, or right-click on a button and select Build Event. The actual code is not important right now, but later, you might want to write similar code or modify this code to add more intelligent processing to your form.

One last element of the form is important. The controls have a tab order that specifies how the focus shifts when the user presses the Enter or Tab keys. Generally, the tab order should be set so that the user's focus moves from the top to the bottom of the form. When you add controls to a form, this order is often altered. Use the View/Tab order option to rearrange the sequence.

Activity: Create Grid Forms

Grid forms are another simple type of form. They are used when a table has a limited number of columns and rows. The columns should all fit on one screen because users find it difficult to edit data if they have to scroll horizontally. The number of rows should be limited because the grid form has few methods for searching, and users should not be forced to scroll through thousands of rows to change one piece of data. Figure 6.7 shows an initial grid form for the SkiBoardStyle table. Notice that the data in this table is generally used only to provide consistent values to other tables. This form will generally be used only by an administrator once in a while to modify or add a style. The data all fit on one screen, making it easy for you to find the items to be altered and to compare the various entries across the rows. In

FIGURE 6.7

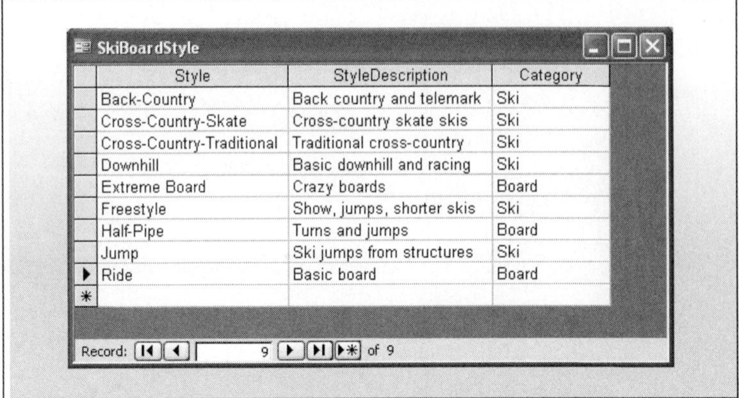

practice, you will use grid forms for similar tasks aimed at administration. Think hard before you use one of these forms for general users. Although you have some control over the form design, your options are limited, so users need to know what they are doing.

You create a grid form in much the same way as a main form. Start the wizard, select the table, and choose the columns you want on the form. As shown in Figure 6.8, the different step is to select the Datasheet option. You could also choose the Tabular style, which provides a few more design

FIGURE 6.8

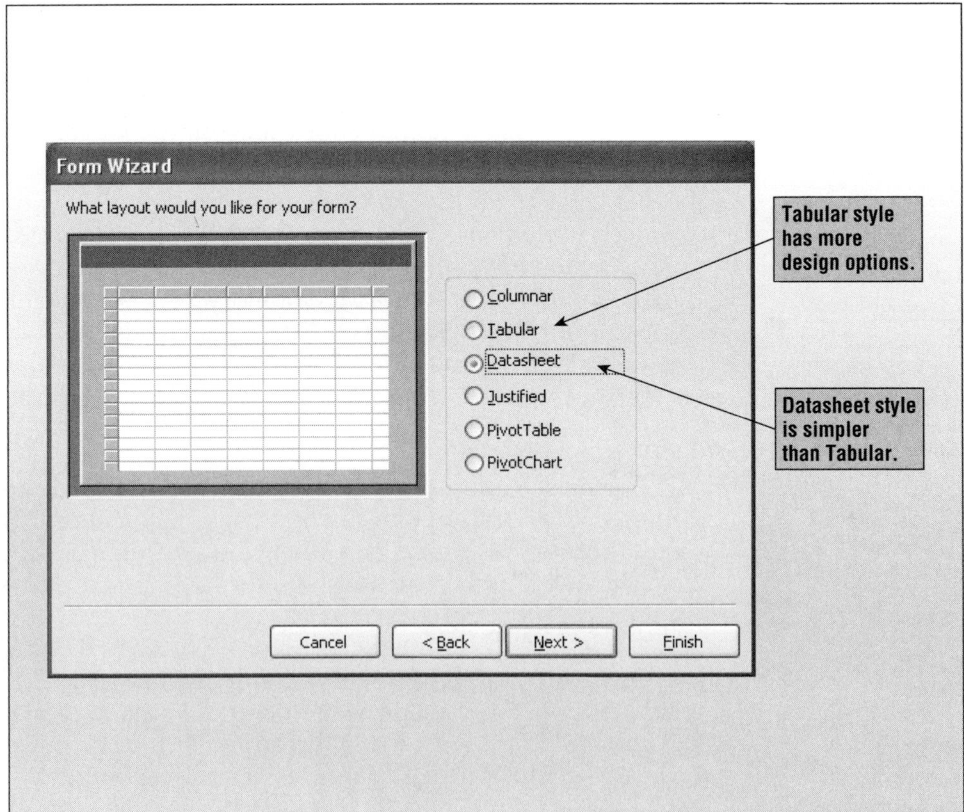

options but tends to have thicker lines between rows and columns. The datasheet style is similar to editing data directly in a table, but you can impose more limits and controls on the user. So, if you find that you want to give users the ability to edit data directly, create a datasheet form instead.

> **Action**
>
> Create a new form with the wizard.
> Table: SkiBoardStyle.
> Columns: All.
> Select the Datasheet layout.
> Test the form.

Look closely at the data in Figure 6.7 and you will see that the Category data actually comes from a second table: ProductCategory. Of course, you should also build a grid form to enable administrators to update this table as well. However, you also need to make it easier for people to enter data into the Category column of the main SkiBoardStyle table. If users have to retype the data for every row, they might abbreviate or misspell the entries—leading to inconsistent data that is difficult to search. Instead, you want to create a combo box on the form that makes it easy for users to select the desired category.

As shown in Figure 6.9, switch the form to Design view and you will see that it looks much like a main form. However, the layout of the form is ignored when it is displayed as a datasheet. In particular, the order of the columns is set by the tab order and not by the position on the form. The goal is to replace the Category text box with a combo box, so the first step is to delete the Category text box and its associated label. Then you can use the toolbox to place a combo box on the form.

FIGURE 6.9

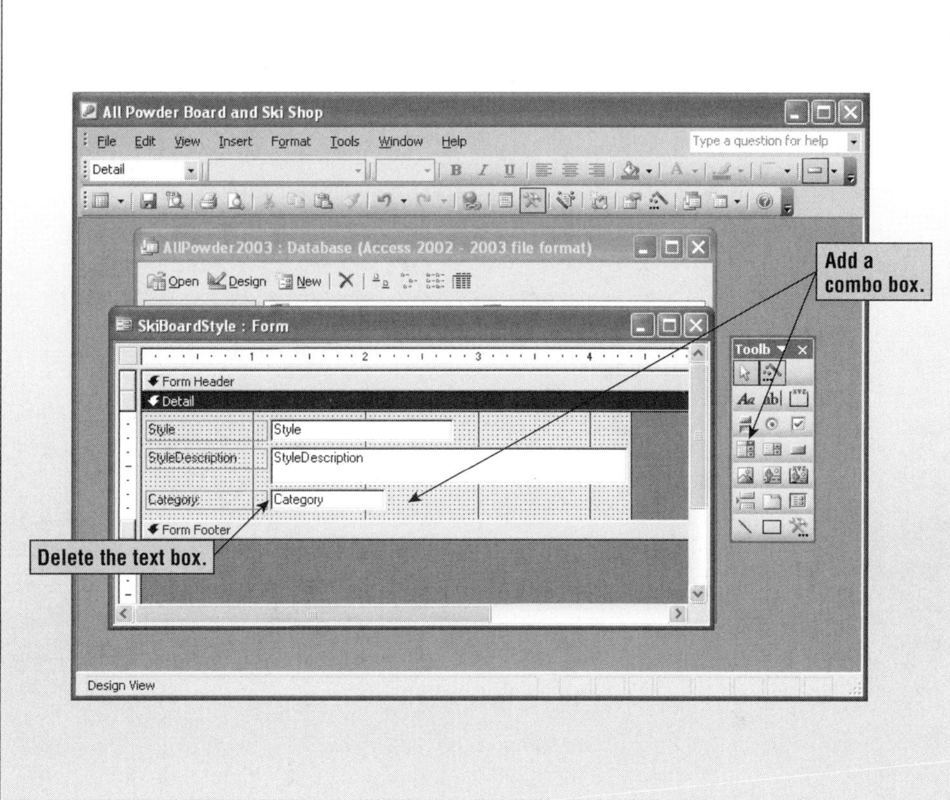

Action
Switch to form Design view.
Delete the box for Category.
Add a combo box.
Select the first lookup option.
Choose the ProductCategory table.
Choose the Category and CategoryDescription columns.
Set column widths.
Select the Category column.
Store value into the Category column.
Rename the combo box.
Set the tab order.
Run the form and test the combo box.

The combo box wizard supports three uses: to look up data from a second table, to select from a fixed list of values, or to search the existing form for matching data. In most cases, you want the first option. You should almost always avoid the second option because it is difficult to change the values later. You generally want to place the values within a separate table and build a form so they can be altered later without having to modify this form. The third option is sometimes useful on main forms but can be confusing because it is used to search for data instead of entering data. The first option is the one needed in this case, so select the table that holds the data that will be displayed in the combo box list (ProductCategory). Choose both the Category and the CategoryDescription columns to be displayed in the combo box list. The wizard gives you the option to hide the key column, which is commonly done for numeric AutoNumber keys. In this case, the key column is text, so make sure it is displayed.

Figure 6.10 shows the role of the combo box and one of the trickiest steps in the combo box wizard. The purpose of a combo box is to display a list of predefined items from a table or query (ProductCategory in this case). To enter data into the SkiBoardStyle table, users select one of the items from the complete list, and the chosen value is entered into the Category column of the SkiBoardStyle table. In the screen of this wizard you specify the Category column of the SkiBoardStyle table as the place to hold the chosen value. The screen immediately prior to this one is where you select the key column in the display list—the Category column in the ProductCategory. The screen in Figure 6.10 is the one that generally causes the most problems. You must be sure to store the value in the appropriate column or the combo box will not work. Once the wizard has completed, you should set the properties of the combo box to give it a better name (cboCategory in this case), and double-check the tab order of all of the controls.

FIGURE 6.10

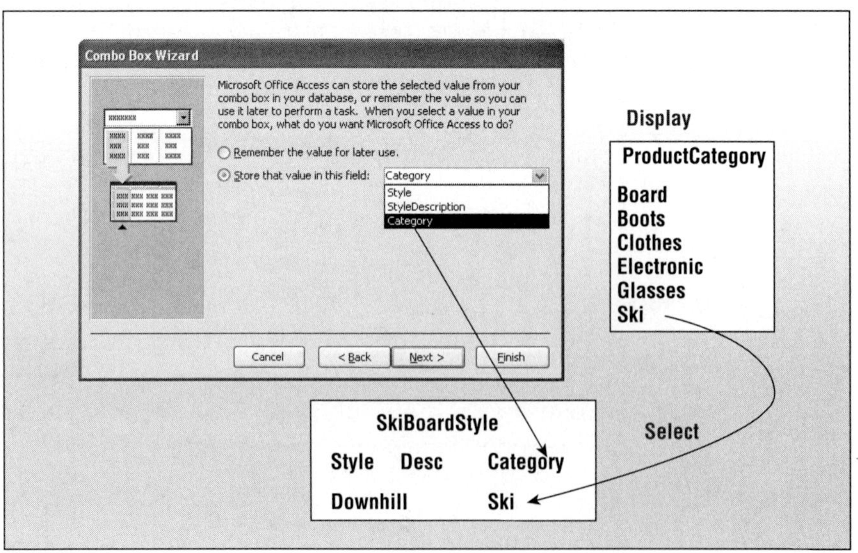

FIGURE 6.11

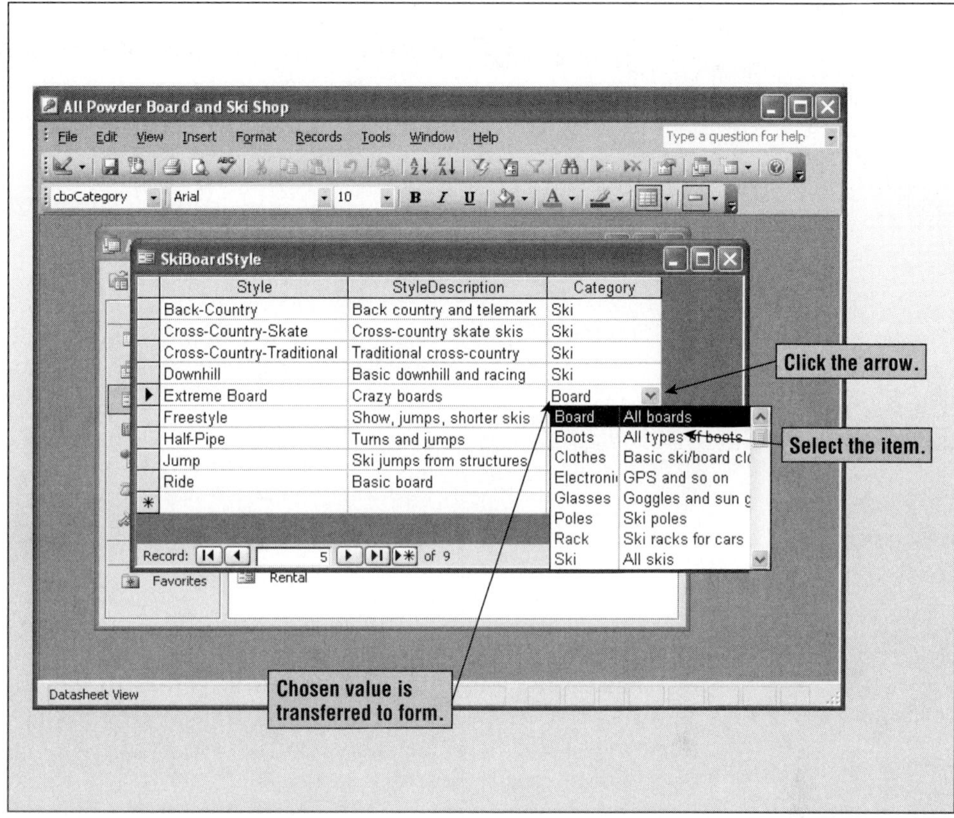

As shown in Figure 6.11, when you run the form, the datasheet rows appear similar to the original version. However, when you click on an entry in the Category column, you will see the arrow box for the combo box. Clicking on the arrow generates the list shown in the figure. Selecting an item transfers it to the form and the table. It is important that you understand the role of the combo box in relational databases. Remember that normalization splits the database into tables that are connected through primary and foreign keys. Generally, these keys are numeric, and often they are generated by the DBMS, so they have no overt business interpretation. It would be difficult for users to remember these numbers, but they have to be entered correctly into many tables. The combo box solves the usability problem by displaying a list of data. When an item is chosen, the matching key value is entered into the foreign key column automatically. With numeric keys, you generally want to hide the key; users do not even need to know that it exists.

Activity: Create Main Forms and Subforms

Now that you understand the main and grid forms, it is time to combine them into a main form and subform. Remember where this process began—with business forms, particularly the sale form. A typical business sale form has data for the sale (SaleID, SaleDate) and customer (name, address, and so on). It also has a section of repeating data to hold the specific items being purchased by the customer. This repeating section was split into the SaleItem table, with some elements placed in the Inventory and ItemModel tables. The

FIGURE 6.12

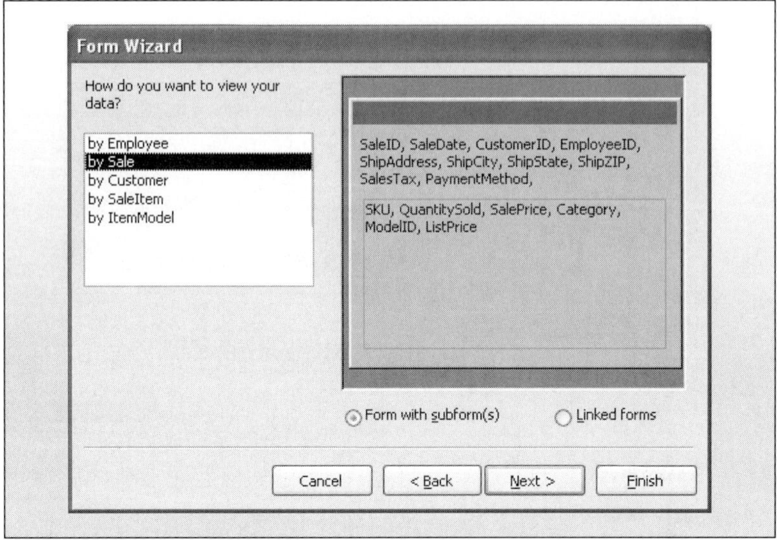

purpose of the main form and subform is to recombine these tables. Keep in mind that each form can be associated directly with only one table. In this case, the sale form will be based primarily on the Sale table, and the subform will be based primarily on the SaleItem table. Additional data from the other tables can be displayed on the forms, but only the primary keys from those two tables will be used.

The wizard is again used to start the forms. Begin by selecting all of the columns from the Sale table. Then select the LastName, FirstName, Phone, and Email columns from the Customer table. Remember, do not use the Customer.CustomerID column. Also, you should add the Employee LastName and FirstName so they can be displayed on the form for the salesperson. Next, use all of the columns from the SaleItem table except the SaleID column, because you do not want to have it repeated on every row of the subform. From the ItemModel table, bring the Category, ModelID, and List-Price columns so they can be displayed as a description on each row of the subform.

The next step in the wizard is to make sure that it recognizes the main/subform relationship by Sale. Figure 6.12 shows the step where you can tell the wizard how to organize the form layout. If your database relationships are correct, it generally picks the correct layout, but sometimes you have to override this choice. Here, the Sale is the main form, and the repeating sections are moved to the sub-form. You can use the default options for the other choices in the wizard.

The initial form generated by the wizard will work, but it usually needs some work. You will have to fix the layout, the widths of the text boxes, and add combo boxes. For subforms that contain numeric data (price and quantity), you will also want to compute the subtotal of the value and display it on the main form. Figure 6.13 shows the initial form. Before trying to improve the form, take a minute to run the form and see how the subform works. Notice that as you switch to a different sale, the subform picks up the items for just

---

Action

Create a new form with the wizard.
Sale table, all columns.
Customer table use name, phone, and e-mail columns.
Employee table, use the name.
SaleItem table, all columns except SaleID.
ItemModel table, use Category, ModelID, and ListPrice.
Finish the wizard and test the form.

FIGURE 6.13

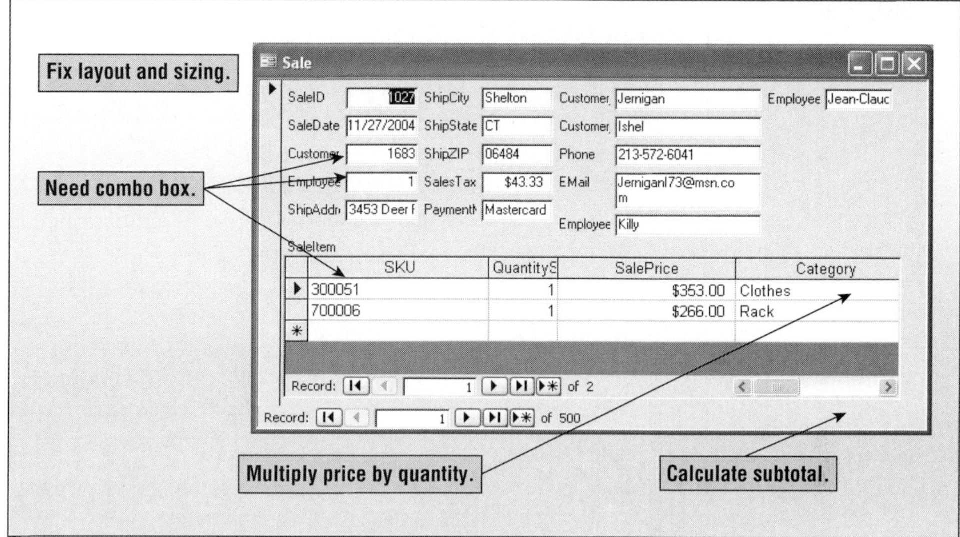

that sale. The subform is linked to the main form through the SaleID, and the form processor knows how to retrieve and display just the matching data.

To improve the form, begin by replacing the foreign key ID text boxes with combo boxes. Make sure that you assign a new name using the combo box properties. Figure 6.14 gives you an idea of how to rearrange and resize the main form controls and add a title. Be sure that you set the tab order. You also might consider adding command buttons to delete and add sales. Also, set the default value for the SaleDate to be =Date( ) so that the current day will always be entered for new sales. Run the form and check that the combo boxes work correctly. If you look closely, you will see that although they work, the customer, employee, and payment options are not sorted alphabetically. There is no automated way to fix this issue, but it is easy to correct if you remember your SQL. Check the properties for the combo box and you will see that the Row Source property contains a SELECT query. Simply add an ORDER BY LastName, FirstName to the end of the query. You can use the Ellipses button (. . .) to open the query in Design view to add the sort order.

The next step is to improve the subform. It is a little challenging because it is difficult to get all of the columns to fit horizontally on the form. You might have to widen the form and the subform box. You set the column widths while the form is running by dragging or double-clicking the column dividing lines. The next changes are often easier if you close the main form and open the subform alone in Design view. First, you should replace the SKU box with a combo box to minimize data entry errors. Next, add a text box to the bottom of the form, and enter "= SalePrice * QuantitySold" as the Control Source. Give it the name "Value" in its properties. Next, expand the form footer and add a new text box

---

Action

Switch to Design view.
Replace CustomerID, EmployeeID, and PaymentMethod with combo boxes.
Use the Row Source property of the combo boxes to set a sort order.
Set tab order and run the form.

Action

Open the subform in Design view.
Insert a combo box for the SKU.
Add a text box to compute
Value = QuantitySold * SalePrice.
Add a text box to the footer to compute the subtotal:
=Sum(QuantitySold * SalePrice).
Set tab order.
Test the subform calculations.
Open the main form in Design view.
Add subtotal text box and use the Expression Builder to copy the subtotal value from the subform subtotal.
Test the form.

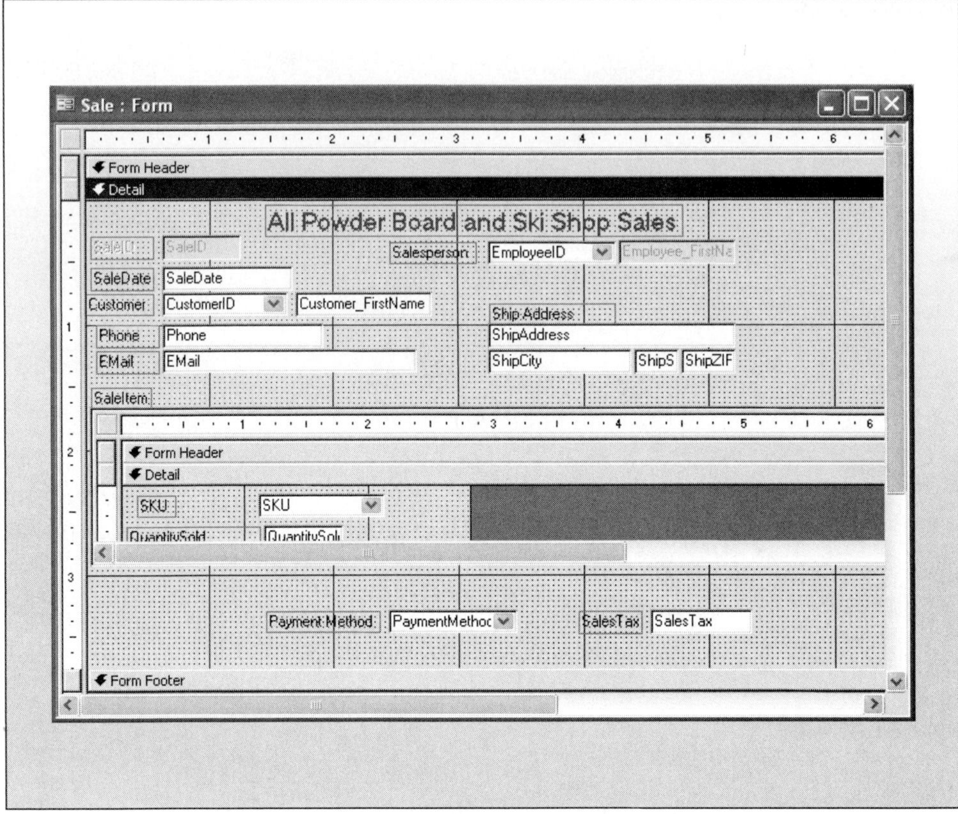

to it. It's formula should be "= Sum(SalePrice * QuantitySold)," and give it the name "SubTotal." Format them both as Currency with two decimal places. Figure 6.15 shows how the forms will appear when you run the main Sale form.

Notice that the subtotal is not displayed on the main form. To get it there, you need to copy its value from the subform. Return to the main form in

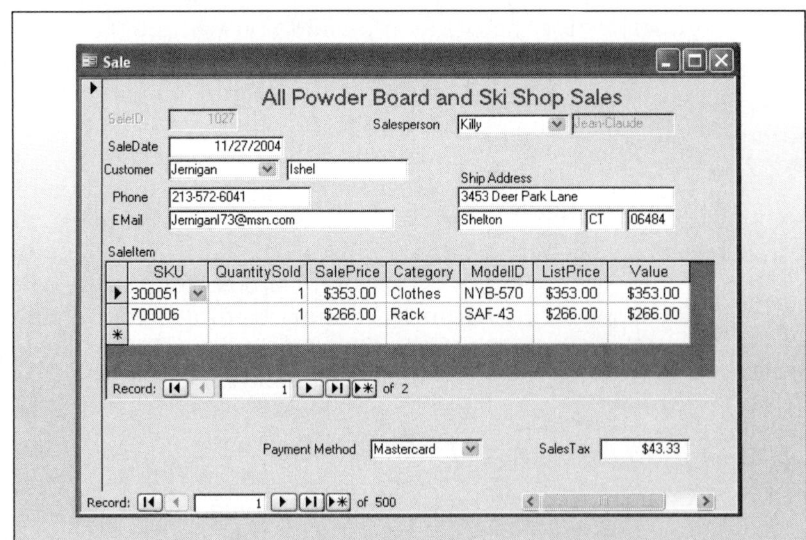

FIGURE 6.16

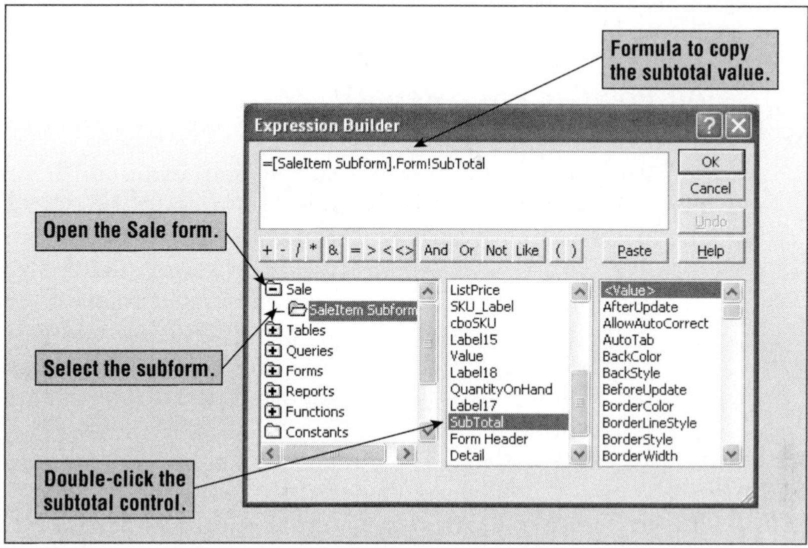

Design view and add a text box beneath the subform. The copy is made dynamically by using a formula, but the formula is slightly complex. Instead of trying to memorize the formula syntax, you can use the Expression Builder to create the formula for you. On the properties for the Sale form Subtotal text box, click the Ellipses button to open the Expression Builder. Figure 6.16 shows the rest of the steps. Open the Sale form and select the subform to see its controls. Find the Subtotal control and double-click it. The proper formula will be entered into the edit box. Click the OK button to return to the properties. Set the format to Currency and run the form to test it. You should also add one more text box to compute the total. Enter the formula as "= SubTotal + SalesTax" and set its format to currency.

Figure 6.17 shows the final form. Your version should be similar to this one, but there is always room for flexibility within a design. Notice that some of the text boxes are disabled to prevent clerks from changing the data. In particular,

FIGURE 6.17

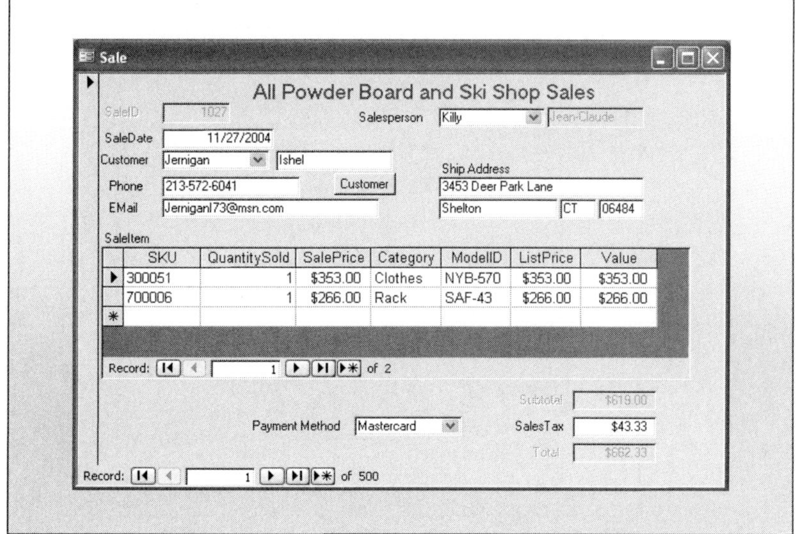

the SaleID and totals are generated by the system and should not be modified by the users. The controls have an Enabled property that you can set to False.

All Powder Basic Reports

Activity: Create Reports with Subtotals

Most managers want reports so they can evaluate the progress of their business. Today, much of the business data could be displayed within forms—if the managers have sufficient access to the online system and if they are comfortable with reading the data on the screen instead of on paper. However, reports are also useful when managers need to see lists of items with subtotals. Remember that queries can print detailed data rows or summary totals, but not both at the same time. And query results are difficult to format. Instead, you want to use the Report Writer to format results, draw lines, and compute subtotals.

<table>
<tr><th colspan="2">Action</th></tr>
<tr><td colspan="2">Create a new report with the wizard.</td></tr>
<tr><td colspan="2">Customer table, use all columns.</td></tr>
<tr><td colspan="2">Sale table, use all columns.</td></tr>
<tr><td colspan="2">SaleItem table, use all columns.</td></tr>
<tr><td colspan="2">Verify the group breaks.</td></tr>
<tr><td colspan="2">Click the Summary Options button.</td></tr>
<tr><td colspan="2">Compute totals for the Quantity.</td></tr>
<tr><td colspan="2">Finish the wizard and switch to Design view.</td></tr>
</table>

The first issue in building a report is to identify the level of detail that will be needed. The Report Writer can always compute subtotals across groups, but you need to ensure that your query retrieves the level of detail desired by the managers. As an example, consider a basic sales report by customer. Managers want to list each customer, followed by the sales placed by that customer. If they also want to include the individual items purchased on each sale, that level of detail is different than if they simply want to see the total value of the sale. For now, assume that they want to see the detailed item list.

You can use the report wizard to build this report. Similar to building forms, your first step is to choose the tables and columns of data that you want on the report. In some ways, queries for reports are simpler because you do not have to worry about keeping the query updatable. Take all of the columns from the Customer table, then all from the Sale table, and all fields from the SaleItem table. If you want to display additional descriptions of the items, you would also have to include the Inventory and possibly ItemModel tables, but for now, leave those out. Figure 6.18 shows one of the more important screens

FIGURE 6.18

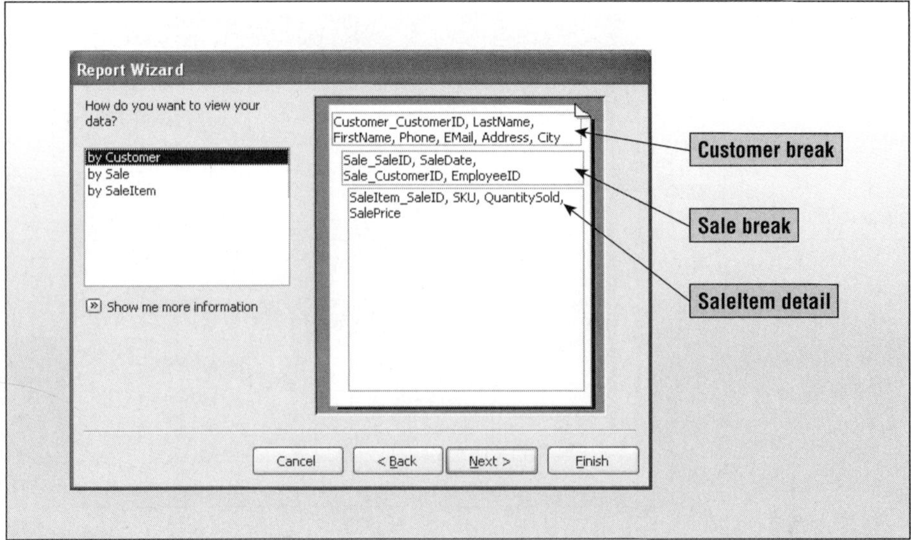

FIGURE 6.19

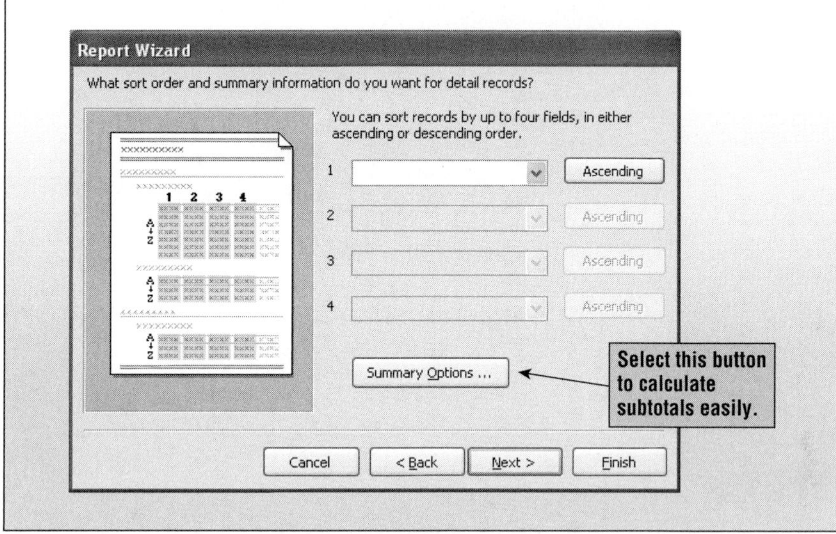

of the report wizard. You need to make sure that the wizard picks up the breaks correctly, and that your detail section is correct.

As shown in Figure 6.19, the next step is a little tricky. It is easy to miss the Summary Options button. Clicking this button gives you options shown in Figure 6.20 to automatically calculate subtotals. The button only appears when you have numeric columns that can be summed or averaged. You then select the columns to compute subtotals or averages.

In this particular example, it does not make sense to sum either of the two numeric columns (quantity and price). You really need to sum the value of price times quantity, which can be done later on the form. If you want to do it at this step, you need to base the report on a query that already computes a column to multiply the two values, then you can sum the resulting column. However, in this case, it is useful to temporarily sum the QuantitySold column and then modify the formula later.

FIGURE 6.20

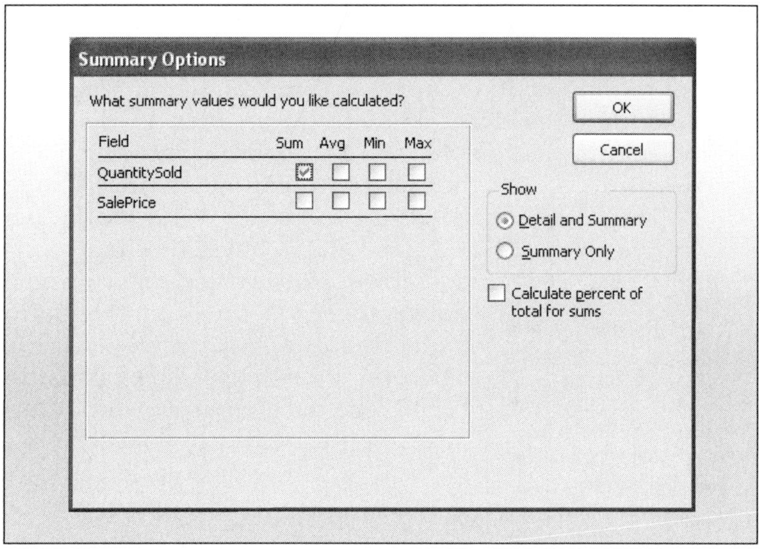

FIGURE 6.21

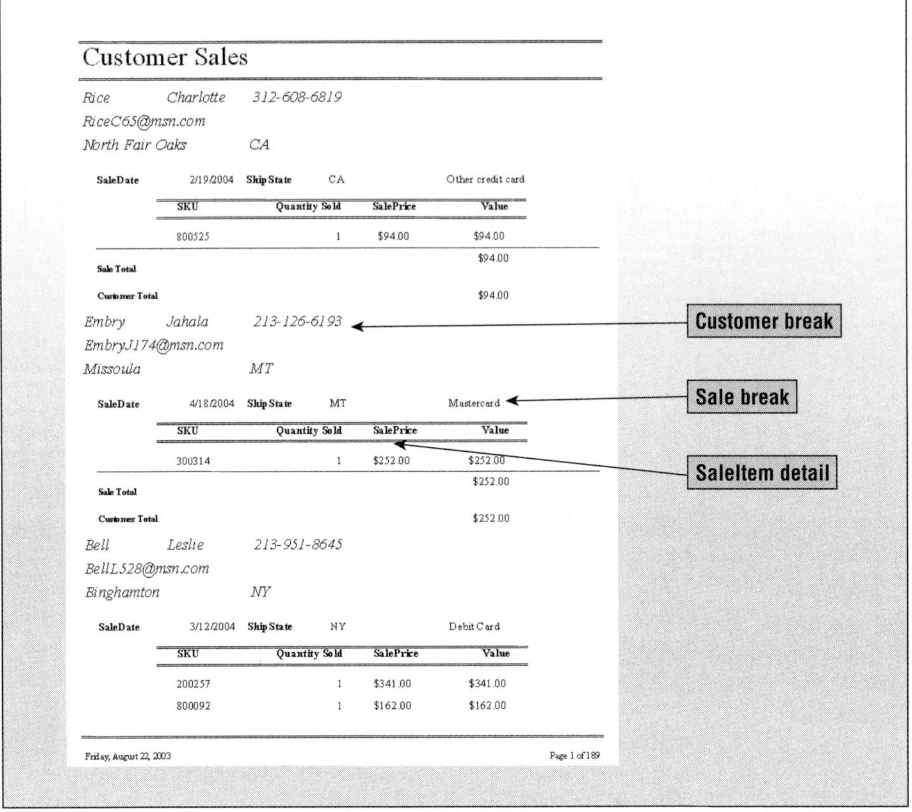

Figure 6.21 shows the initial report created by the wizard. Notice that it has the three sections defined by the group breaks. However, the report is a little messy—largely because it attempts to include all of the columns from three tables. It also needs a column in the detail section to multiply price by quantity, and then compute the total in the footer sections. It would also be useful to split the output so that sales for each customer appear on separate pages.

The report can be cleaned up by switching to Design view. You can create some extra space by removing some of the unneeded columns and a few of the labels. Figure 6.22 shows some of the ways to rearrange the form. Notice that sections correspond to the group breaks. The Customer and Sale breaks have headers and footers. The titles are displayed in the headers, and the sum in the footers. The figure also shows the addition of the Value text box in the detail section. It computes QuantitySold * SalePrice to get the value of the items being purchased.

Figure 6.23 shows the final design for the Customer Sale form. Notice the cleaner layout of the controls. Also, notice the page break at the bottom of the Customer footer. It ensures that each new set of customer data will begin on a new page. The calculations for the sum have been corrected so that they total QuantitySold * SalePrice instead of just QuantitySold. The interesting aspect of the sums is that the formula for all three controls is exactly the same. The only difference is the section on the report.

Action

Delete some unnecessary columns.
Move items around to improve the look.
Add a text box in the Detail section called Value to compute [QuantitySold] * [SalePrice].
Set currency format.
Edit the Sum calculations to be Sum([QuantitySold] * [SalePrice]).
Run the form and clean up the layout.

FIGURE 6.22

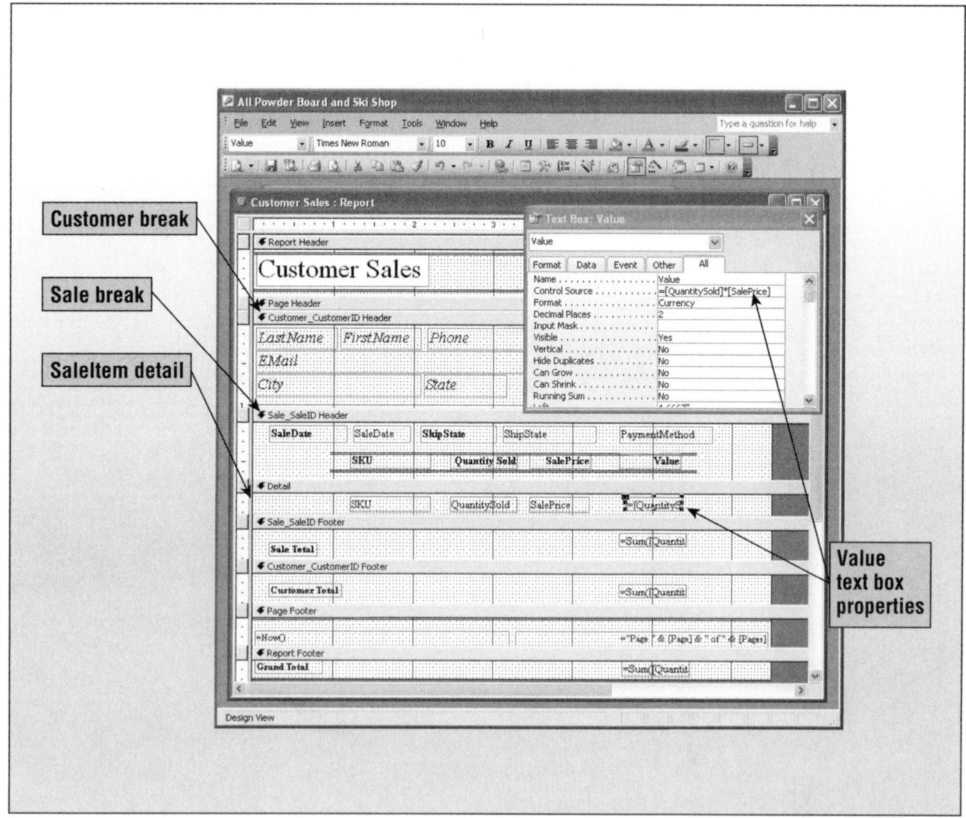

The total on the Sale footer computes the sum just for that sale, while the total control on the Customer footer computes the total for the customer, across all sales for that customer. The total control on the Report footer computes and displays the total for all sales printed on the report.

Figure 6.24 shows a portion of the final version of the report. Notice that the page shows sales for only one customer. The Value calculation is correct, and the sums for the Sale and Customer are correct. Although the report will use a considerable number of pages, the details and summary values can be read easily. If the managers truly want this level of detail, the report should work well.

It is possible that managers do not need the detailed list of items sold. Perhaps they need only the total value of the sale for each customer. The report would certainly be shorter. Because this level of report requires a different level of detail, you will first have to create a query that extracts the main data and computes the sales value and the total value for each sale. The Report Writer will then compute the totals per customer.

Figure 6.25 shows the query used to create the total value of the items for each sale. The design is straightforward—add the desired columns from the Customer, Sale, and SaleItem table. Then add the computed column Value to compute SalePrice by QuantitySold. Save the query and build the report based on that query. Be sure that the wizard

> ### Action
> Create a new query to total sales by customer.
> Save the query.
> Create a new report based on the query.
> For the Customer group, set the Keep Together property to Whole Group.
> Run the report.

FIGURE 6.23

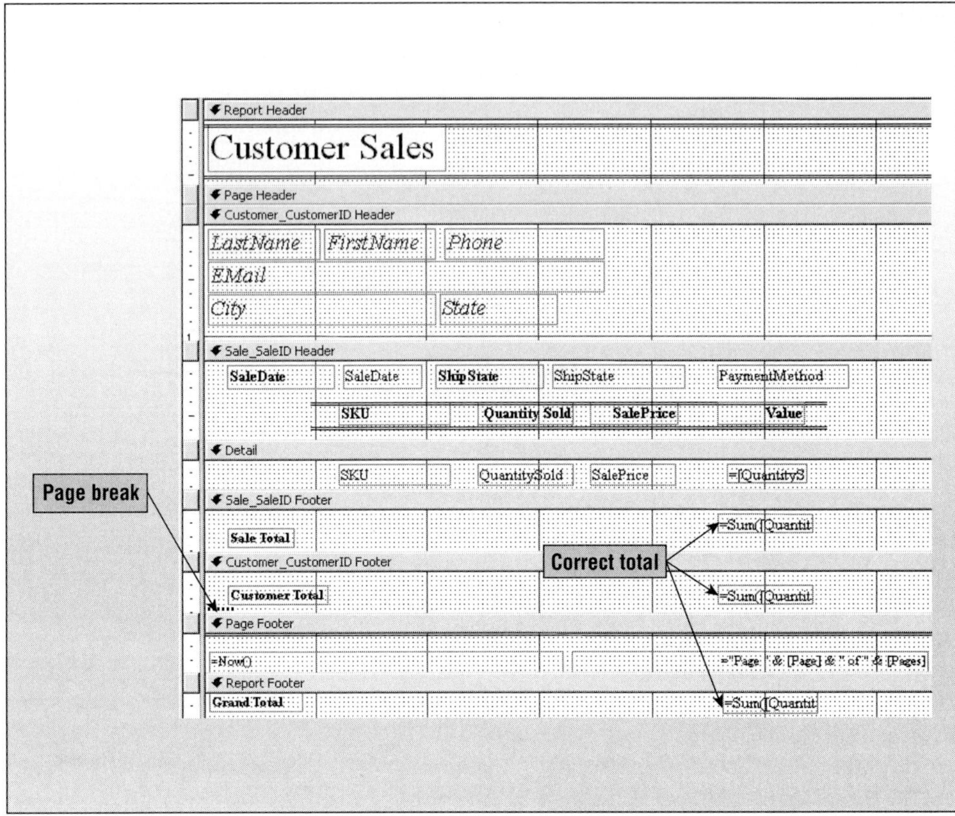

creates a group break based on the CustomerID. You can clean up the report in Design view. Move the columns for LastName, FirstName, Phone, and Email from the detail section to the Customer header section.

Figure 6.26 shows the Design view for the new report after it has been cleaned up. Clicking the Sorting and Grouping button on the tool bar brings up the options to control how the grouping is handled. In this case, for the CustomerID, set the Keep Together option to Whole Group. This value tells the Report Writer to avoid splitting customer data across pages. If data for a customer would be split by a page break, the Report Writer will move the entire group to a new page. These options are useful and can provide detailed control over the report layout. However, you have to be careful. If a customer has so many sales that the data will not fit on one page, the system will still be forced to spread the data across multiple pages. The options are particularly useful for relatively small groups of data.

Activity: Create Subreports

Access supports subreports, which are similar to subforms in that a repeating group can be displayed as a linked report within the main report. It is primarily useful when you need two or more repeating groups of data. For example, for each customer you might want to display a list of sales and a list of rentals. With subreports, you can display the lists side by side. The two subreports are linked by CustomerID to the main customer group, but not to each other since sales and rentals are not necessarily related.

FIGURE 6.24

Forbes   Horace   213-757-9252
ForbesH610@msn.com
Chattanooga   TN

SaleDate	1/12/2004	**Ship State**	TN		Check
SKU		**Quantity Sold**	**SalePrice**		**Value**
600016		1	$32.00		$32.00
100115		1	$308.00		$308.00
800419		1	$166.00		$166.00
Sale Total					$506.00

SaleDate	5/10/2004	**Ship State**	TN		Cash
SKU		**Quantity Sold**	**SalePrice**		**Value**
800272		1	$262.00		$262.00
100046		1	$647.00		$647.00
800131		1	$202.00		$202.00
600057		1	$42.00		$42.00
Sale Total					$1,153.00
Customer Total					$1,659.00

Action

Create a simple report based on the Customer table.

Create a Sale subreport from the Sale and SaleItem tables, grouping it by SaleItem.

Create a Rental subreport from the Rental and RentalItem tables.

Open the Customer report in Design view.

Drag-and-drop the two subreports onto the Detail section of the Customer report.

Use properties of the subreports to set the Link Child and Link Master Fields to CustomerID.

Run the report.

The wizard does much of the work, but not all of it. This report needs to be built in three sections: (1) the Customer report, (2) the Sales subreport, and (3) the Rentals subreport. You can use the wizard to build each report, and then drag the subreports onto the main Customer report. Begin by creating the Customer report with some of the basic data from the Customer table. Then build the Sale subreport with the SaleID, CustomerID, and SaleDate from the Sale table and the columns from the SaleItem table. Group the report by SaleItem instead of the Sale table. Third, build the Rental subreport in a similar manner using the RentalID, CustomerID, and RentalDate from the Rental table, along with the columns from the RentalItem table.

To build the final report, open the new Customer report in Design view. Expand the detail section so it has room to hold the subreports. Drag the SaleItem subreport onto the detail section and resize it horizontally and vertically so it fits on the page. On the subreport, delete and shrink any report and page header and footer sections. Add a text box to compute and display the value = SalePrice * QuantitySold, and resize the width of the lines and the page so you will be able to fit the two reports on the page. To link the subreport to the main report, you need to set the link properties

FIGURE 6.25

```
SELECT Customer.CustomerID, Customer.LastName,
Customer.FirstName, Customer.Phone, Customer.EMail,
Sale.SaleID, Sale.SaleDate, Sale.ShipCity, Sale.ShipState,
Sum([SalePrice]*[QuantitySold]) AS [Value]
FROM (Customer INNER JOIN Sale ON Customer.CustomerID =
Sale.CustomerID) INNER JOIN SaleItem ON Sale.SaleID =
SaleItem.SaleID
GROUP BY Customer.CustomerID, Customer.LastName,
Customer.FirstName, Customer.Phone, Customer.EMail,
Sale.SaleID, Sale.SaleDate, Sale.ShipCity, Sale.ShipState
ORDER BY Customer.LastName, Customer.FirstName;
```

on the subreport. Carefully, right-click on the border of the subreport and open the property list. Then set the master and child properties to CustomerID, which tells the subreport (child) to display only the data for the matching customer. Figure 6.27 shows the layout of the form and the property values needed to link the forms. The next step is to add the subreport for rentals following the same process. Be sure to set the link master and child properties. You will also want to rearrange the text boxes so that the two subreports fit side by side on one page. You should also consider adding a border around each of the subreports to highlight them on the main report. You will probably want to add totals on each of the subreport report footers.

FIGURE 6.26

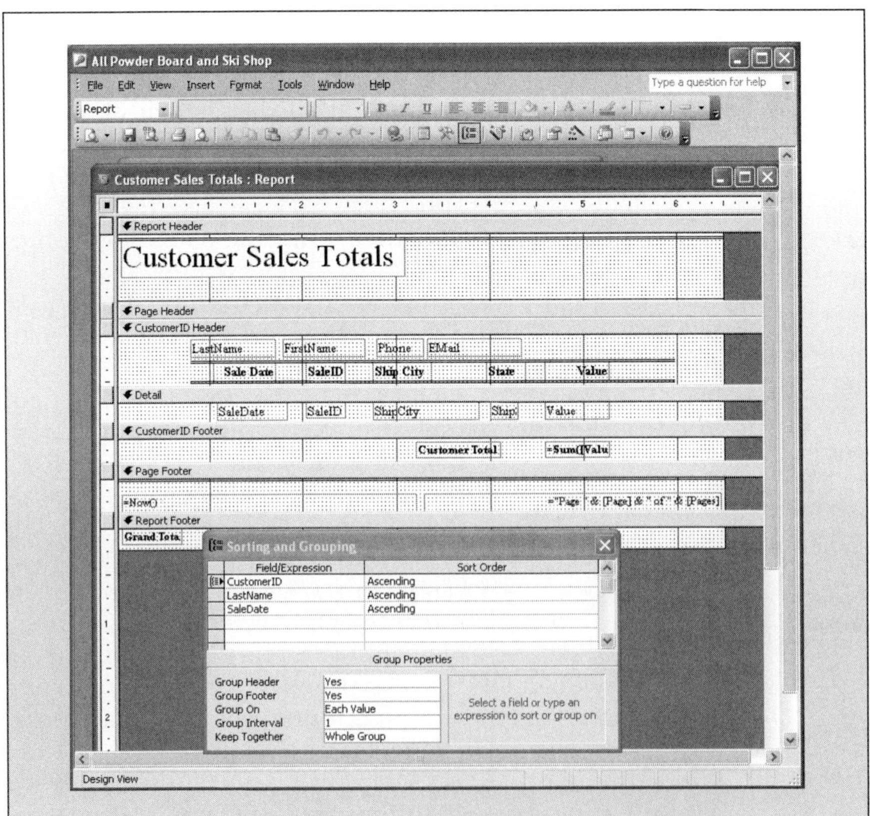

FIGURE 6.27

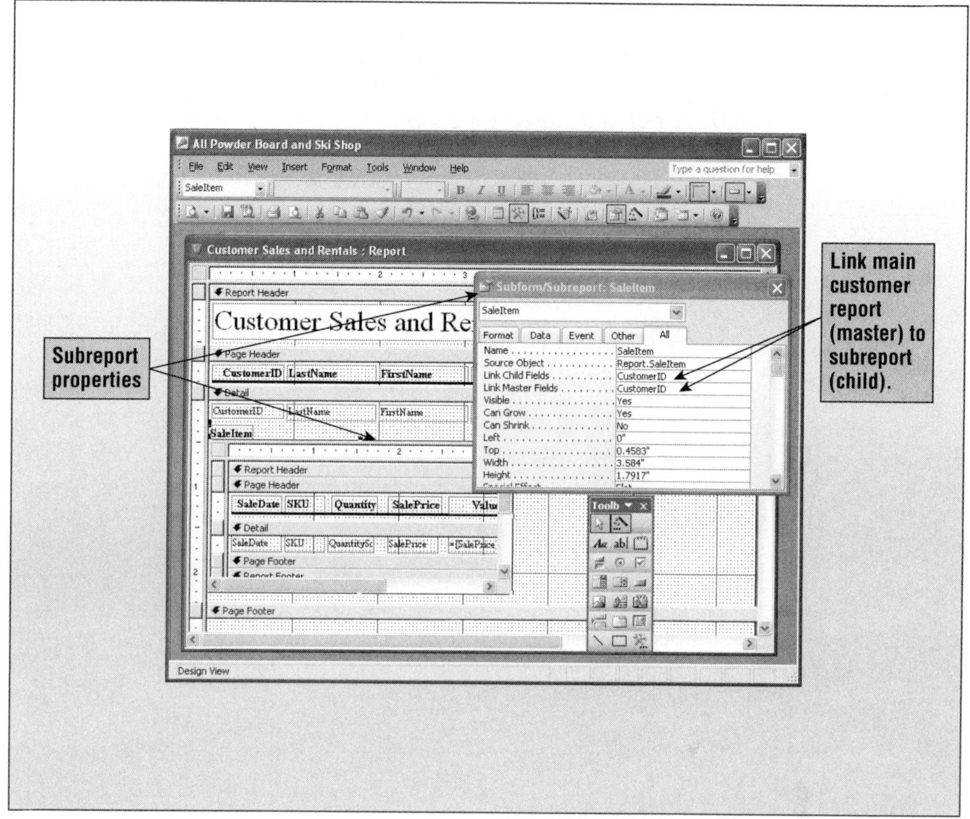

Figure 6.28 shows a sample page from the new report. The subreport also supports properties to control automatically expanding the report to handle additional rows, or autosizing to restrict it if there are only a few rows in the report. You also might want to include a page break at the bottom of the detail section so that each customer report is printed on a separate page, but that decision will depend on the sizes of the subreports, which depend on the number of items purchased or rented. One of the most time-consuming elements in creating reports is setting the layout, sizing, and design elements to make the report compact, yet readable. The main aspect of this report is the dual column layout to show the separate sale and rental items.

Building the All Powder Application

Activity: Create the Switchboard Form

Once you have created the forms and reports, you need to combine them into an application. A Startup or Switchboard form is a key element of an application. It is a form that contains links to the other forms and reports. Generally, it is easy to create; the challenge lies in determining how to organize all of the forms and reports. In most cases, users will see the application only through your forms. They will almost never want to open forms directly from the Access forms list. You have to create a structure, beginning with the Switchboard form that guides them through their tasks. This process will often include links on other forms as well. You will have to test this sequence with the users to make sure that it matches their job workflow.

FIGURE 6.28

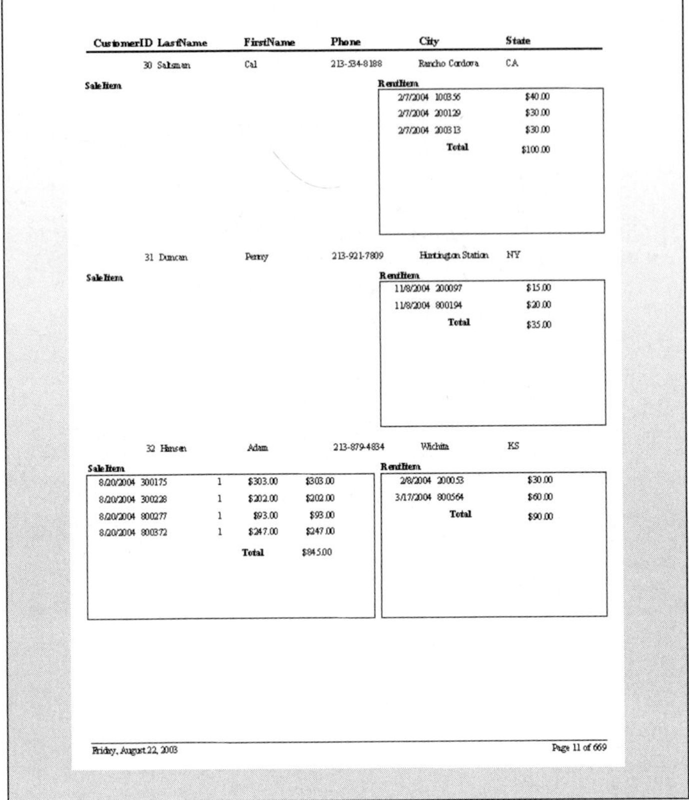

<table>
<tr><td colspan="6">

CustomerID	LastName	FirstName	Phone	City	State
30 Salzman		Cal	213-534-8188	Rancho Cordova	CA

</td></tr>
</table>

To create a switchboard form, begin with a new form in Design view. Avoid the wizard because it severely limits your form. Add labels to place a title on the form. Use the form's properties to improve the appearance of the form, removing the navigation buttons and perhaps adding a picture. Then add buttons that open the initial forms and reports.

In large applications, you might want to create additional forms that would function as submenus. For instance, you might have a special menu form just for administrators. This approach reduces clutter on the main form and hides details from other users to make their job easier. Figure 6.29 shows the main steps used to add a command button. In the subsequent steps, you choose the form to be opened (Sales), and give the button a descriptive label instead of an icon. The wizard also gives you the opportunity to name the function to match the button (cmdSales). Note that if you delete a button, the corresponding code is not deleted, so you will have to switch to Code view and delete the associated code yourself. Giving the functions meaningful names makes it is easier to find the appropriate routines. You should also add command buttons to the other forms so the users have all of the necessary commands readily available. For example, you should include a button on the Sales form to open the Customer form. In this case, use the wizard option to open the form for the matching customer. With the menu Tools/Startup, you can assign the new Switchboard form to open automatically whenever the database file is opened.

FIGURE 6.29

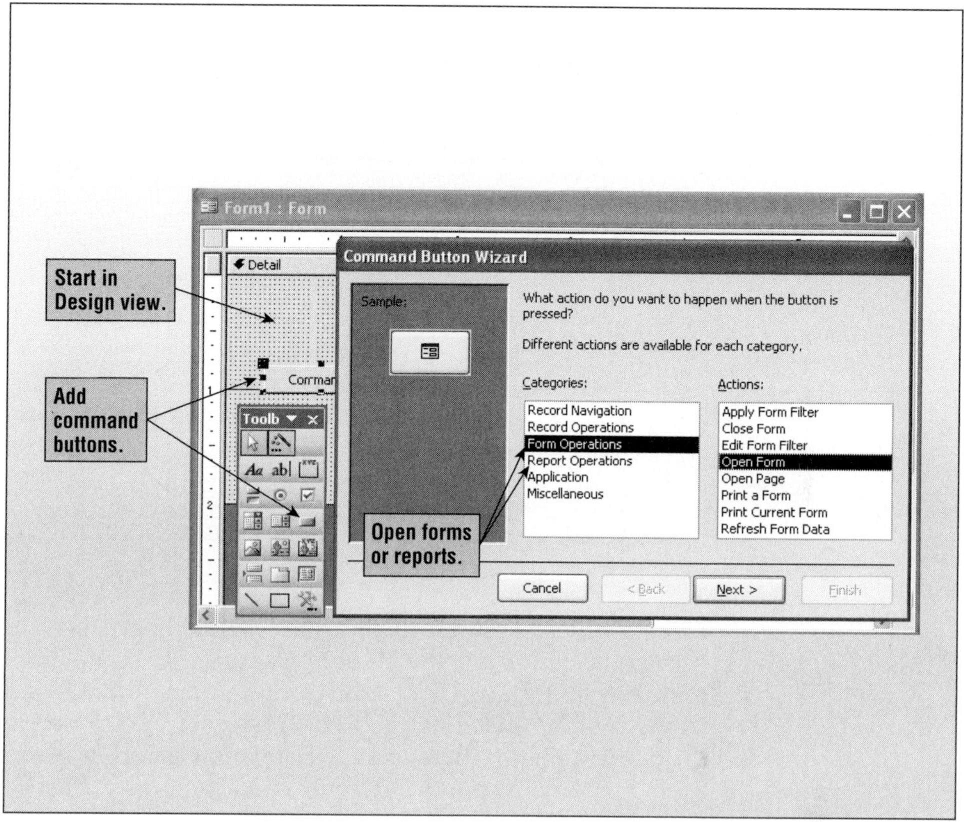

Activity: Build Menus and Toolbars

Switchboard forms and command button links help users navigate from one form to another, but in complex applications, users might need additional support. Menus and toolbars are another method of displaying available actions to the users. Toolbars are often displayed at the top of the application to provide quick links to common activities that are needed in any form. For instance, you can include a Print button for all reports, so users always know they can click one button to print whatever report they are viewing. You can also create secondary toolbars that are customized for each form. Access includes tools that make it easy to create toolbars and menus. The challenge is to identify the tasks and options that users need to have available on the toolbar.

Toolbars can contain icons or drop-down menu lists. As shown in Figure 6.30, you create a toolbar with the menu option View/Toolbars/Customize to create a new toolbar. Look closely at your screen and you will see a small empty toolbar. One of the first things you should do is give it a recognizable name (AllPowder). At this point, you select the Commands tab to display a list of the items you can place on the toolbar. To add an item to the toolbar, find the desired item in the right-hand list and drag it onto the toolbar. To begin, go to the All Forms option and drag the switchboard (AAMain) to the toolbar. With this icon, users will be

---

Action

Choose View/Toolbars/Customize.
On the Toolbars tab create a new toolbar.
Click the Commands tab.
Drag the Main Form icon onto the toolbar.
Add a Customers menu option and drag the Customer forms and reports onto it.
Add the Help icon.
Test the toolbar.

FIGURE 6.30

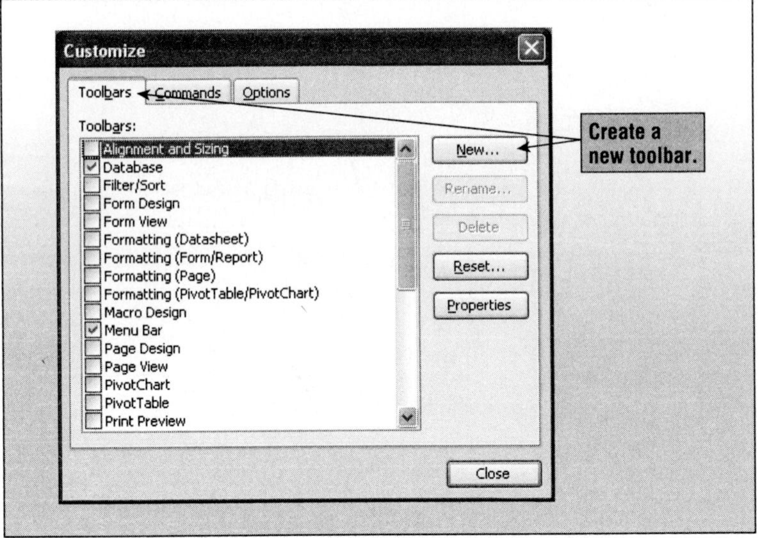

able to quickly return to the main switchboard even if several reports and forms are cluttering the screen. Next, select the Windows and Help options and drag the main Help icon to the toolbar. Finally, add a New Menu item to the toolbar and rename it as "Customer." Click on the toolbar to open the drop-down menu, then add the Sale and Customer forms. Next, add the three main customer reports. You can add a separator line between the forms and reports by right-clicking the list and selecting the Begin Group option. Figure 6.31 shows the resulting toolbar. Close the customization form and test the toolbar.

Activity: Write Help Files

A finished application also needs customized Help files. Users should be able to press the F1 key or select the Help menu option and receive additional information to help them perform a task or understand the data that needs to be entered. Detailed Help systems can become complex, with large applications requiring hundreds of pages of Help text and instructions. On large projects, companies often hire a special team just to create and edit the Help files. For these situations, you will want to purchase a dedicated Help System editor. However, Microsoft has a free Help Compiler system that can be used to create Help files. You can write the Help text without this system, but you need it to compile the files into a Help package. Search the MSDN site for the htmlhelp.exe file. Figure 6.32 shows the basic steps involved in creating a Help system. First you write individual Help pages as HTML text files. These pages can have links to each other and to external websites. One of the pages should be the startup page, and each page should contain a list of keywords. You also create a mapping file that assigns a number to each page. The Help Compiler converts all of the pages into a single chm file. Finally, in each Access form, you

Action
Create at least three HTML Help files for the All Powder forms using an HTML editor or Wordpad.
If necessary, download and install the HTML Help workshop.
Create a new project in the workshop.
Add the HTML files.
Edit the HTML files to add keywords.
Create the mapping file with a text editor and add it to the project.
Set project options to build the TOC and index files.
Compile and test the Help file.
Edit the database forms and add the Help file name and ContentID.
Run the form and press the F1 key to test the Help files.

FIGURE 6.31

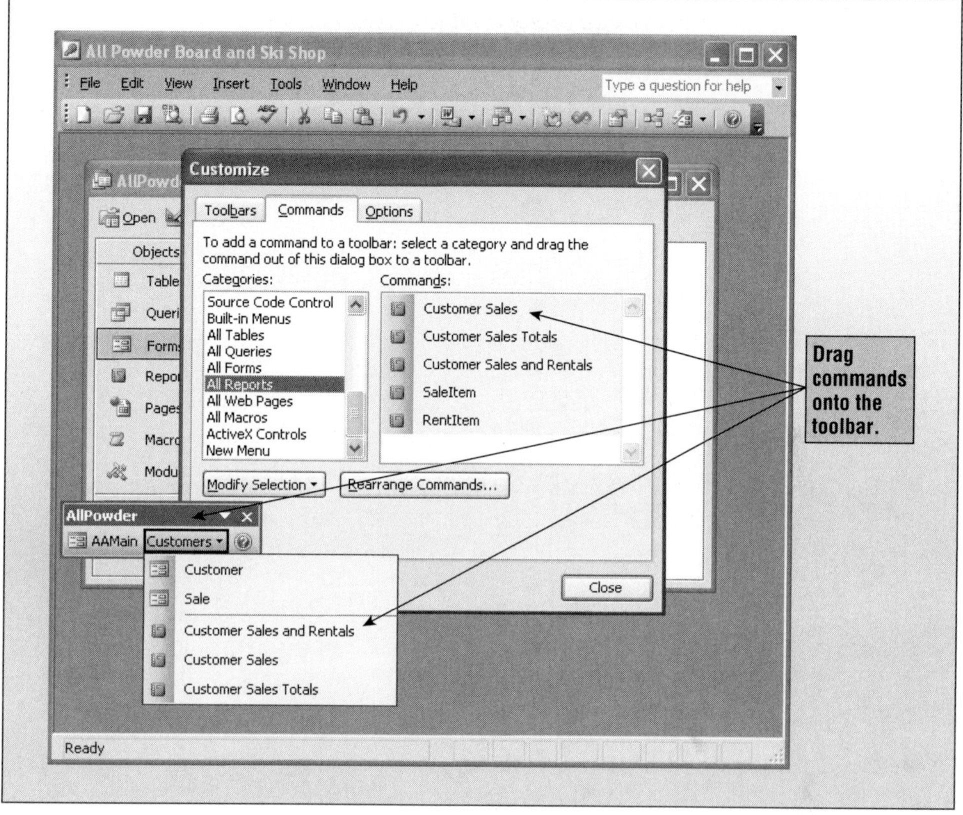

set the properties to the name of this compiled form, and the number of the topic associated with that page or even a particular control. When the user presses the F1 key, the system looks up the page that matches the number and displays it in the Help viewer. Users can also search by table of contents or by keywords.

FIGURE 6.32

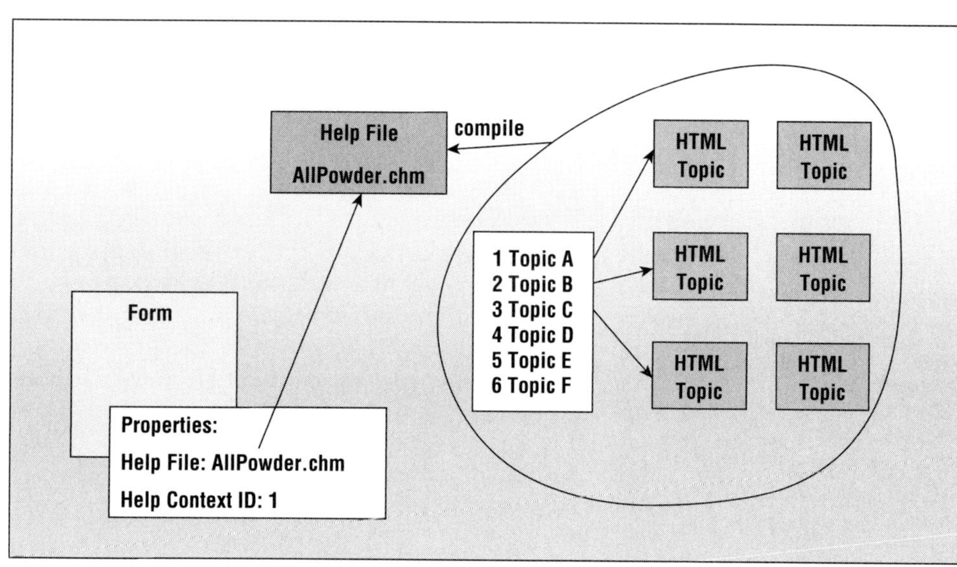

FIGURE 6.33

```
<Object  type="application/x-oleobject"
classid="clsid:1e2a7bd0-dab9-11d0-b93a-00c04fc99f9e">
 <PARAM  name="Keyword"  value="Contents">
 <PARAM  name="Keyword"  value="Introduction">
 <PARAM  name="Keyword"  value="Start">
 <PARAM  name="Keyword"  value="Management">
</OBJECT>
<HTML><HEAD>
<TITLE>All Powder Board and Ski Shop</TITLE>
<LINK rel="stylesheet" type="text/css" href="Styles.css">
</HEAD><BODY>
<H1>Introduction to the All Powder Board and Ski Shop</H1>
<TABLE><TR>
<TD><IMG SRC='BoardLogo1.gif' border='0'></TD>
<TD>All Powder Board and Ski Shop sells and rents snowboards
and skis for all levels of riders and skiers.</TD>
</TR></TABLE>
<H2>The Board and Ski Shop</H2>
<UL>
<LI><A HREF='Customers.html'>Customers</A></LI>
<LI><A HREF='Sales.html'>Sales </A></LI>
</UL>
</BODY></HTML>
```

Figure 6.33 shows that you can create Help pages using a simple text editor, or you can use most HTML editors. You should create a style sheet to ensure consistency across all of the files. More importantly, use the H1, H2, and H3 heading tags to define the major topics covered in each page. These headings can be used by the Help compiler to generate the table of contents. The keywords are entered in the special <OBJECT> tag. This tag can be created using the Microsoft HTML Help editor, or you can copy, paste, and edit the keyword information. At this point, you should create two or three HTML files and test the pages and the links to make sure they work together.

Once you have created the individual HTML pages, you should create the mapping file that assigns a number to each topic. In HTML, you refer to each topic by the name of the file, but Access references topics by a number. As shown in the sample in Figure 6.34, you can assign almost any number (it uses a long integer), but it helps if you group the numbers by topic to make them easier for you to find later. This data is stored as a simple text file. It is typically named "topics.h," but that is not a strict requirement. Be careful with the entries in the topics.h file: You must separate the names from the numbers with at least two spaces and you cannot use tabs.

Once the pages have been created, you compile the files into a single chm file that is distributed with the Access mdb file. The Help compiler does most of the work; you simply add the files to the system and set a few options. Begin by starting the HTML Help Workshop and creating a new project file. Use the Menu button to add the html topic files to the project.

FIGURE 6.34

```
#define  AllPowder       100
#define  Customers     10000
#define  Sales         20000
```

FIGURE 6.35

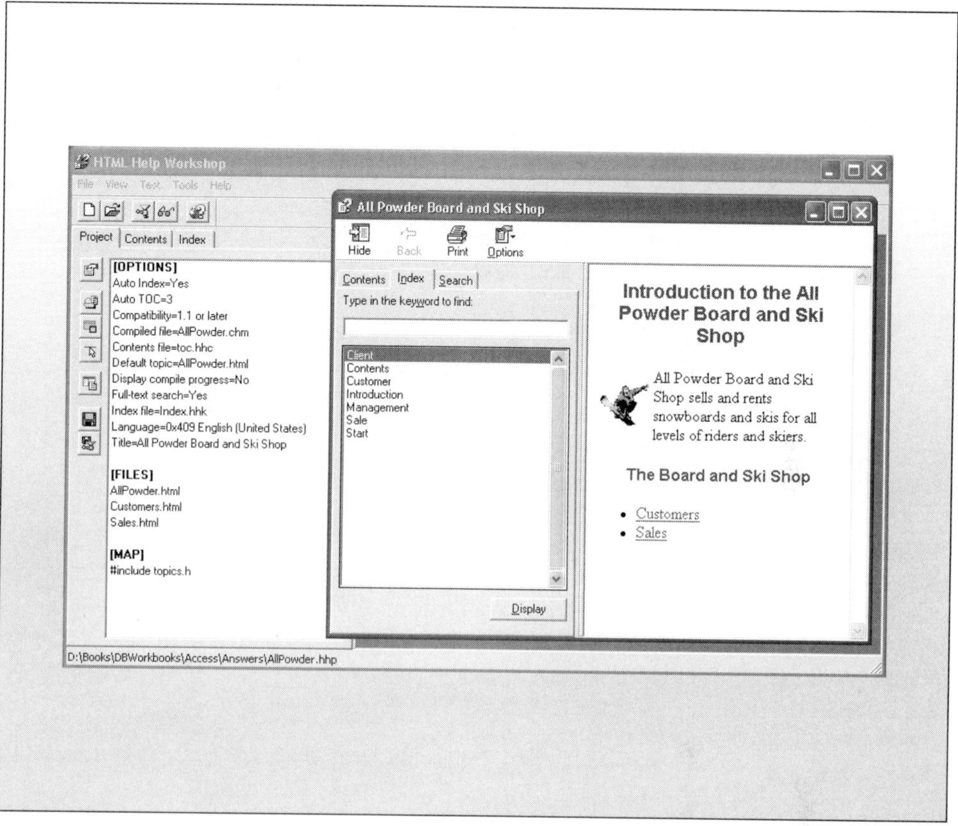

Use the API menu button to add the topics.h header file to the project under the Map option. Use the Options menu button to set the title and default file for the project. Use the Files tab to tell it to automatically create the contents file and include the keywords from the HTML files to build the index. You might have to click the tabs for Contents and Index to force the compiler to create new versions of these files. Figure 6.35 shows the basic elements of the HTML Help compiler and the resulting compiled Help file.

The final step is to set up the Access forms so that they open the correct Help file to the correct page. Keep your list of mapping numbers handy; you will have to enter them into the form properties. Figure 6.36 shows the two properties (filename and topic number) that have to be set. These values have to be entered onto every form. You can also assign different topics to individual controls on a page, but remember that this means you have to write more Help topics. Make sure that you place the Help file in the same folder as the database file. When you have set these properties for all of the forms, you should run the application and test each page to ensure that it brings up the correct topic. Someone should also proofread all of the topics to make sure they contain no errors.

Exercises

Crystal Tigers

The Crystal Tigers club is mostly interested in tracking members and events. The officers who will use the system do not know much about computers, but

FIGURE 6.36

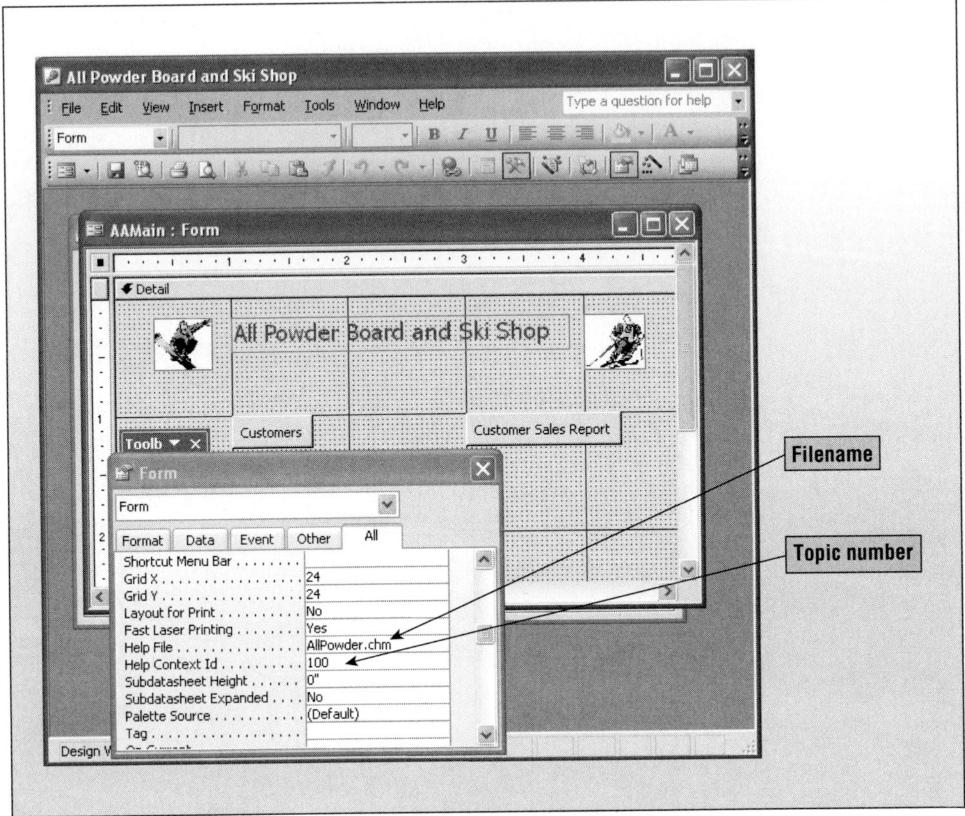

they can enter data into forms. They are also interested in a few key reports. For instance, they want to be able to get totals for the amount of hours their members devoted to charity events. They also want monthly summaries of the amount of money raised. The vice president also wants to be able to print a simple listing of the officers with their phone numbers and e-mail addresses. Sometimes she also wants a similar list of members who have participated in the initial steps of an event. She wants to be able to carry the list with her when the event starts so she knows who to contact if problems arise.

1. Create the basic forms needed to enter data into the database.
2. Build a form similar to the one defined in Chapter 2.
3. Create the main reports needed by the organization.
4. Build the forms and reports into an application with a startup form.
5. Create the Help files for the system; remember that the users have limited computer experience.

Capitol Artists

Job tracking is the most important aspect of the application needed by Capitol Artists. In particular, the employees need to be able to quickly select a job and enter the time and expenses for the task performed. This data is then used to create a monthly billing report for the client. Consequently, you need to focus on creating the forms to capture this data. You need to make sure they are fast and easy to use. The managers also want weekly reports showing the hours and money generated by each employee so they can use the data for personnel evaluations.

1. Create the basic forms needed to enter data into the database.
2. Build a form similar to the one defined in Chapter 2.
3. Create the main reports needed by the managers.
4. Build the forms and reports into an application with a startup form.
5. Create Help files for the system.

Offshore Speed

Special orders have always been a complex problem for the Offshore Speed managers. Customers come to the shop because it is one of the few that can obtain the custom parts they want. But the company has always had problems training employees to collect all of the order data and to keep track of getting the orders placed and delivered in a timely manner. Some of these orders include contracts with other local firms to perform customization and finish work on the boats. Although these firms do excellent work, most are terrible at keeping records. Consequently, the managers want to use the system to generate reports on individual boats for each contract shop that can be used to remind the other owners of the details. The company also needs reports on the inventory status of the specialized parts. They have trouble keeping some items in stock, and other items seem to sit on the shelves forever. They have no good way of keeping track at the moment.

1. Create the basic forms needed to enter data into the database.
2. Build a form similar to the one defined in Chapter 2.
3. Create the main reports needed by the managers.
4. Build the forms and reports into an application with a startup form.
5. Create Help files for the system.

Final Project

The main textbook has an appendix with several longer case studies. You should be able to work on one of these cases throughout the term. If you or your instructor picks one, perform the following tasks.

1. Create the main forms needed for the database, including forms that will be used by administrators.
2. Build the forms similar to the ones used to define the project. That is, build database forms that match the existing user forms.
3. Create the main reports needed. Think about the analysis that managers will want to do and provide reports that help them. Consider adding charts to compare data.
4. Build the forms and reports into an application with a startup form.
5. Build a toolbar that makes the application easier to use.
6. Create Help files for the system.

Database Integrity and Transactions

Chapter Outline

Objectives
Program Code in Microsoft Access
Case: All Powder Board and Ski Shop
Lab Exercise
All Powder Board and Ski Data
Database Cursors, Keys, and Locks
Exercises
Final Project

Objectives

- Define customized functions.
- Improve forms by responding to form events.
- Execute customized SQL statements from code.
- Define transactions.
- Create new rows and use the generated key value.
- Write cursor-based programs that compare data across rows.
- Set up and handle optimistic and pessimistic locking conditions.

Program Code in Microsoft Access

Access supports code modules that contain functions that you can use throughout your application. Access also supports detailed code behind each form that is activated in response to events on the form. However, Access does not support data triggers that attach to database events. Because of this emphasis on forms, data integrity code, locking, transactions, and key generation are handled within the necessary forms. For instance, you will generally have to write code within a sales form to handle transactions and data locking. In some ways, this approach is easier to understand because you write the code within each form. On the other hand, similar code might have to be written several times, and it is up to each application developer to ensure that problems are handled correctly in every form.

To understand how the code and event models work, this chapter begins with some easy examples. Pay close attention to the code and where it is located. For example, code written in a module can be accessed throughout the application, but code written within a form is generally only called in response to events on that form.

Case: All Powder Board and Ski Shop

Figure 7.1 shows the Sales form developed in the last chapter. Notice that it has a box to enter the sales tax. If you look at the underlying Sale table, you will see that it contains a column to hold the sales tax amount for each sale. You could argue that the sales tax does not have to be stored, since it can always be computed from the other sales data. But what happens if the tax rate changes? Or, what if the round-off computation is modified? Then the company's sales tax records will no longer exactly match the data filed with the state and local governments. It is safer to store the actual tax amount collected to ensure consistency. However, now you need a method to compute the sales tax on each sale—you certainly cannot expect clerks to compute the amount or even to look it up correctly in a table. Instead, you need to write a function

FIGURE 7.1

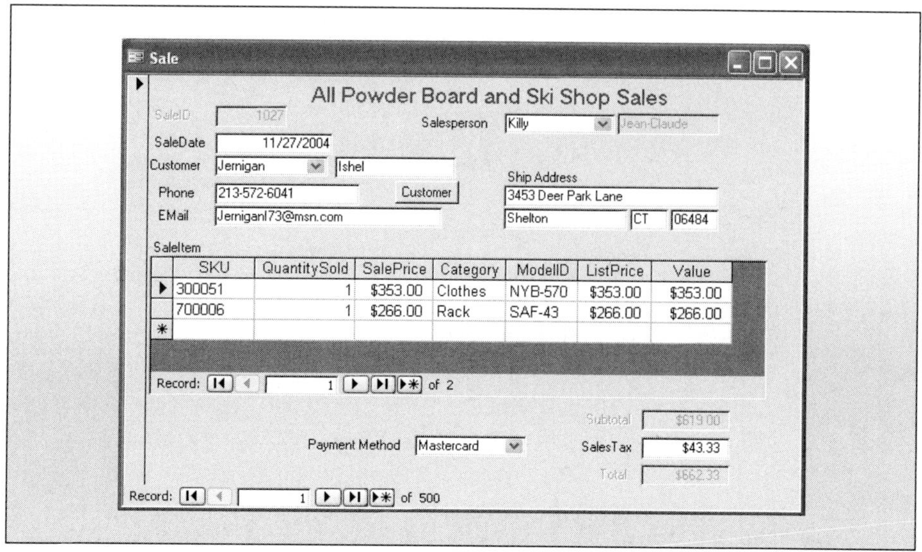

	SKU	QuantitySold	SalePrice	Category	ModelID	ListPrice	Value
▶	300051	1	$353.00	Clothes	NYB-570	$353.00	$353.00
	700006	1	$266.00	Rack	SAF-43	$266.00	$266.00
*							

that will compute the sales tax correctly and transfer it to the form and the database. Sales taxes can be highly complex. Some items are taxable, while others are not. Since each state and local district is different (and there are several thousand tax districts in the United States alone), this presentation is simplified and assumes a single tax rate to be applied to all sale and rental items.

The first question you must answer when creating custom code is to determine where it belongs. In this example, you might consider putting it on the Sales form, but since the code will also be useful for rentals, it makes more sense to generalize it and place it in a module so that it is available to any form, query, or report within the application. Placing the code in a special module also makes it easier to find later.

Lab Exercise

All Powder Board and Ski Data

Most applications require some amount of programming. Code is used to improve data integrity and to make the application easier to use. Functions and modules are used to centralize code so it is easy to find and change elements later.

Activity: Create Sales Tax Function

Begin by creating a new module, which brings up the Visual Basic editor. Before defining the function to create the sales tax, add the command Option Explicit at the top of the module. This option forces you to declare (Dim) all variables that you use, and helps spot typographical errors. Figure 7.2 shows

FIGURE 7.2

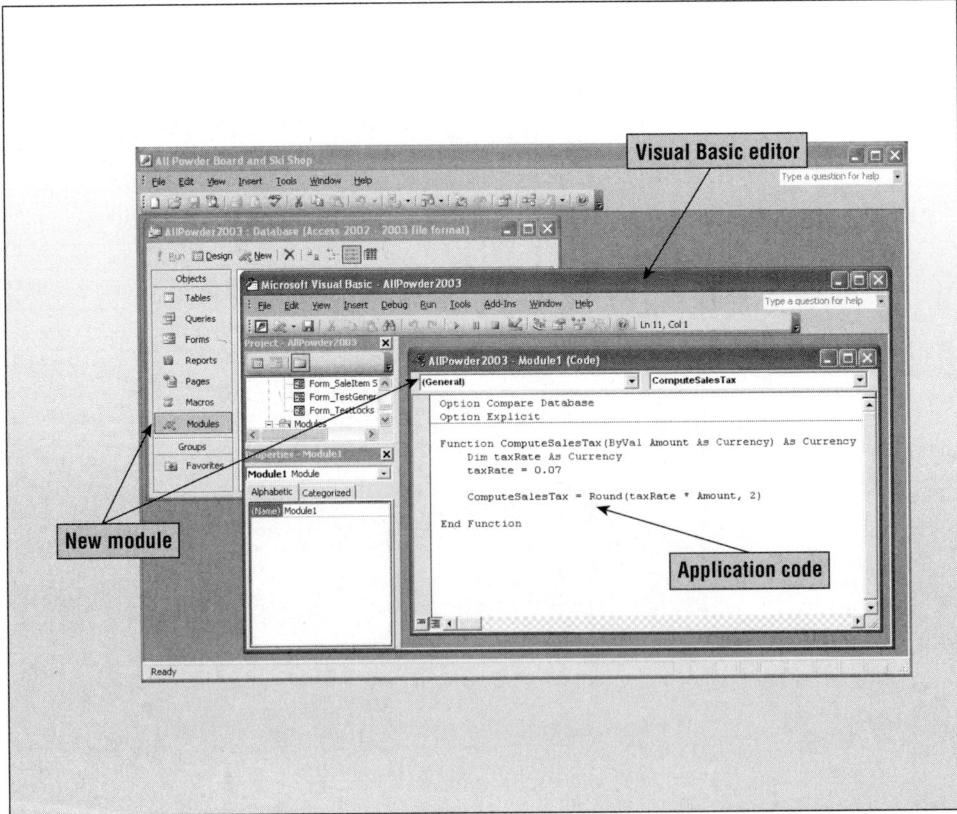

that the function is a simple calculation. Be sure to use a variable for the tax rate, since it makes the code easier to understand and reduces errors when someone tries to modify it later. Also, make sure you use the Round function to truncate the tax due at two decimal places. Save and close the module. You can now use this function in queries and forms just as you would use any other function.

> **Action**
>
> Create a new module.
> At the top add: Option Explicit.
> Add the function ComputeSalesTax.
> Use Debug/Compile to find errors.
> Close the module.

The next step is to use the formula to automatically compute the sales tax on the Sales form. The challenge at this step is to identify when you want to compute the tax. Why does that matter? The problem is that there are times you do not want to compute the tax. For example, if a sale has been completed and a manager is simply reviewing the form, you should not recompute the tax because the rate might have changed. So, you only want to compute it for a new sale. Realistically, it only needs to be computed when all of the sale items have been selected, but the form has no way to know when the sale is completed. Probably the easiest solution is to compute the sales tax due when the user clicks on the SalesTax box. For new orders, a simple click generates the correct value and the order total.

You need to attach a line of code to the Enter event of the SalesTax box (see Figure 7.3). Right-click on the text box and choose the Build Code option. Use the Code Builder option to open the Visual Basic editor. Select the Enter event from the drop-down list of events. Enter the computation as "SalesTax = ComputeSalesTax(SubTotal)," where SubTotal is the name of the box on the form that copies the subtotal amount from the subform.

FIGURE 7.3

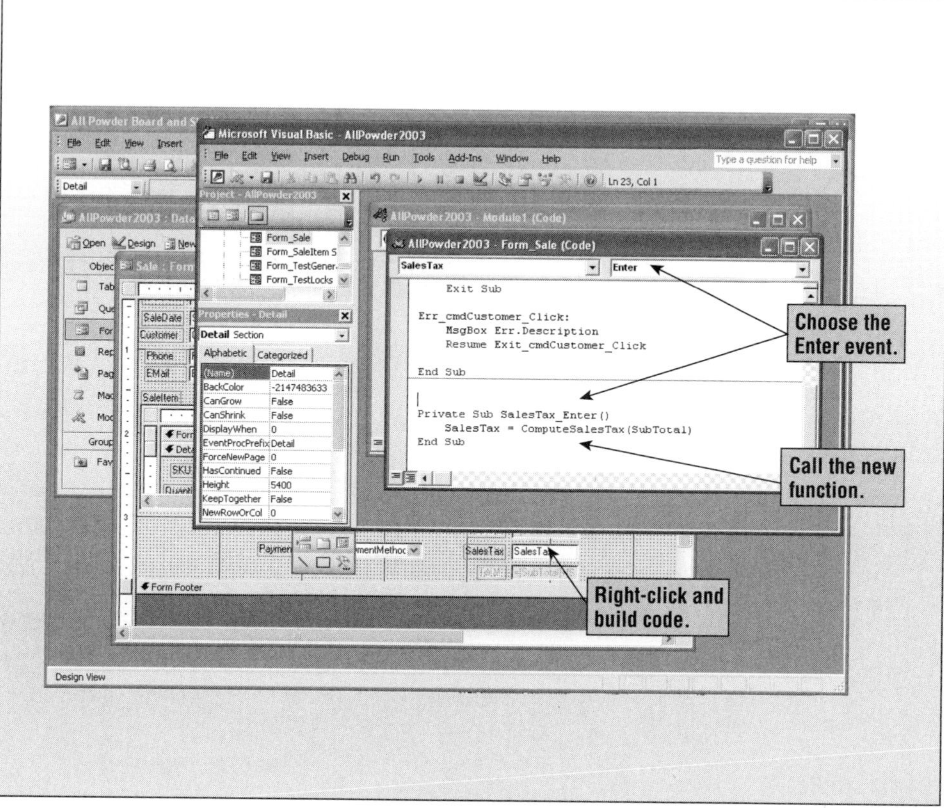

The Enter event is fired whenever the user clicks on or tabs to the specified text box.

To test the code, run the form and create a new order. Select an employee as the salesperson and choose the customer from the list. Select a product to sell (100003), enter the QuantitySold (1) and the SalePrice (300). Initially, the Sales Tax entry will be empty. Click on the box and the 7 percent tax will be computed and entered. The total sale value will also be updated.

In real life, program code rarely runs correctly the first time. To find mistakes, you need to use the debugger. Open the Sales form in Design view and return to the code (View/Code from the menu). Click on the gray column just to the left of the calculation line in the subroutine. The line should be highlighted in red as a break point. Return to the form and run it so that you can click on the Sales Tax box. Figure 7.4 shows that this time, the Visual Basic editor pops up, with the interpreted stopped on the break line. You can use the F8 debug key to step through line-by-line to see how the program behaves. Rolling the cursor over a variable displays its current value.

> **Action**
>
> Edit the Sale form in Design view.
> Right-click the SalesTax box and select the Build Code option.
> Select the Enter event.
> Add the line: SalesTax = ComputeSalesTax(Subtotal).
> Run the form.
> Click on the SalesTax box to test the calculation.

Activity: Update Inventory with Form Events

Maintaining quantity-on-hand statistics for inventory is one of the trickiest elements in programming business forms. Reexamine the Inventory table

FIGURE 7.4

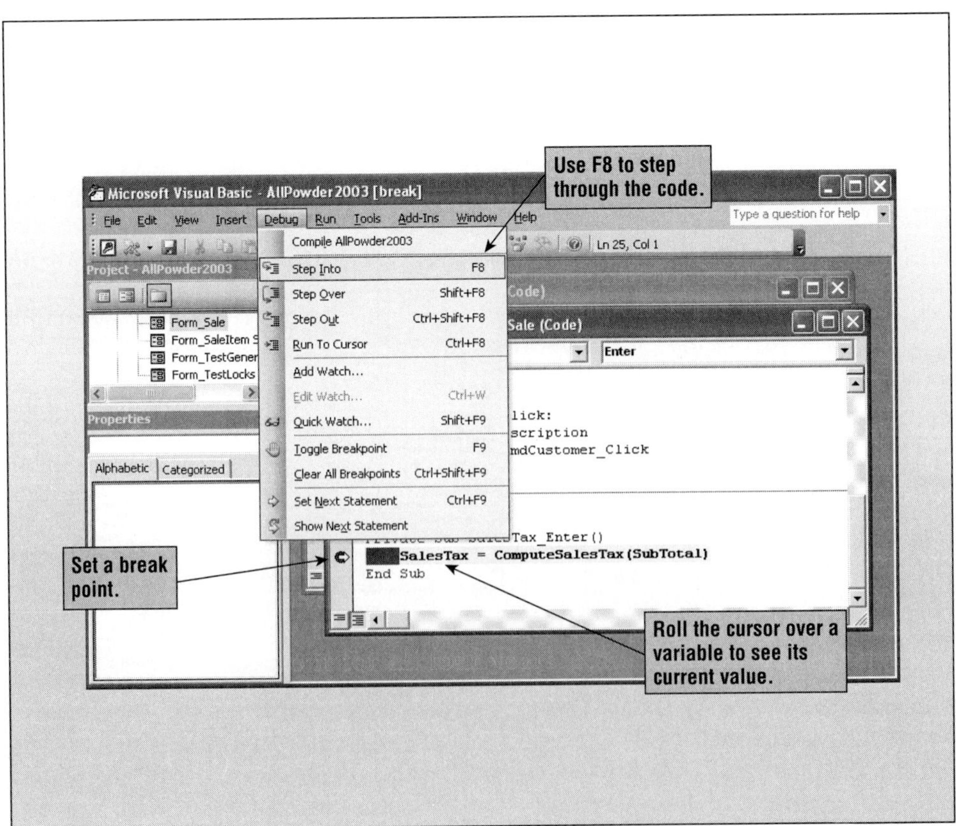

Action
Open the SaleItem subform in Design view. Open the form properties and modify the Record Source query to add the QuantityOnHand column. View the Field List box. Drag QuantityOnHand onto the form. Run the form and improve the layout.

and notice that it contains the column QuantityOnHand. This value represents the current number in stock for a specific item. The value of the column is that clerks can quickly check the column to see if certain sizes are available. Also, managers can get a quick look at the list of items that might be under- or overstocked. Technically, this value would not have to be stored in the database—if you have a complete list of all purchases, sales, and adjustments, you could use a query to compute the total number currently in stock. However, with thousands of items and sales, this query might take too long to run. Consequently, you need a mechanism to update this value on the fly. Whenever an item is sold, the corresponding quantity should be subtracted from the quantity on hand. In Access, this subtraction has to occur on the Sale form.

The first step in modifying the Sale form is to add the QuantityOnHand column to the SaleItem subform so clerks can see the status of each item. Since QuantityOnHand is already in the Inventory table, you simply have to modify the subform to display it. Open the SaleItem Subform and right-click on the Form Properties button. Click the Ellipses button on the Record Source property to build the query. Add the QuantityOnHand column from the Inventory table. Close and save the query, which returns it to the form. Figure 7.5 reviews the steps needed to add the field to the subform. You will need to resize the Sale form to display the new column.

FIGURE 7.5

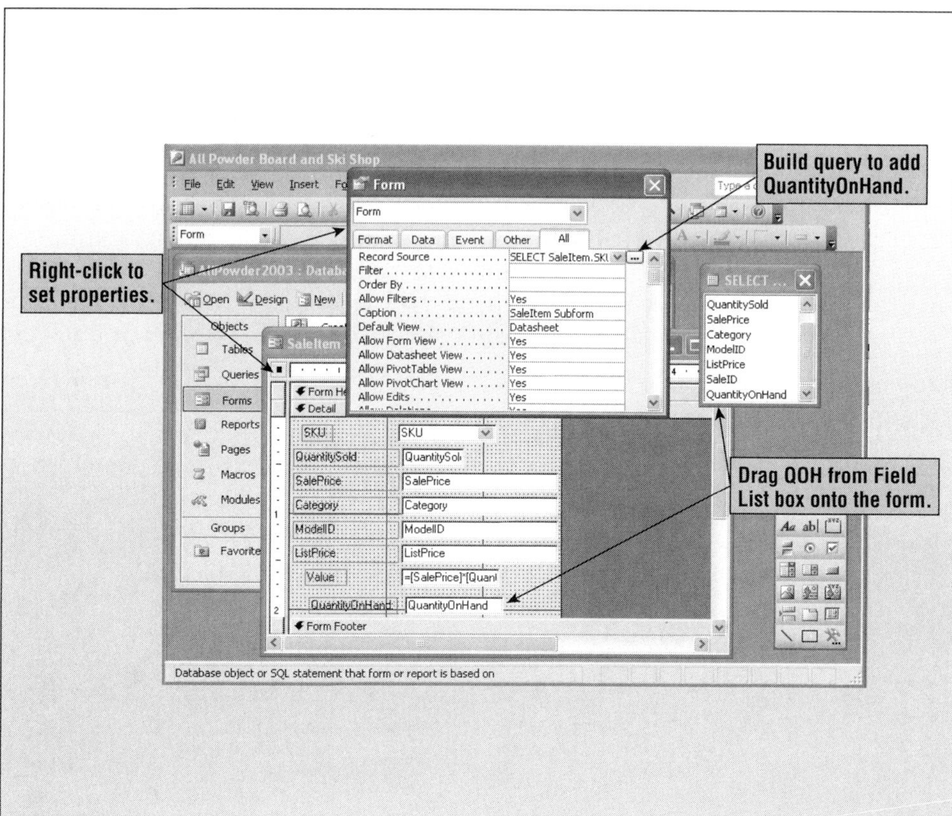

FIGURE 7.6

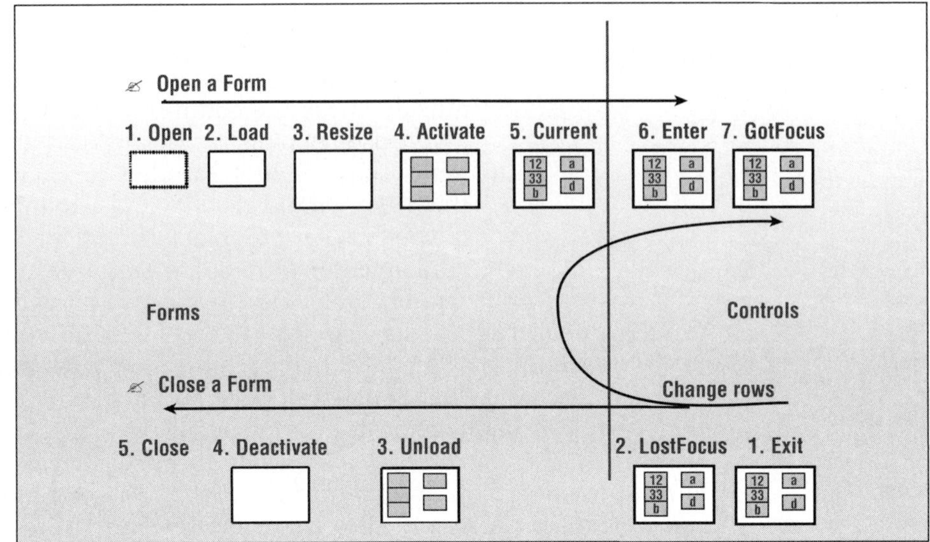

Now that the QuantityOnHand is displayed on the sale subform it is relatively easy to update as items are selected. Remember that you can attach code to any event on the form or events on specific controls. Before attempting to write the code to modify the QOH, it is best to look at some of the form events. The Visual Basic editor gives you a complete list of form and control events through the drop-down lists. However, the editor does not explain the sequence of events. Figure 7.6 shows the primary events that are triggered as a form is opened and closed. The Current event of the form fills the form with data from the current row. Then controls trigger Enter and GotFocus events. Controls also experience BeforeUpdate and AfterUpdate events, which are triggered just before and just after the data is transferred to the database when it is changed.

It is important to understand the event sequence for a control being edited. Figure 7.7 shows the main events as sample data is changed in a text box. You can write code that is activated in response to each event. The trick is to determine the proper event. In many cases, the BeforeUpdate and AfterUpdate events are useful. The BeforeUpdate event is often used to

FIGURE 7.7

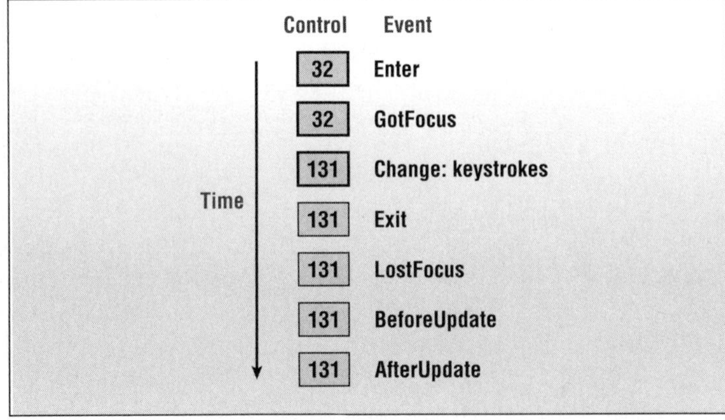

FIGURE 7.8

```
Private Sub QuantitySold_AfterUpdate()
Me.Refresh  ' Save data for new rows '
QuantityOnHand = QuantityOnHand – QuantitySold
End Sub
```

All Powder Board and Ski Shop Sales

perform complex validation checks on the value before writing it to the database. You can cancel the update if something is incorrect. The AfterUpdate event is used when you want to make sure that the change was correctly recorded and need to take some action in response to the change. The AfterUpdate event is useful for handling the change to QuantityOnHand. The inventory level will be changed only when the initial item selection has been successful.

You begin by adding the subtraction code to the AfterUpdate event of the QuantitySold field. Figure 7.8 shows the two lines of code you need to enter at this stage. The Refresh command forces newly added rows to be saved before attempting to change the QOH. You should open the Sales form and create a new order; select a salesperson and a customer. Choose product 950049 because it has a QOH of 10. Next, enter a value of two for the QuantitySold and see what happens to the QuantityOnHand column. When you exit the QuantitySold column, the value is written to the database, your new code is executed, and two units are subtracted from the QuantityOnHand.

> **Action**
>
> Edit the SaleItem subform in Design view.
> Right-click the QOH box and build code.
> Select the AfterUpdate event.
> Add code to refresh the row and subtract QuantitySold from QuantityOnHand.
> Test the form.

Before celebrating and moving on, you need to think about some potential problems. These problems may highlight the event-driven nature of the form, but they also exist with a database trigger approach. In particular, you should determine what happens if the clerk makes a mistake: Although he enters two items sold, he meant to enter one, so he returns to the QuantitySold box and changes the value. Try this and see what happens. Although your code dutifully subtracts another unit from the QuantityOnHand, the new value of seven items in stock is wrong. Since the company really sold only one item, it should be nine units. The problem is that you have to add the original two units back to the total. In more general terms, if the QuantitySold value is not zero, your code must add that original value back to the total, and then subtract the new QuantitySold. That is, your calculation should be

QuantityOnHand = QuantityOnHand − QuantitySold + OldQuantity. The only problem is to find the OldQuantity.

Look again at the Figure 7.7 events. If you wait until the AfterUpdate event, the only value you can get is the new number that was entered. In fact, any event after the Change event is too late—the original value will be gone. Actually, GotFocus is even too late, because someone might change the data, leave the text box and return, triggering a new GotFocus event and losing the original value. That leaves the Enter event. When the user first enters the box, you can obtain the original value. But it does not do you any good within the Enter event. As soon as the event is finished, the subroutine ends and the number will be discarded. The AfterUpdate event cannot refer to data in other events. You need a place to temporarily store the OldQuantity value so that it will be available to the AfterUpdate calculation. The solution is to create a new variable on the form code page that is outside of all of the events, making it accessible to all of them. Before modifying the code, you should open the Inventory table and correct the total to nine units.

Figure 7.9 shows the new code to update the inventory. The value for OldQuantity is assigned in the Enter event. By declaring the variable outside of the individual routines, it is global to the form and exists as long as the form is open, and can be used by any routine on the form page. Notice the use of the condition to handle the case where the QuantitySold is missing (null). Without this test, the code might crash if the data is missing. Null values in operations lead to more null values, or sometimes a total crash if Null cannot be converted to an integer. When you have entered the code, save and close the subform. Run the Sale form and return to the new sale. Change the QuantitySold value from one to two and watch the QuantityOnHand change from nine to eight, just as it should.

This trick with events is impressive, but not perfect. What else could go wrong? Think about other possible changes. What happens if the clerk selects a different SKU after the QuantitySold has been updated and the QuantityOnHand has been changed? To handle this problem, you would

FIGURE 7.9

```
Option Compare Database
Option Explicit


Dim OldQuantity As Integer


Private Sub QuantitySold_AfterUpdate()
  Me.Refresh                'Save data for new rows
  QuantityOnHand = QuantityOnHand − QuantitySold + OldQuantity
End Sub


Private Sub QuantitySold_Enter()
  If IsNull(QuantitySold) Then
    OldQuantity = 0
  Else
    OldQuantity = QuantitySold
  End If


End Sub
```

<table>
<tr><td>

Action

Open the SaleItem subform in
Design view.
Choose View/Code.
Add and modify the code as specified to
handle changes in quantity.
Test the form.

</td></tr>
</table>

have to add the quantity back to the QuantityOnHand for the original SKU, and then subtract it for the new SKU. Or what if the user deletes the SKU item or even the entire order? You need to add the original QuantitySold back to the QuantityOnHand before the row is deleted. Although these issues seem to be similar to the first problem, they are harder because they require changing a QuantityOnHand value for an SKU that is no longer displayed on the form. You will have to write SQL commands that can execute changes directly to the database.

Activity: Building and Executing SQL Commands in Code

Remember the power of the DML SQL commands (INSERT, UPDATE, and DELETE). In most cases, they are too powerful to trust to typical users. (Oops, half the database has just been deleted!) On the other hand, they are useful within your code when you need to make changes automatically. You might have a form that collects a few pieces of information and then builds an SQL command that can be executed immediately. Or, as in the inventory case, your code might have to update a row of data that is not displayed on the form. This latter situation arises when a clerk changes the value of the SKU item being sold. Figure 7.10 shows the changes needed in the Inventory table. When the first SKU (950049) is entered, your code subtracts the two units from the quantity on hand. When the clerk changes the SKU to 950050, you need code to add the two units back to the 950049 row and subtract them from the 950050 row. The code for subtracting the two units from the new row is straightforward because it is the current row and the corresponding quantity on hand is directly accessible. The catch is that the old row (950049) is no longer active, and you will have to write an SQL statement to change the value.

Again, you need to keep track of the original value of the SKU. As shown in the first part of Figure 7.11, your code for the combo box Enter event stores the current SKU value in a temporary variable. Be sure you create the new variable at the top of the form. Then, if the SKU is changed in the combo box, the code first updates the QOH for the current SKU (950050). It then creates an SQL statement to update the QOH for the prior SKU. Before attempting to write the code, think about how you would write the SQL

FIGURE 7.10

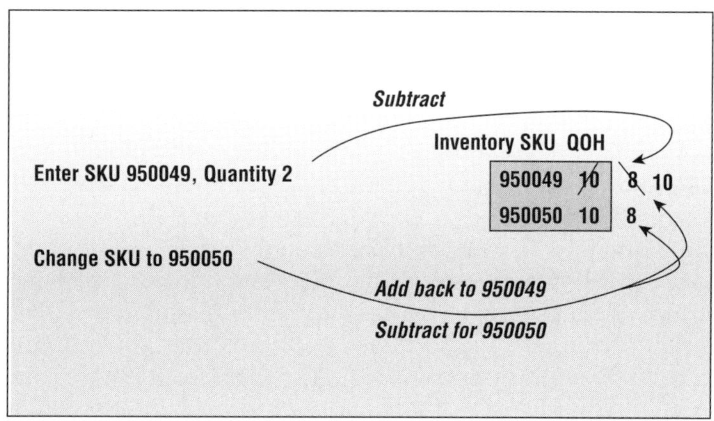

FIGURE 7.11

```
Private Sub cboSKU_Enter()
  If IsNull(cboSKU.Value) Then
    OldSKU = "-1"
  Else
    OldSKU = cboSKU.Value
  End If
End Sub
Private Sub cboSKU_AfterUpdate()
  If OldSKU <> "-1" And Not IsNull(QuantitySold) Then
    QuantityOnHand = QuantityOnHand - QuantitySold
    Dim sql As String
    sql = "UPDATE Inventory SET QuantityOnHand = QuantityOnHand + " _
      & QuantitySold & "WHERE SKU='" & OldSKU & "'"


    Dim cmd As ADODB.Command
    Set cmd = CreateObject("ADODB.Command")
    cmd.ActiveConnection = CurrentProject.Connection
    cmd.CommandText = sql
    cmd.Execute
  End If
End Sub
```

statement by hand. If you want to add two units back to QuantityOnHand for the 950049 SKU, it would be: UPDATE Inventory SET QuantityOnHand = QuantityOnHand + 2 WHERE SKU = '950049'.

The UPDATE statement is straightforward, but you have to be careful to include the quotes around the SKU value. The table definition declares the SKU as a text column—just in case the store wants to use nonnumeric codes in the future. Consequently, all SKU values have to be enclosed in quotes within an SQL statement. Figure 7.11 shows how the SQL string is built in pieces. First, the literal portion "UPDATE . . ." is created. Next, the value of the QuantitySold is appended with an ampersand (&), followed by more literal text "WHERE . . ." that also includes the first single quote mark. The old SKU value is then appended, followed by the trailing single quote character. To test this code, you should place a breakpoint on this line, then examine the string that gets assigned to make sure it is correct. In particular, double-check that there are spaces between the words. If you have a complex SQL statement that does not seem to work but you cannot identify the problem, you can display the value in the Immediate window. Then copy the statement and return to Access to build a new query. Paste the SQL statement into the SQL query window and run it. Access will give you more detailed error messages. The final part of the code simply creates a new Active Data Object Database (ADODB) command. It connects to the current database and runs the SQL statement.

Maintaining quantity on hand is a good way to learn the details of form events. It forces you to think about how users interact with the form and the

---

Action

Open the SaleItem subform in Design view.
Add the oldSKU variable.
Add the SKU event code as described.
Place a breakpoint in the code before the Execute line.
Test the form by changing an SKU number.
Examine the SQL line before it runs.
Add the delete code as shown.
Test multiple changes to validate the code.

effects of user changes. As a developer, you must always think of different ways that people will use your application. Always assume that someone will follow a different path and consider how that will affect the data. Now, what happens if a user deletes an item from the list of sale items? If your code has already subtracted units from inventory, you must restore those values. This process is similar to the two cases already examined. But it is more difficult because Access allows users to delete multiple rows at one time. You need code that captures each SKU and the corresponding quantity. Then, when the rows are deleted, your code goes through the list of deleted items and restores the quantity on hand for each entry. Handling this list efficiently requires a dynamically created array. A complete description of the code would be too long for this lab. However, Figure 7.12 shows the code so your application can be complete. Notice that two events are used: Delete and AfterDeleteConfirm. The Delete event is triggered once for each row being deleted, so this is where the SKU and QuantitySold values are collected and stored in temporary arrays. The AfterDeleteConfirm event is fired once— when users agree to delete the rows. At this time, a loop updates the QOH for each of the saved values, using an SQL statement that is executed in a separate routine.

FIGURE 7.12

```
Dim DelQuantity() As String
Dim DelSKU() As String
Dim nDel As Integer
Private Sub Form_Delete(Cancel As Integer)
  If IsNull(cboSKU.Value) Or IsNull(QuantitySold) Then Exit Sub
  If (nDel = 0) Then
    ReDim DelQuantity(Me.CurrentView)
    ReDim DelSKU(Me.CurrentView)
  End If
  DelSKU(nDel) = cboSKU.Value
  DelQuantity(nDel) = QuantitySold
  nDel = nDel + 1
End Sub
Private Sub Form_AfterDelConfirm(Status As Integer)
  Dim i As Integer
  For i = 0 To nDel - 1
    DeleteOneRow DelSKU(i), DelQuantity(i)
  Next i
  nDel = 0
End Sub
Private Sub DeleteOneRow(ByVal SKU As String, ByVal Qty As String)
  Dim sql As String
  sql = "UPDATE Inventory SET QuantityOnHand = QuantityOnHand + " _
    & Qty & "WHERE SKU='" & SKU & "'"
  Dim cmd As ADODB.Command
  Set cmd = CreateObject("ADODB.Command")
  cmd.ActiveConnection = CurrentProject.Connection
  cmd.CommandText = sql
  cmd.Execute
End Sub
```

FIGURE 7.13

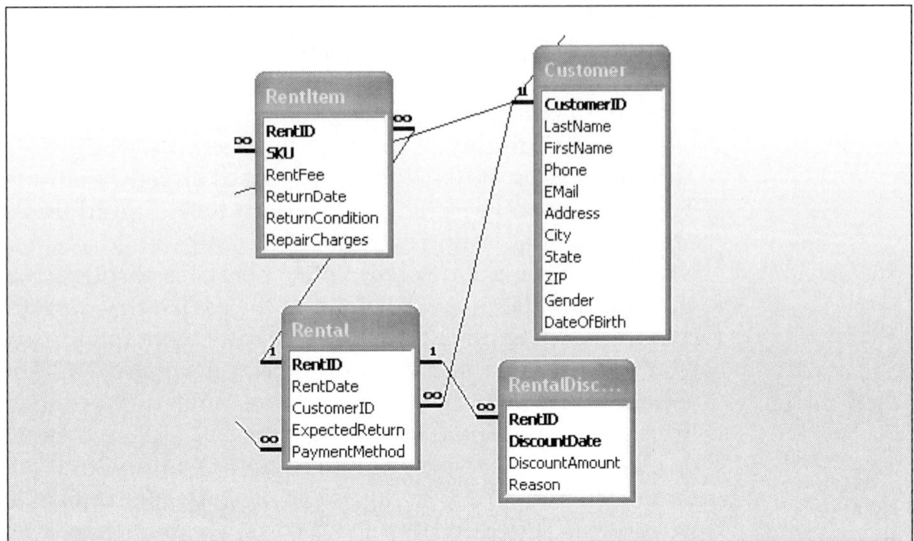

Activity: Define Transactions

Transactions consist of multiple changes that must succeed or fail together. Access provides some support for transactions using the ADODB transaction code. However, you need to know that Access does not provide a backup journal log. If the system crashes in the middle of a transaction, it wipes out the transaction point. That is, all of the updates will fail; there is no easy way to find the point at which they failed or to know which transactions to restart. But at least you will not end up with half a transaction completed and the rest missing.

Katy, the manager at All Powder, has noticed that many customers do not like being charged for damages caused to the rental equipment. Some of them believe that the equipment has simply worn out and failed. She has also noticed that there can be several complaints about a specific rental—particularly when it involves multiple items. David, the rental manager, agrees, but still wants to be able to track the cumulative charges. He has suggested that any reduction in the damage charge be recorded as a discount to that customer. That way, he can track the total damages, as well as which customers might receive the most discounts. Katy also likes the discount idea because she wants to implement a discount program for employees who rent equipment. Since multiple discounts can be applied to a single rental, a new table is needed. Figure 7.13 shows the table keyed by both RentID and DiscountDate.

You can build a form to handle data entry for the employee discounts, but do not do that now. It is a little more complicated to correctly handle the customer discounts for disagreements over the damage charges. You need a transaction that decreases the repair charges and adds a row to the RentalDiscount table for the same amount. To begin, you need to create a Rental form similar to the Sales form. Figure 7.14 shows a standard Rental form. Notice that it needs subtotals for the rental amount and for the charges. Any repair charges would be entered

Action
Create the Rental Discount form in Design view.
Add the text boxes and button.
Save the form.
Open the Rental form in Design view.
Add a button to open the Discount form.
Modify the open code as indicated.
Run the form and test the button.

FIGURE 7.14

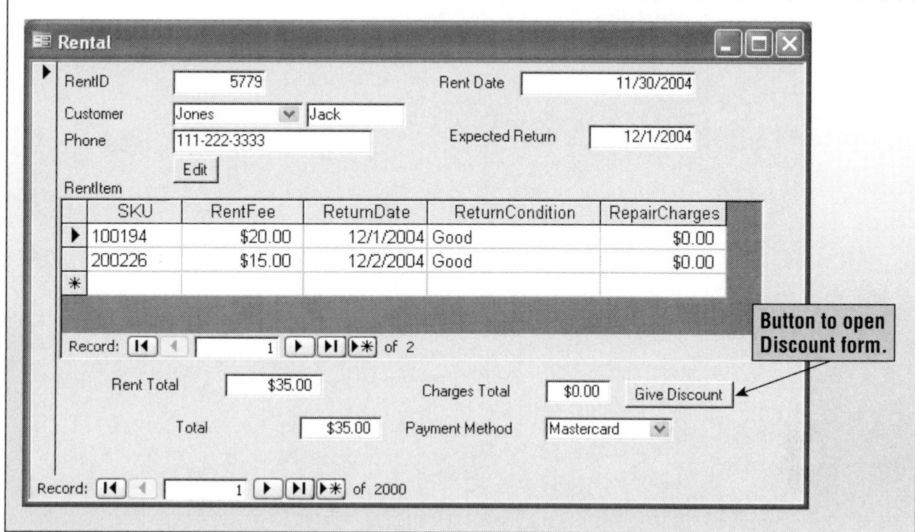

when the items are returned. Eventually, you also need to add a standard command button to open the form to give the discounts, but it is easier to create the form first and then return to add the button on the Rental form.

Figure 7.15 shows the Discount form (GiveRentDiscount). It is built from the Design view and not tied to the database. Add the text boxes by hand and be sure to give them names, such as txtRentID. Set the default value on the date field to Now( ), so the current date and time are entered by default. You can manually add the button, but if the wizard creates any code for the Click event, keep the subroutine, and delete all of the code from inside of it. Save the form.

The next step is to place a button on the Rental form that will open this Discount form and transfer two values automatically: RentID and Amount. Figure 7.16 shows the code used on the Rental form button. The wizard to

FIGURE 7.15

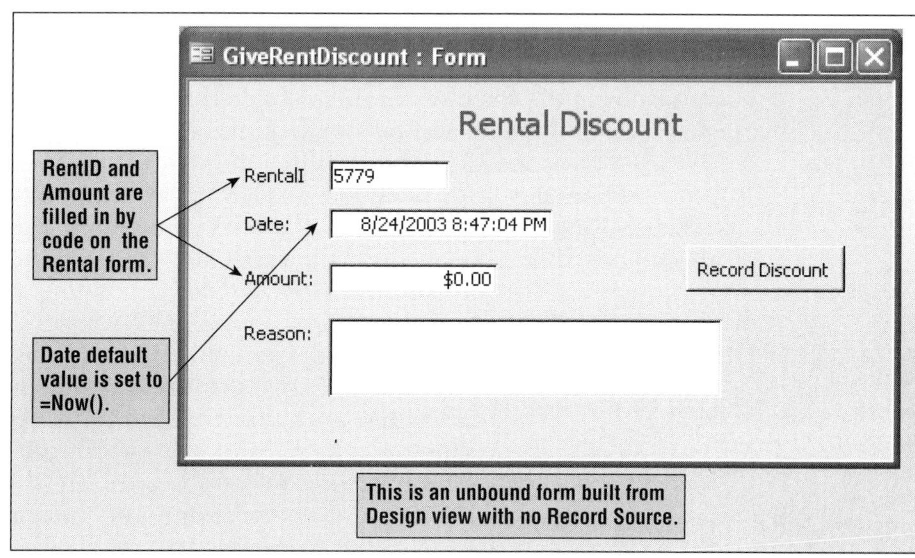

FIGURE 7.16

```
Private Sub cmdDiscount_Click()
On Error GoTo Err_cmdDiscount_Click
  Dim stDocName As String
  Dim stLinkCriteria As String

  stDocName = "GiveRentDiscount"
  DoCmd.OpenForm stDocName, , , stLinkCriteria
  Forms!GiveRentDiscount!txtRentID = RentID
  Forms!GiveRentDiscount!txtDiscountAmount = SubTotalCharges

Exit_cmdDiscount_Click:
  Exit Sub

Err_cmdDiscount_Click:
  MsgBox Err.Description
  Resume Exit_cmdDiscount_Click
End Sub
```

open a form generated most of the code automatically. You only have to add the two lines that transfer the RentID and Charges to the Discount form. You do that by assigning the values on the current Rental form to the corresponding text boxes on the discount form by using the name of the Discount form and the desired text box. Save the forms and test the data transfer.

The code for handling the actual discount is a little more complex. One complicating factor is the question of how to apply the discount. Should the charges be subtracted from one of the rental items or several of them? If the managers want to subtract only some of the charges, you will need to implement a mechanism on the Discount form to identify which charges should be reduced and by what amount. You might add a drop-down list to do one item at a time, or a subform with text boxes on each line. Either way, the process becomes too complicated for this lab. The code in Figure 7.17 assumes that all repair charges are being reduced to zero. The first SQL statement updates the RentItem table and sets the repair charges to zero for the specified RentID. The second SQL statement records the change by inserting a new row into the Discount table. The string is built by appending the values from the form text boxes. Notice that the date is surrounded by pound signs (#), and the reason by single quotes ('). Since the code requires changes to two tables, the BeginTrans function is called on the database connection to establish the start of the transaction. If no problems arise, the code executes linearly and commits the two changes to the database. A simple message is then displayed on the form and the code exits.

Notice the use of the **ON ERROR GOTO** statement to handle potential errors. This line states that if something goes wrong in the processing, the computer will immediately jump to the specified location in the code (Err_DiscountTrans). Here, the error message is written to the form, and the transaction is rolled back. The code then exits the subroutine. This error control structure is commonly used in this version of Visual Basic. In fact, the command button wizards write this code for all of the routines. However, you will have to add

FIGURE 7.17

```
Private Sub cmdDiscount_Click()
  Dim cmd As ADODB.Command
  Dim SQL1 As String, SQL2 As String
  Set cmd = CreateObject("ADODB.Command")
  cmd.ActiveConnection = CurrentProject.Connection
  SQL1 = "UPDATE RentItem SET RepairCharges=0 WHERE RentID=" & txtRentID
  SQL2 = "INSERT INTO RentalDiscount (RentID, DiscountDate, DiscountAmount,
  Reason)" & _
    " VALUES (" & txtRentID & _
    ",#" & txtDiscountDate & "#" & _
    "," & txtDiscountAmount & _
    ",'" & txtReason & "')"

  On Error GoTo Err_DiscountTrans
  cmd.ActiveConnection.BeginTrans
  cmd.CommandText = SQL1
  cmd.Execute
  cmd.CommandText = SQL2
  cmd.Execute
  cmd.ActiveConnection.CommitTrans
  lblMessage.Caption = "Changes recorded."

Exit1:
  Exit Sub

Err_DiscountTrans:
  cmd.ActiveConnection.RollbackTrans
  lblMessage.Caption = Err.Description
  Resume Exit1
End Sub
```

customized code to the error routines. For example, (you should) at least display the error message so you and the users know something went wrong. Also try to handle the error and clean up the database where possible.

Database Cursors, Keys, and Locks

Activity: Read Rows of Data

Direct SQL commands are useful for DML issues where you need to change or delete rows of data. When you need program code that has to examine several rows of data, you should use database cursors. Consider the business question of sales by week. Katy wants to know if weekly sales increase more in the first part of the year or in the last part. In particular, she wants to know the average percent increase in weekly sales for the first weeks (1 to 15) compared to the last 15 weeks (38 to 52). Remember that SQL can perform calculations on data within the same row. SQL can also compute subtotals for groups of data. However, it is difficult to get SQL to compare data by subtracting values across two rows. Instead, it is easier to write a query that does the main computations, and then use cursor code to do the comparisons.

Action
Create a new query in Design view.
Tables: Sale and SaleItem.
Create column SaleWeek:
Val(Format([SaleDate],"ww")).
Create column Value:
[QuantitySold] * [SalePrice]).
Sum the Value column.

FIGURE 7.18

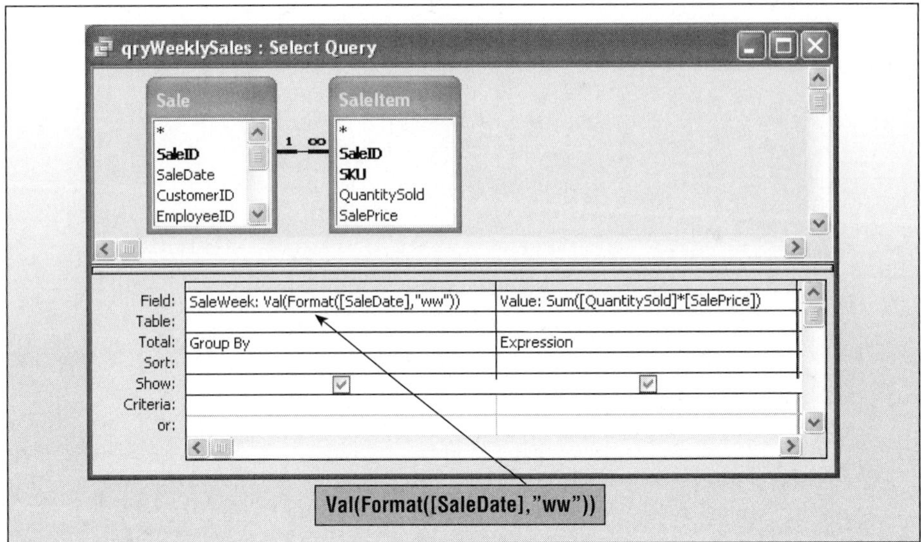

Action
Create a new form in Design view.
Add a button.
Add a text box named txtAverage.
Add the specified code to the button.
Run the form and test the code.
Place a breakpoint and step through the code as it runs.

Begin by creating a query that computes total sales by week. Figure 7.18 shows that the query is slightly tricky. You can use the Format(SaleDate, "ww") statement to convert the date to week of the year. However, because the Format function returns a string for the week number, it does not sort correctly. So you have to use the Val function to convert the weeks into values that are sorted numerically. Run the query and you will see that it returns the total value of sales for each week of the year. Note that there are 53 weeks instead of the expected 52, but the last week does not have seven days. The issue of 52 and 53 weeks per year is important when setting up accounting systems for retailers but can be ignored for this lab. Save the query as "qryWeeklySales" and close it.

The next step is to compute the percentage change between the rows. Because you will need code for this step, begin by creating a new form in Design view. Add a command button and a text box to display the result. Give meaningful names to both controls, such as txtAverage. Figure 7.19 shows the basic form.

FIGURE 7.19

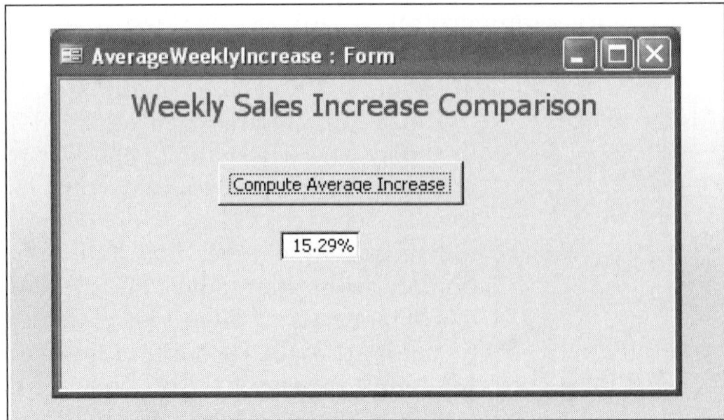

FIGURE 7.20

```
Dimrst As ADODB.Recordset
Set rst = CreateObject("ADODB.Recordset")
Dim SQL As String
SQL = "SELECT SaleWeek, [Value] FROM qryWeeklySales"
rst.OpenSQL, CurrentProject.Connection, adOpenStatic, adLockReadOnly
Dim avg1 As Double, n As Integer              ← Open the SQL statement or table.
Dim prior As Currency
prior = -1
Do Until rst.EOF
  If (prior > 0) Then ←                        Skip the first week because
      avg1 = avg1 + (rst("Value") - prior) / prior   there is no prior value.
      n = n + 1
  End If                                        Compute the percent change
  prior = rst("Value")                          and keep a running total.
  rst.MoveNext ←
Loop                                            Save the current value
rst.Close                                       and move to the next row.
Me.txtAverage = avg1 / n
```

The next step is to write the code that computes the average percent increase. For each pair of rows, the code needs to subtract the two values and divide by the value in the prior row to yield a percentage change. This percentage needs to be summed and eventually divided by the number of calculations to obtain the average percent increase. Figure 7.20 shows the main code. The SQL statement is opened as a recordset, which retrieves one row of data at a time. The avg1 variable keeps the running total of the percentage increase, while n counts the number of operations. The role of the "prior" variable is the most important. At the end of the loop, it is assigned the value obtained from the current row. When the next row is retrieved, the program can now compare the current (new) value to the old (prior) value. This trick is useful for many cursor-based programs, so you should study the code until you understand it. You should also place a breakpoint at the start of the code and then step through it line by line so you can see how it operates.

Activity: Generate and Use Keys

Access uses the AutoNumber field type to indicate when a key should be generated. For standard forms, the process is relatively automatic. For example, the Customer table uses AutoNumber for the CustomerID. Whenever a new customer is added in the Customer form, a new value is generated and stored automatically. For many common operations, this process works well and is mostly invisible to the user and developer. However, some cases cause more problems—particularly when you need to perform operations outside the common forms. Consider a case where you need custom code to generate each sale and enter the sale items. For example, perhaps you have a barcode scanner and want to automate as much of the checkout process as possible.

Figure 7.21 outlines the basic events that will occur. Notice that when the new Sale is created, Access will generate a new key value. You need to get this value so that you can save it in the SaleItem table for each scanned item. The immediate question is, How do you get this value? This question is somewhat challenging to answer and highlights one of the biggest problems with

FIGURE 7.21

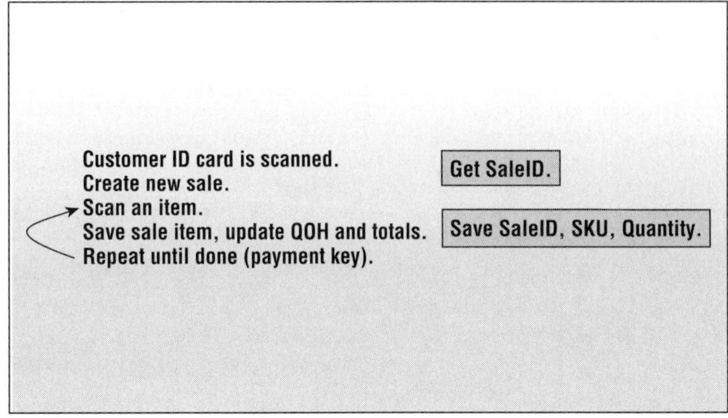

using AutoNumber. The other issue with AutoNumber is that the techniques are not portable to other systems.

Action
Create a new form in Design view.
Add boxes for CustomerID, EmployeeID, SKU, and txtSaleID as the generated key.
Create a command button and add the indicated code.
Test the form.
Place a breakpoint at the top of the code and step through the code.

The most important issue to recognize is that you cannot get a reliable value for the generated key if you use an SQL DML command. For example, if you issue an INSERT command on the Sale table, Access will automatically generate and insert a new key value for SaleID. However, there is no way to know what value was generated. You may consider issuing a select statement using the other columns in a complex where clause. But if you do, there is no guarantee that those values are unique, so you cannot be completely certain that you will obtain the correct SaleID value. However, there is a way to use cursor code to obtain the newly generated value.

Even if you have a scanner handy, you probably do not want to write the interface code for it. To simulate the data from the scanner, begin by creating a form in Design view that has text boxes for the three main keys: CustomerID, EmployeeID, and SKU. Figure 7.22 shows a sample form with default values that will work. Add a command button and delete the main wizard code. Also, add a text box to display the SaleID that will be generated within the code.

FIGURE 7.22

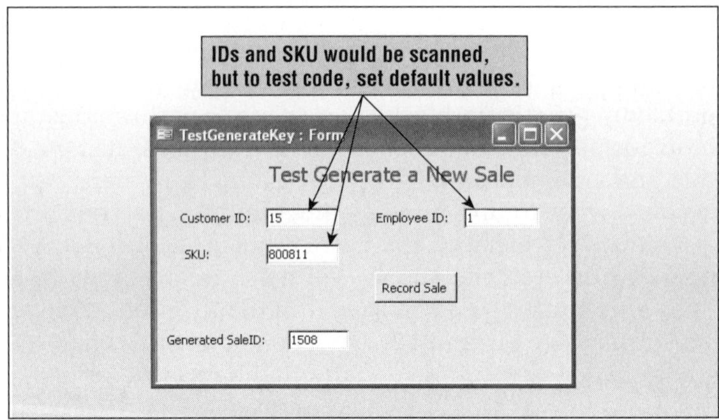

FIGURE 7.23

```
Dim sqlSale As String, sqlItem As String, sqlSaleItem As String
Dim rstSale As ADODB.Recordset, rstModel As ADODB.Recordset
Dim rstSaleItem As ADODB.Recordset
Set rstSale = CreateObject("ADODB.Recordset")
Set rstModel = CreateObject("ADODB.Recordset")
Set rstSaleItem = CreateObject("ADODB.Recordset")

sqlSale = "SELECT SaleID, CustomerID, EmployeeID, SaleDate FROM Sale"
sqlItem = "SELECT ModelID, ListPrice FROM Inventory INNER JOIN ItemModel ON " & _
    "Inventory.ModelID = ItemModel.ModelID WHERE SKU='" & SKU & "'"
sqlSaleItem = "SELECT SaleID, SKU, SalePrice, QuantitySold FROM SaleItem"

Dim cnn As ADODB.Connection
Set cnn = CurrentProject.Connection
'Get the List Price for the SKU
rstModel.Open sqlmodel, cnn, adOpenStatic, adLockReadOnly
Dim ListPrice As Currency
ListPrice = rstModel("ListPrice")
rstModel.Close
'Open the Sale table and create a new sale
rstSale.Open sqlSale, cnn, adOpenDynamic, adLockOptimistic
Dim SaleID As Long
rstSale.AddNew
rstSale("SaleDate") = Now
rstSale("CustomerID") = CustomerID
rstSale("EmployeeID") = EmployeeID
SaleID = rstSale("SaleID")
rstSale.Update
rstSale.Close
'Add the SKU to the SaleItem table using the new SaleID
rstSaleItem.Open sqlSaleItem, cnn, adOpenDynamic, adLockOptimistic
rstSaleItem("SaleID") = SaleID
rstSaleItem("SKU") = SKU
rstSaleItem("SalePrice") = ListPrice
rstSaleItem("QuantitySold") = 1
rstSaleItem.Update
rstSaleItem.Close
txtSaleID = SaleID
```

Figure 7.23 shows the code that runs the process. First, a query is used to look up the ListPrice of the scanned SKU. Second, a new sale row is created and the foreign key values of CustomerID and EmployeeID are entered into the row along with the current date. When these values are added, Access generates the new SaleID key value, so you need a line of code to capture this value and save it in a variable. Otherwise, the value will disappear when the sale recordset is closed. Third, a new SaleItem row is added. The SaleID stored in the temporary variable is placed into the data row, along with the values for the SKU, ListPrice as the SalePrice, and a QuantitySold of one unit. Calling the Update method saves the data to the database, and the recordset can be closed. The last step is to display the newly generated SaleID on the form so you can see it. If you open the main Sale form and go to the last record, you should see this new sale with one item having been sold. Of course, you

FIGURE 7.24

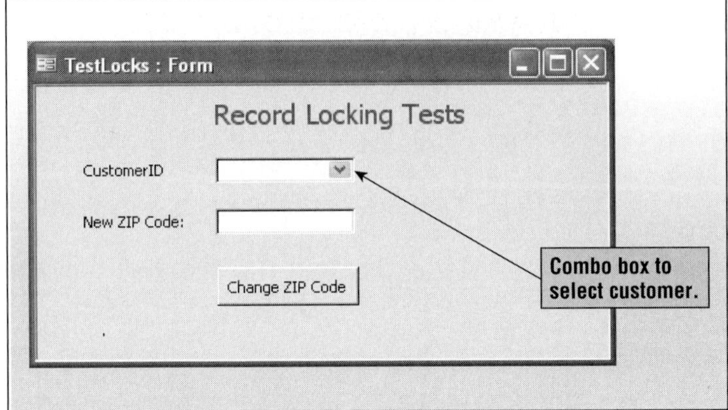

could modify the code to handle multiple items scanned, along with a screen to add the payment data, but they are not needed at this point. This trick of using cursor code to add a row and entering at least one column value is the only way to guarantee that you get the generated key value in Access.

Activity: Compare Pessimistic and Optimistic Locks

The issue of locking records to prevent concurrency errors could be applied to the rental discount form. Think about the possible errors if one clerk enters new values for damages while a second one is offering a discount. However, the differences between pessimistic and optimistic locking are difficult to understand, and it is better to start with a simple problem that is independent of the other forms. Consider a program that changes ZIP codes for customer data.

<table>
<tr><td>

Action

Create a new form in Design view.
Add a combo box to select customers.
Add a text box to enter a new ZIP code.
Create a button and add the indicated code for it.
Test the form.

</td></tr>
</table>

Create a new form in Design view that is not bound to the database. As shown in Figure 7.24, add a combo box to select a customer. Add a text box to enter a new ZIP code. Create a command button that will execute the code to change the ZIP code for the selected customer. If you use the wizard to add the button, edit the wizard code to leave the error-handling code, but remove the one or two lines of working code.

Figure 7.25 shows the code used to update the ZIP code for the selected customer. The SQL statement selects the desired customer through the WHERE clause, and the new ZIP code is assigned using the data cursor.

FIGURE 7.25

```
Dim rst As ADODB.Recordset
Set rst = CreateObject("ADODB.Recordset")
Dim SQL As String
SQL = "SELECT CustomerID, ZIP FROM Customer " & _
  "WHERE CustomerID=" & cboCustomerID
Dim cnn As ADODB.Connection
Set cnn = CurrentProject.Connection
rst.Open SQL, cnn, adOpenDynamic, adLockOptimistic
rst("ZIP") = NewZIPCode
rst.Update
rst.Close
```

FIGURE 7.26

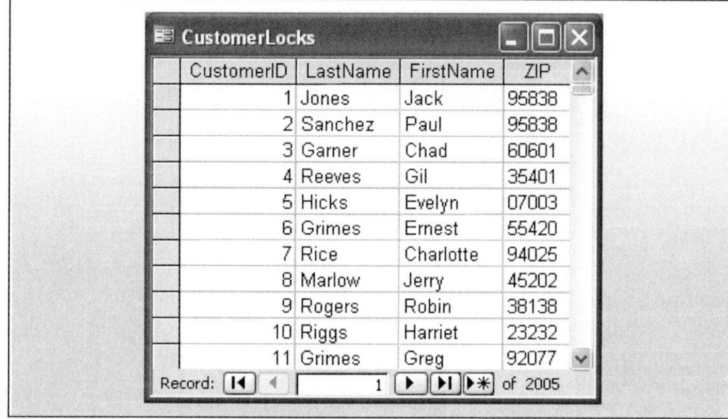

You need two processes that change the same data to test the data locks and concurrency. To be able to see the effects of locks, create a quick and simple form to view a few of the columns of the Customer table. Use the form wizard to create a form based on the Customer table showing CustomerID, LastName, FirstName, and ZIP. Choose the datasheet view so you can see several rows at one time. Figure 7.26 shows the basic form. Keep the form small so you can display it on the screen along with the TestLock form. By default, Access forms are set to optimistic locking, and it is the form locking that is easiest to test. Open both forms and position them on the screen so you have easy access to both of them. Click on the ZIP code for the first customer and change the last digit. But keep the cursor inside the ZIP box; that is, do not press the Tab or Enter keys.

Action
Create a CustomerLocks form as a datasheet into the Customer table.
Run the form.
Edit a ZIP code, but do not leave the cell.
Switch to the new form and run it for the same CustomerID.
Return to the table and press the Tab key.

Switch to the CustomerLocks form, select the first customer in the combo box. Enter a new ZIP in the text box. Then click the button to submit the changes. You should not receive any error messages. Return to the Customer-Locks forms and press the Tab key to accept the changes. Figure 7.27 shows the error message you will receive, indicating that another process (the TestLocks form) has changed the same data before you finished editing the value. You are given the choice of accepting the new value (Drop Changes) or of forcing your changes to over-write the change made by the TestLocks form (Save Record). The key to understanding that this process uses optimistic locks is to recognize that even though you began by editing the form, Access still allowed the TestLocks program to change the underlying data.

You can set pessimistic locks on any form by setting its properties. Switch the CustomerLocks form in Design view and find the Record Locks property. Currently, it is set to "No Locks." Change this value to "Edited Record," which will assign a pessimistic lock to any row edited on the form. Close the Properties window and return to the runtime view of the form. Again, make a change to the ZIP code for the first customer, then click on the TestLocks form. Make sure the first customer is selected and a new ZIP code is specified, then click the Change button. Figure 7.28 shows the result of these steps. The code on the TestLocks form is prevented from making changes to this row of the customer data because the row is locked. The error trapping on

FIGURE 7.27

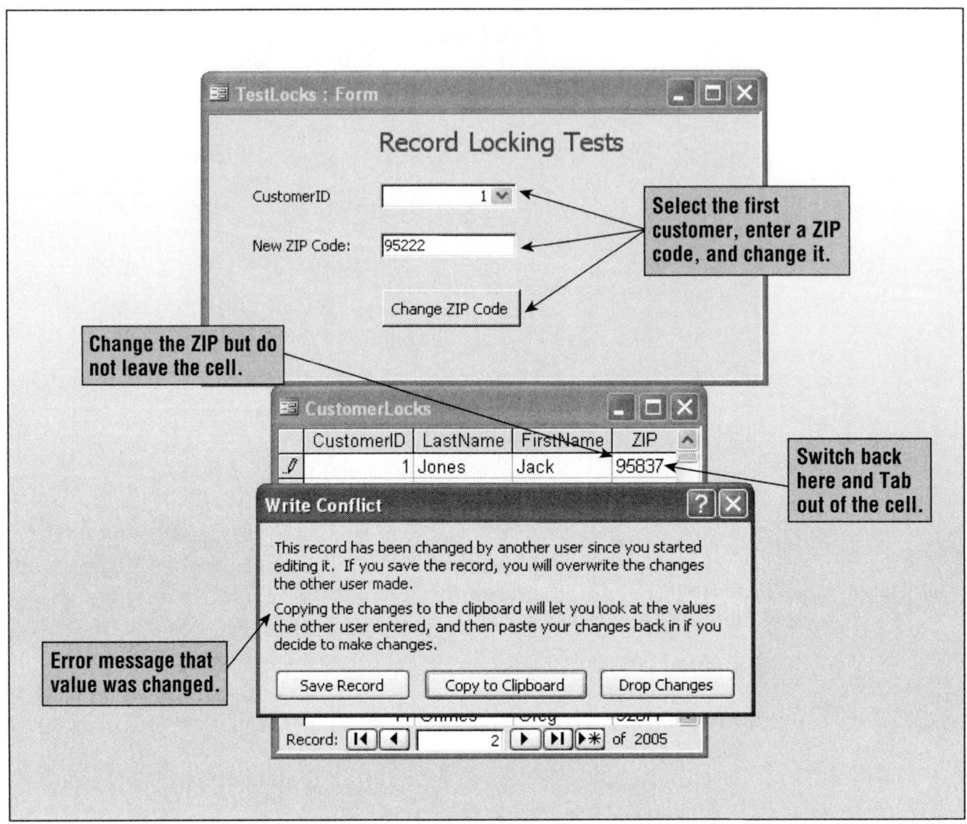

<table>
<tr><td>

Action

Switch to Design view on the change form and add the specified error-handling code.

Open the CustomerLocks form in Design view and set the Record Locks property to Edited Record.

Run both forms.

Change a ZIP code in CustomerLocks. Enter a new ZIP code in the change form for the same customer.

</td></tr>
</table>

the TestLocks form catches the error, skips the update, and displays the error message. If you check the underlying Customer table, you will see that the data has not been changed. Close the error message box and return to the CustomerLocks form. Press the Tab key to switch to a new row and complete the update.

The choice of pessimistic or optimistic locking depends on how often you expect collisions to arise and on how you want to handle them. Optimistic locking is considerably more efficient and is the preferred solution. However, all of your update code will need an error-handling section that recognizes an update has occurred and makes a decision of how to proceed. Figure 7.27 shows that forms automatically handle the problem by displaying the two main choices. Essentially your code would have to create the same form. For example, you could create a more sophisticated message box in the Test-Locks error section that offers the two main choices. Figure 7.29 shows the foundations of the code. The error handler displays the message and lets the user choose to retry or cancel the operation. The Cancel option discards the current changes and allows the changes made by the other process to remain. The Retry option cancels the current operations to be safe and then restarts the changes which should now succeed (unless some process intervenes again).

FIGURE 7.28

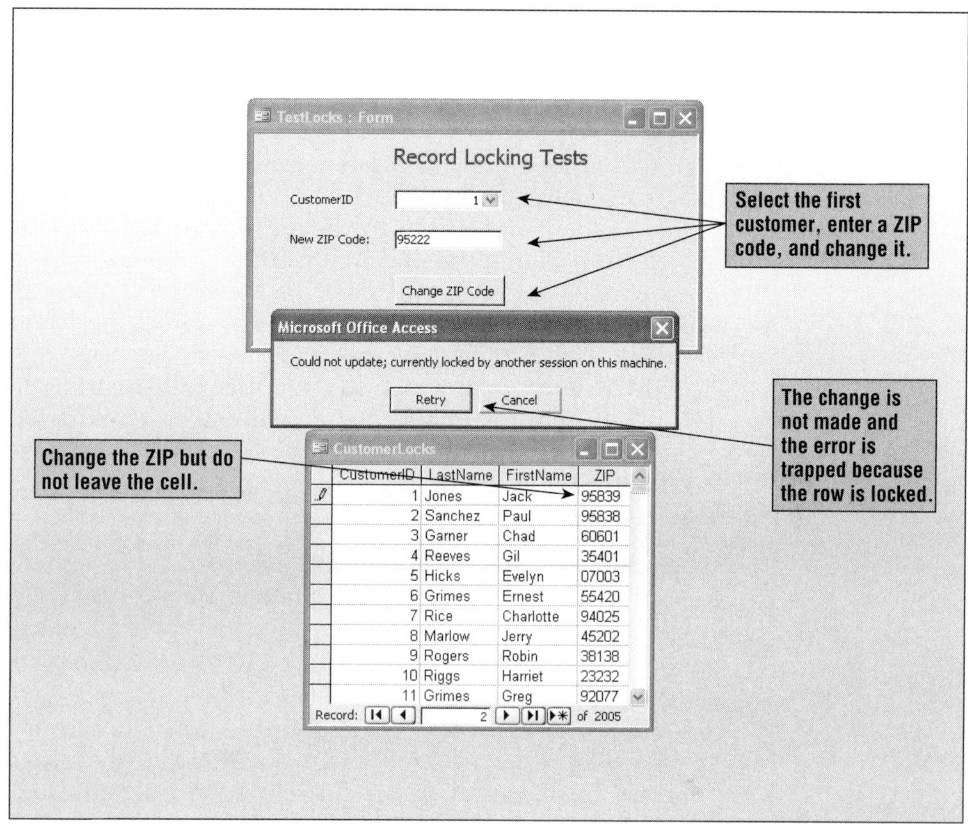

This code is difficult to see in operation and hard to test. To trigger the error, you would have to add a delay in the middle of the update code, which would give you enough time to switch to the other form and make an intervening change. Unfortunately, Access does not have an internal Wait function, so you would have to write one using the Timer function. But if you have time, you should test the code to see that it correctly handles changes under optimistic locking.

FIGURE 7.29

```
RetryUpdate:
  rst.Open SQL, cnn, adOpenDynamic, adLockOptimistic
  rst("ZIP") = NewZIPCode
  rst.Update
  rst.Close

Exit_cmdNewZipCode_Click:
  Exit Sub

Err_cmdNewZipCode_Click:
  If (MsgBox(Err.Description, vbRetryCancel) = vbCancel) Then
    Resume Exit_cmdNewZipCode_Click
  End If
  rst.Cancel
  rst.Requery
  Resume RetryUpdate
```

Exercises

Many Charms

Inventory control is a critical success factor for determining profitability at Many Charms. Madison and Samantha need to watch the quantity on hand— particularly for the high-cost items. The suppliers are a complicating factor. Some of them are known for being inconsistent in delivering items ordered. As a result, Samantha and Madison have to carefully check every shipment they receive and cross-match it to the orders. Many times the shipment is missing items, and once in a while, the companies send items that were not ordered. These items have to be returned, but the supplier billing is just as bad. Madison has to watch the supplier bills continually to ensure that they are billed only for items they actually ordered and received. As a result of problems, she also wants to track the unordered items that were sent back, so if they show up on a bill, she can provide the details of when the item was returned.

1. Create a form to handle purchase orders to suppliers. Create a second form to handle received shipments. Be sure that it can handle receipt of partial orders and track the day that each partial order arrives. It must also handle receipt of unordered items (which should be stored in a separate table).

2. Add a button to the Received Orders form so that if they receive an interesting unordered item, it can be added to the orders and inventory and paid for. Create it as an entirely new order and be sure to handle optimistic locks and transactions.

3. Create a form that enables Madison to select product and metal categories, and then enter a percentage price increase. Write the SQL update code so that this increase is applied to the list price of the selected categories.

4. The company ships orders to three states, each of which charge different rates of sales tax. Write a function that takes the state code and the amount and returns the tax due.

5. Create a form and write a program that for a given type of charm and type of metal, computes the average of (1) the number of days between sales of that item, and (2) the average number of days between purchase orders for that item.

Standup Foods

Although food items and celebrities are important aspects of the business, the day-to-day operations depend on managing the employees. In particular, Laura wants to reward the workers who continue to do well. The evaluation and rating system she has implemented is a major component of this plan. Now, she has to set up the system to make it easy to use so everyone can enter the necessary data. She also needs a way to analyze the data to help managers select the best employees for the next job, and to reward people who do well.

1. Create a form to enter data about an event, with an emphasis on the jobs performed by the employees and their evaluations. Make sure the form includes the revenue received from the event, the costs, and the dates involved. Create a separate form to enter and display data about employee specializations.

2. Create a form for Laura that lets her select a job category and then displays the top-rated employees in that category. (*Hint:* Create a subform and modify its Record Source query using code.) Create a text box so Laura can enter an average rating as a cutoff value. Create a second text box so Laura can enter a percentage raise increase. Add a button and write the code to give that raise increase to all of the selected employees.

3. Sometimes managers need to hire part-time workers on the spot. Create a simple form that lets managers add basic employee data without allowing them to see or change data for other employees.

4. Workers often want to estimate how much money they will make after all withholdings are deducted. Calculating withholdings is a complex process, but create a simple version to use as an estimate. The function should include number of exemptions, wage rate, and hours worked as inputs. It returns an estimate of the take-home pay. Use sample paychecks or research the Internet to estimate the tax withholding based on the number of exemptions. Create a simple form so employees can plug in these three values and receive the estimate.

5. Laura needs to provide some documentation to the bankers regarding the firm's growth. Create a new table with columns for month, revenue, costs, and percent change for revenue and cost. Write a query to compute the total revenue and costs per month and insert those values into the new table. Write a cursor-based program to compute the percent changes and insert the values into the appropriate columns.

EnviroSpeed

Tracking the knowledge of the workers and experts along with recording the experiences obtained in the many cleanup situations is a primary element of the company. You need to create forms that make it easy for workers to enter the data and knowledge gained. However, for the company to stay in business, you also need to track costs and revenue. Revenue is generally straightforward—the company bills based on the underlying costs, but payments are generally received over time. You will need a form to record receipt of payments by the customers.

1. The company is trying to standardize its fee structure. Write a function that has inputs for the cost of the crews, the cost of expert time, the cost of chemicals, transportation costs, the cost of equipment, and miscellaneous costs. Compute a billing fee based on a percentage profit from each of these costs (crews: 20 percent, experts: 30 percent, chemicals: 15 percent, transportation: 10 percent, equipment: 50 percent, miscellaneous: 15 percent). Also include a $50,000 fixed cost for overhead.

2. Create a form that enables managers to quickly put together a crew in an emergency. The form will have selection boxes for specialty and years of experience (subtract date hired from today). Clicking a button will retrieve a list of crew members meeting the desired conditions. Double-clicking on a name should add that person to the crew required for this disaster.

3. In the middle of an incident, crew members still need to record all of the details so they can be retrieved later. Create a form that enables them to enter the needed information. Be sure to include a way to quickly add a list of chemicals encountered in the incident. They should primarily be able to select from a known list, but they sometimes encounter new

chemicals. Be sure to control for concurrency, since several people may be entering data at the same time.

4. Write a program that evaluates payments by each customer. Assuming payments are due at the end of each month, assess an interest charge of one-half percent of the outstanding balance. Also, assess a late fee of $200 for each month that a payment is late. Automatically add these values to the customer's balance. *Note:* You will have to enter several payments and late or missing payments to test the function.

5. Enter enough sample incident data to cover at least a year. Write a cursor-based program to calculate and display the percent increase in revenue per month.

Final Project

The main textbook has an appendix with several longer case studies. You should be able to work on one of these cases throughout the term. If you or your instructor picks one, perform the following tasks.

1. Make the forms easier to use by automating as many tasks as possible.
2. Examine the case for situations where you can use SQL to update records selected by the users. For example, consider price increases, employee raises, and automated inventory orders.
3. Look for potential reports that require comparing data over time. Write the cursor-based code to generate the necessary change data.

Data Warehouses and Data Mining

Chapter Outline

Objectives

Data Warehouse

Case: All Powder Board and Ski Shop

Lab Exercise

All Powder Board and Ski Shop Introductory Data Analysis

Exercises

Final Project

Objectives

- Extract data from spreadsheets and import it into a data warehouse.
- Create and browse an OLAP cube.
- Analyze time-series data.
- Analyze geographic data.
- Analyze data with statistical tools.

Data Warehouse

Data warehouses have evolved because of the need for online analytical processing (OLAP) and its conflicts with online transaction processing (OLTP). The goal of a data warehouse is to hold consistent data, possibly obtained from several sources, which can be quickly searched and analyzed. Unfortunately, Access was never designed to function as a data warehouse, and it does not include much in the way of analysis functions. However, it is extremely flexible at importing and exporting data, which makes it easy to extract and transform data from other sources. In particular, it can interact with Microsoft Excel, which does have many tools for analyzing data. Also, either as a stand-alone tool or in conjunction with Excel, the PivotTable is a powerful OLAP cube browser.

Case: All Powder Board and Ski Shop

Like most businesses, the managers of All Powder need to analyze data to spot trends and to solve problems. One of the most challenging aspects of a board and ski shop is the huge variety of inventory needed. As vendors produce even more styles and variations, it becomes difficult to stock all of the items in a collection of sizes. Yet, if the store does not have the desired items in stock, it will lose sales. This balancing act between inventory costs and sales revenue has destroyed many other firms. The owners of All Powder are committed to running a large enough shop so that they can afford to carry a good selection of snowboards and skis. However, managers need to constantly evaluate styles and products so items can be cleared out if needed. For that analysis, one of the main tools they need is an OLAP cube browser or PivotTable that shows sales split by several features and categories. Figure 8.1 lists some of the main dimensions that managers want to examine in terms of sales. Because they are not certain about the validity of the last three, they are displayed with question marks.

Managers also occasionally raise some more challenging statistical questions, such as whether customers who rent equipment are likely to buy that

FIGURE 8.1

Sales Dimensions
State (ship)
Month
Category
Style
SkillLevel
Size
Color
Manufacturer
BindingStyle
WeightMax?
ItemMaterial?
WaistWidth?

equipment, and whether skiers buy specific types of poles or boots with their skis. They also need to forecast sales by categories. In particular, they often argue about whether certain styles are increasing or decreasing in popularity. Some of these analyses might require the help of a statistician to build a formal model, but the managers would at least like to see some rough analyses.

Lab Exercise

All Powder Board and Ski Shop

As organizations grow over time, the internal processes undergo changes, data also changes, systems improve, and number systems rarely stay the same. Consequently, most information systems consist of a mix of technologies and databases. Rarely is the data consistent across all of these systems. Before the database was created for the All Powder shop, the managers kept limited records in Microsoft Excel. These records are not perfect. They are organized by Sales and by Rentals, and the data is not normalized. Also, the records focused primarily on the equipment and did not keep data on customers. From our modern database perspective, the records are a pain—but at least they are electronic and not paper so you do not have to enter all of the data by hand.

Nonnormalized data is common in business, and you will often be asked to convert this data into a relational database. Fortunately, you can use the power of SQL as a magical "super tool" to impress mere mortals with your skills.

Activity: Extract and Transform Data

Figure 8.2 shows the layout of the data in the two worksheets. Again, notice that lack of normalization. Each row represents an item being sold or rented. Fortunately, the worksheets repeat the SalesID and RentalID so you can still recover which items are grouped onto a single sale or rental. Likewise, they repeated the descriptive item data for each time the model was sold. To be really safe, you should eventually check to see that they were consistent in recording this data. For example, ModelID BVG-290 might have been given different descriptions at different times. If there are many inconsistencies of this type, it will be difficult and time-consuming to clean up this data. Most of the corrections would have to be handled manually, unless you have a third source of data that you know is correct. These are the types of problems you often face when extracting data from diverse systems.

The first step in extracting and transforming this data is to get it into the database where you can use SQL to work on it. Fortunately, Access can quickly read a worksheet into a new table. Use File/Get External Data/Import to find the spreadsheet, select the worksheet, and read it into a new table. You should give the table a simple name, such as OldSales because spaces and hyphens will make it harder to type later. Read the sales and rental worksheet data into separate temporary tables.

Looking through the temporary Sales table, you will see that the data needs to be split into four tables: SaleItem, Sale, Inventory, and ItemModel. Go back and examine the relationships for those tables, and you will see that because

<table>
<tr><td>

Action

Choose File/Get External data/Import.
Read the Sales spreadsheet into a new table.
Read the Rental data into another new table.
Create new entries for CustomerID and EmployeeID equal to zero.

</td></tr>
</table>

FIGURE 8.2

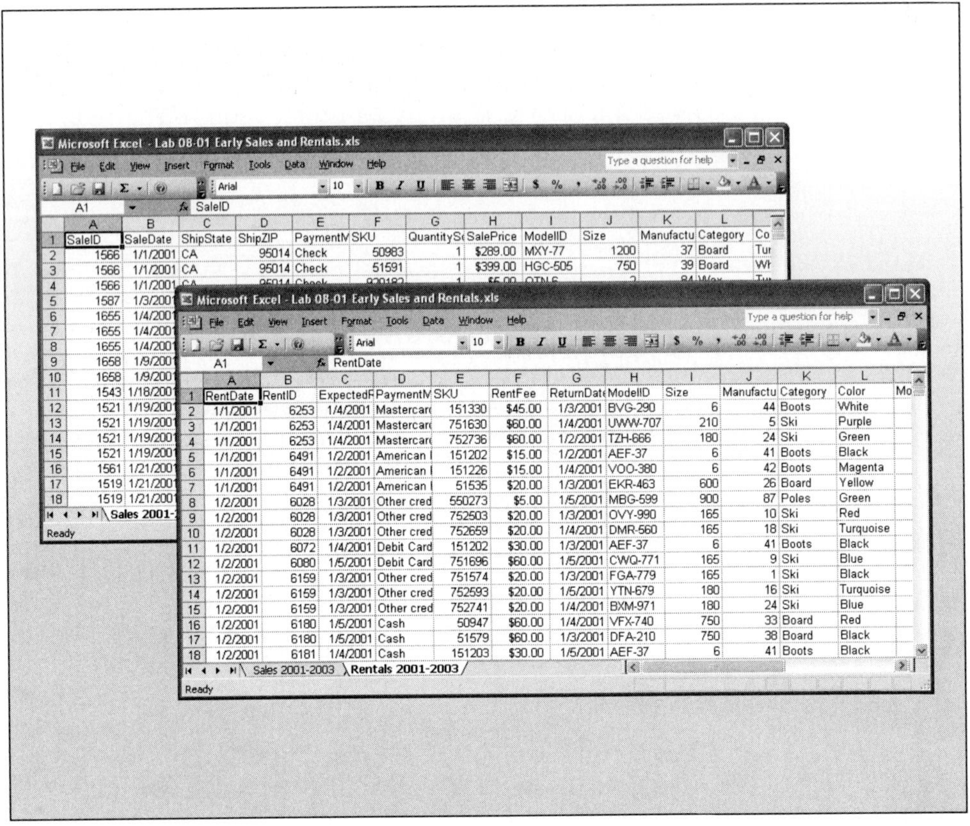

of the dependencies, you will have to enter data first into the tables for Item-Model, Inventory, Sale, and finally SaleItem. The relationships and foreign keys require that data be entered in that order. You must also be careful with the Customer and Employee data. If you try to create a row in the Sale table, the system will automatically try to set a value of zero for the CustomerID and EmployeeID. But there is no matching data for a zero ID in either of these tables. So either you try to force a blank CustomerID and EmployeeID, or you create a new Customer and new Employee called "walk-in" and "staff." This latter approach is slightly better than relying on blank data. Your first task, therefore, is to create these new entries in the respective tables. As shown in Figure 8.3, if you use SQL in a Design View query, you can force the ID values to zero, which makes these anonymous entries easy to find.

Before moving on to the next steps that will alter the data in your main tables, it is critical that you make a backup copy of the database. Go to Windows now and copy the database file so you can return to this point if anything major goes wrong.

FIGURE 8.3

```
INSERT INTO Customer (CustomerID, LastName)
Values (0,'Walk-in')


INSERT INTO Employee (EmployeeID, LastName)
Values (0,'Staff')
```

FIGURE 8.4

ModelID	ManufacturerID	Category	Color	ModelYear	Graphics	ItemM
ABF-878	23	Ski	Magenta	2002	Linear	Compos
AEF-37	41	Boots	Black	2001		Leather
AFZ-41	57	Clothes	Blue	2001		Nylon/G
AGE-77	22	Ski	Turquoise	2002	Geometric	Compos
AHX-640	28	Board	Orange	2002	Pop-Art	Compos
AIB-457	54	Clothes	White	2002		Wool
AKC-953	71	Clothes	Green	2003		Leather
AMJ-792	70	Clothes	Green	2003		Leather
ANO-456	73	Glasses	Turquoise	2002		
ANU-625	84	Wax	Green	2003		Wax
ANV-783	12	Boots	Turquoise	2003		Plastic
APA-554	29	Board	Turquoise	2003	Space	Wood
APX-230	26	Board	Red	2003	Landscape	Compos

Record: 1 of 1099

```
SELECT DISTINCT OldSales.ModelID, OldSales.ManufacturerID,
OldSales.Category, OldSales.Color, OldSales.ModelYear,
OldSales.Graphics, OldSales.ItemMaterial, OldSales.ListPrice,
OldSales.Style, OldSales.SkillLevel, OldSales.WeightMax,
OldSales.WaistWidth, OldSales.BindingStyle
FROM OldSales;
```

Action

Create a new query in Design view.
Retrieve DISTINCT data from the new Sales table.
Retrieve DISTINCT data from the new Rental table.
Connect the two queries with a UNION.
Save the query.

SQL makes it relatively easy to extract the new model data and copy it to the ItemModel table. The first step is to create a SELECT query that retrieves the model data from the temporary tables and removes the duplicates. This process is slightly complicated because of the two tables. It is possible that a product has been sold but not rented and vice versa. The easiest way to handle this problem is to write two queries and use UNION to combine the results. Figure 8.4 shows the basic query to retrieve the model attributes from the OldSale table. Recall that you have to add the DISTINCT keyword by hand. Move this query to the side and build a similar one from the OldRentals table. Be extremely careful to list the columns in exactly the same sequence.

Add the data rows from the two queries with the UNION statement. Figure 8.5 shows the basic structure of the query, but yours will contain several more columns. Save this query as qryOldModels so you can use it as one set of data.

Now that you can retrieve the new model data, it is relatively easy to write a query to insert these rows into the base ItemModel table. Build a new SELECT query using the qryOldModels query with all of its columns. Add the DISTINCT keyword to be absolutely certain that all duplicates are removed. Run the query to make sure it retrieves the data. As shown

FIGURE 8.5

```
SELECT DISTINCT ModelID, ManufacturerID, Category, . . .
FROM OldSales
UNION
SELECT DISTINCT ModelID, ManufacturerID, Category, . . .
FROM OldRentals
```

FIGURE 8.6

```
INSERT INTO ItemModel (ModelID, ManufacturerID, Category,
Color, ModelYear, Graphics, ItemMaterial, ListPrice, Style,
SkillLevel, WeightMax, WaistWidth, BindingStyle)
SELECT DISTINCT qryOldModels.ModelID,
qryOldModels.ManufacturerID, qryOldModels.Category,
qryOldModels.Color, qryOldModels.ModelYear,
qryOldModels.Graphics, qryOldModels.ItemMaterial,
qryOldModels.ListPrice, qryOldModels.Style,
qryOldModels.SkillLevel, qryOldModels.WeightMax,
qryOldModels.WaistWidth, qryOldModels.BindingStyle
FROM qryOldModels;
```

Action

Create a new query that retrieves DISTINCT values from the saved UNION query.
Verify that it works.
Add an INSERT INTO statement above the SELECT statement to copy the data to the ItemModel table.
Run the query.
Use a similar process to add SKU, ModelID, and Size to the Inventory table.
Follow a similar process to copy the Sales, Rental, SalesItem, and RentalItems tables.

in Figure 8.6, switch to SQL view and at the top of the query, add the phrase: INSERT INTO Item Model (ModelID, . . .). Because you do not have data for all of the columns, you must list them in the parentheses, in the order of the columns being selected. Run the query and all of the new models will be added to the ItemModel table.

Follow a similar process to add the SKU, ModelID, and Size columns to the Inventory table. Note that you should set the QuantityOnHand to zero for each of these items since the store probably does not have any of the old models in stock. If they do happen to have a few of the older items around, the quantity can be entered by hand later. Figure 8.7 shows the final step that inserts the data into the Inventory table. Notice the use of the column alias to force a zero value into the QuantityOnHand column for each row.

The Sale and Rental data is considerably easier because they are separate, and you will not need the UNION command to merge the two sets of data. In fact, you can copy the Sales (or Rental) data with one SQL command. First, build a query to retrieve the distinct sales data from the OldSales table. Be sure to include the DISTINCT keyword in the SELECT statement. After you test the SELECT statement, add the INSERT INTO line above it. Figure 8.8 shows an additional trick that is often helpful. Remember that the SaleID column is AutoNumber, so if you added new rows of data to your Sale table, it might have generated values that would conflict with the values from this older dataset. To avoid this problem, you can add an offset number to the old SaleID (+5000 in this example). If you choose a large enough offset, this step will ensure that all of the new ID values will be safe. However, you must also remember to add the same calculation in the final step of transferring the SaleItem rows.

FIGURE 8.7

```
INSERT INTO Inventory (ModelID, SKU, Size, QuantityOnHand)
SELECT DISTINCT qryOldInventory.ModelID, qryOldInventory.SKU,
qryOldInventory.Size, 0 As QuantityOnHand
FROM qryOldInventory;
```

FIGURE 8.8

```
INSERT INTO Sales (SaleID, SaleDate, ShipState, ShipZIP, PaymentMethod)
SELECT DISTINCT OldSales.SaleID+5000, OldSales.SaleDate,
OldSales.ShipState, OldSales.ShipZIP, OldSales.PaymentMethod
FROM OldSales;
```

Figure 8.9 shows that the query for the SaleItem table is almost identical to the query that copied the sale data, but with slightly different columns. Remember that if you transform the SaleID in the Sale table, you must make exactly the same transformation for the SaleItem table. Otherwise, the data will never match and cannot be joined. If you forget, you will most likely receive several error messages. But some of the data might be joined to your existing Sales data, making it difficult to reverse the query. Finally, you need to do the same two steps for the Rental and RentalItem tables. At this point, you have successfully imported the old data and cleaned it up so it can be used within your database.

Activity: Create PivotTable to Browse the Sales Cube

Investigating sales by a variety of dimensions is an important task for the managers and owners of All Powder. It would be difficult to train all of them to build queries to examine all of the items that might be of interest. A faster and more flexible solution is to create an OLAP cube that contains the sales value (Price * Quantity) as the factor, along with the dimensions. Using Microsoft's PivotTable technology, the cube can be manipulated to see subtotals and sort or filter the dimensions. PivotTables can be displayed and manipulated on Access forms, in Excel spreadsheets, or even on Web pages generated from within Access. You can also create PivotCharts that let managers select the data to be displayed.

Action
Create a new query in Design view.
Tables: Sale, SaleItem, Inventory, ItemModel, Manufacturer.
Columns: ShipState, PaymentMethod, SaleMonth with a format of "yyyy-mm", and Value = QuantitySold * SalePrice.
Sum the Value column.
Test the query and save it.

Begin the process by creating a query that includes all of sale and model dimensions needed by the managers. Then add the value column. As shown in Figure 8.10, the SaleDate column needs to be formatted to display just the year and the month. The format "yyyy-mm" displays the month as a number so that it sorts correctly. The PivotTable does not directly support hierarchies of data (such as year, quarter, and month) so you have to format the date as the lowest level that you want displayed, then build groups later to provide rollup capabilities. Compute the sum of the value column and leave everything else as Group By columns. You should sort the data by year and month, but it can also be sorted later. Save the query as "qryMonthlyPivot."

FIGURE 8.9

```
INSERT INTO SaleItem (SaleID, SKU, QuantitySold, SalePrice)
SELECT DISTINCT OldSales.SaleID+5000, OldSales.SKU,
OldSales.QuantitySold, OldSales.SalePrice
FROM OldSales;
```

FIGURE 8.10

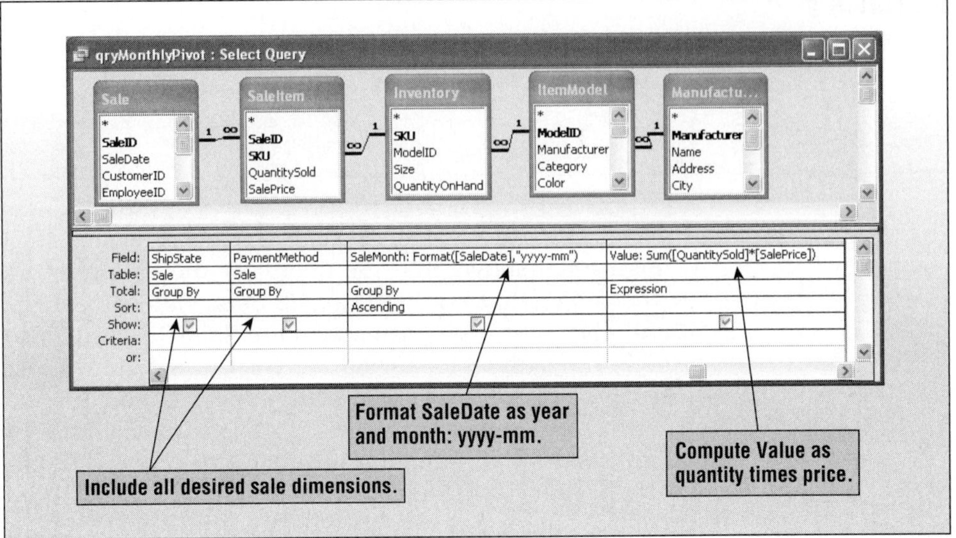

With the query in place, you can create the PivotTable form. The easiest approach is to use the PivotTable form wizard. On the main menu, select Insert/Form, then choose AutoForm: PivotTable and select the qryMonthlyPivot as the data source. Figure 8.11 shows the initial wizard screen. It is important that you create the query before you start the wizard.

As shown in Figure 8.12, the PivotTable wizard creates a blank screen with four sections and a list of the columns from the query. The four sections are (1) filter fields, (2) column fields, (3) row fields, and (4) the value field. The first three represent the dimension elements; the fourth is the fact data that you wish to sum. Because of the way the table dynamically adjusts to changes, be sure to place the fact field last.

In this example, begin by placing the SaleMonth field to create the columns. Simply drag it from the list and drop it on the area indicated for

FIGURE 8.11

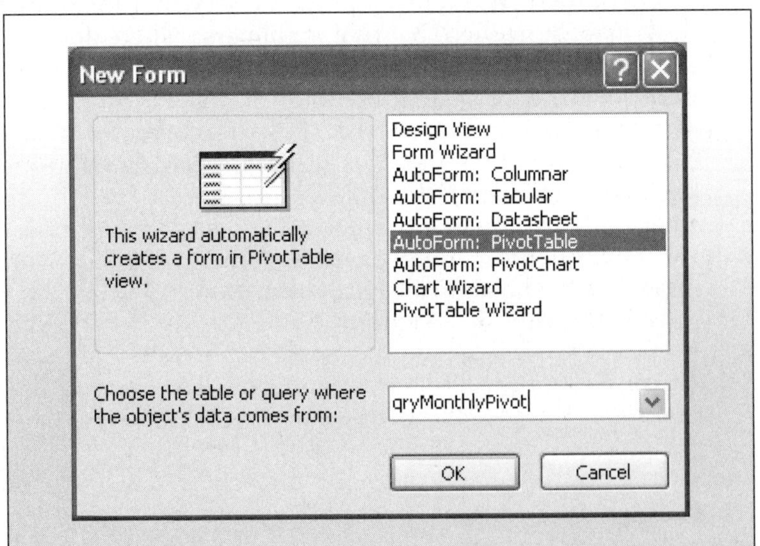

FIGURE 8.12

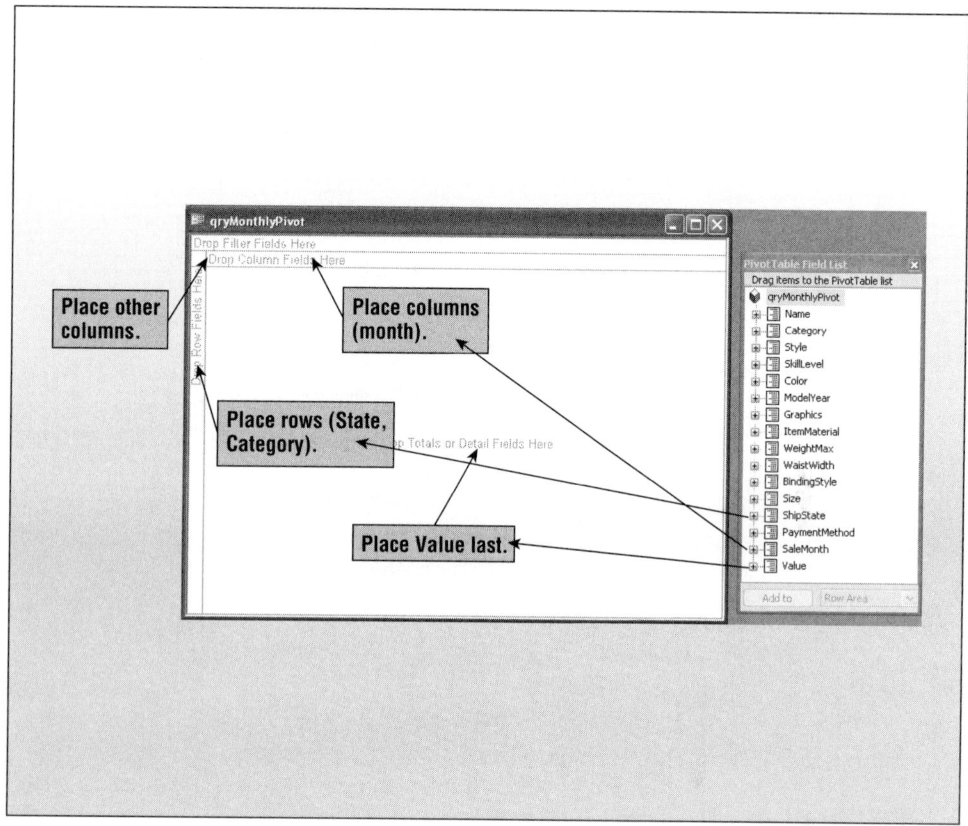

columns. The managers primarily want to see the Category and SaleState as rows of the cube. Drag each of those fields to the left side of the screen. If you drag them one at a time, simply drop the remaining fields on top of the first ones you placed. If they are not displayed in the order you want, you can drag them to rearrange the sequence. The other fields, such as Color and Style, might also be used by the managers, but including them would make the table too large. Place all of the other dimensions (not Value) onto the filter location at the top of the table. From here, managers can choose to restrict the display based on various conditions. They can also change the composition of the table by replacing Row or Column fields with a Filter field. Finally, drag the Value field onto the middle of the table.

The next step is to scroll to the right edge of the PivotTable and notice that the Total column is empty. You also have to drag the Value field and drop it onto this column to be able to see subtotals. However, by default, the PivotTable shows too much detail—it tends to compute subtotals for every single item. To hide this unnecessary detail, right-click on the SaleMonth heading to select all of the columns, then choose the Hide Details option. Figure 8.13 shows the initial structure of the PivotTable.

The next step is to create the time hierarchy (year-quarter-month) to enable managers to roll up the data or drill down, depending on the detail they want to see. The PivotTable uses Groups to establish the year and quarter elements. You highlight the columns that belong together,

FIGURE 8.13

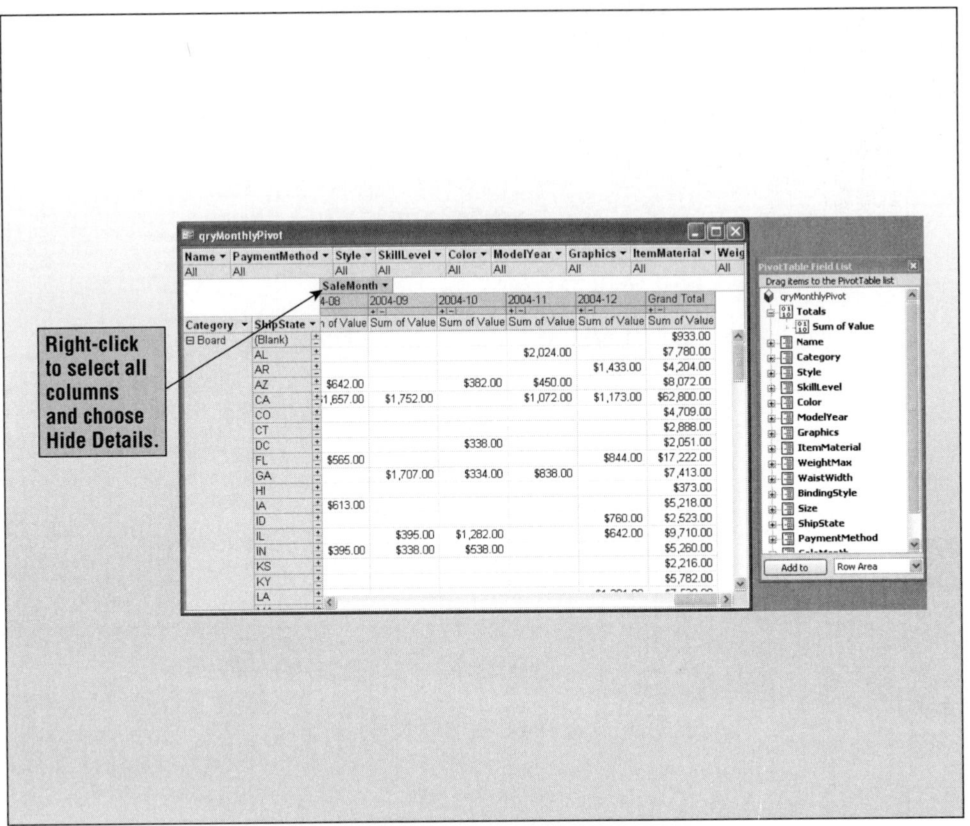

<table>
<tr><td colspan="3">**Action**</td></tr>
</table>

Action
Choose Insert/Form.
Select AutoForm: PivotTable.
Select the saved query.
Drag the SaleMonth and drop it on the column fields position.
Drag the Category and ShipState fields and drop them on the row fields position.
Drag the Value field and drop it in the middle Detail section.
Drag the other fields and drop them at the top as filter fields for future use.
Scroll the main grid to the far right. Drop the Value field in the Totals column.

right-click the highlighted area and choose the group option. It is also important that you use the properties to rename the individual cells so they are meaningful to the managers. To begin the process, you must build the lowest-level groups first (quarters). Click the cell 2001-01, then shift-click the cell for 2001-03 to highlight the first three months. Right-click the highlighted area and choose the Group Items option. A new cell labeled SaleMonth1 will be added to the left of the original SaleMonth cell. Right-click on this new cell, select Properties, click the Captions tab, and rename the caption to Quarter. Immediately below that cell, you will see a new cell labeled Group 1. Change its caption to 2001-Q1 because it represents the group you just created. Repeat the same process for each three-month interval. Be careful to label the quarters correctly. It is easy to make mistakes: The process becomes tedious because you have to do it for all four years. Note that the last quarter will already be grouped under the "Other" label; you only have to change the label to 2004-Q4. Once the quarters are defined, you can aggregate them into years using the same process. Click the 2001-Q1 cell and right-click the 2001-Q4 cell to highlight all four quarters. Right-click to group the items. Notice that a third grouping cell has been added at the top of the

<table>
<tr><td colspan="2">Action</td></tr>
<tr><td colspan="2">Create quarterly groups.</td></tr>
<tr><td colspan="2">Click on the first month and right-click on the third month to highlight them.</td></tr>
<tr><td colspan="2">Right-click and select the Group/Group Items option.</td></tr>
<tr><td colspan="2">Right-click on the new cell SaleMonth1 and change its Caption property to Quarter.</td></tr>
<tr><td colspan="2">Right-click on the Group1 cell and set its caption to 2001-Q1.</td></tr>
<tr><td colspan="2">Repeat the process for all quarters.</td></tr>
<tr><td colspan="2">Use a similar process to group the four years.</td></tr>
<tr><td colspan="2">Use the Collapse option to reduce the grid display.</td></tr>
</table>

form. Rename it to "Year," then rename the Group 1 cell to "2001." Repeat the grouping process for 2002 and 2003. The 2004 data is already grouped; you need only to rename the cell.

To see the purpose of the groups, scroll back to the left side and click on the Year cell. On the PivotTable toolbar, click the Collapse icon (yellow minus sign), or right-click the year cell and choose Collapse from the menu. The Collapse option rolls up the data and displays the group (year) totals instead of the details (months). Figure 8.14 shows the PivotTable collapsed on the years and on the Category row dimension. Managers can expand or contract individual years and quarters. They can also use the drop-down boxes on any of the dimensions to quickly display the subtotals for combinations of attributes.

If the managers prefer graphical displays, you can use a similar process to create a PivotChart. Just be careful not to put too many items on the chart at one time—it quickly becomes unreadable. Instead, focus it to one or two of the major dimensions and place the rest into the filter area. From there, managers can move the dimensions onto the chart to see exactly the combinations of data that interest them. For even more flexibility, you can build the same PivotTable in Excel. Managers can use familiar Excel tools to format, chart, or manipulate the data. You can even include a button on a form to open the Excel file directly from the database application.

Also, you should always remember the power of SQL when analyzing data. Although the queries are difficult for managers to create, as a developer you can build some standard queries for them to run. For instance, managers might be interested in seeing a list of customers who have rented but not purchased any skis.

FIGURE 8.14

qryMonthlyPivot

Name ▾	PaymentMethod ▾	Style ▾	SkillLevel ▾	Color ▾	ModelYear ▾	Graphics ▾	ItemMaterial ▾	WeightN
All	All	All	All	All	All	All	All	All

		Year ▾	Quarter	SaleMonth		
		⊞ 2001	⊞ 2002	⊞ 2003	⊞ 2004	Grand Total
Category ▾	ShipState ▾	Sum of Value	Sum of Value	Sum of Value	Sum of Value	Sum of Value
⊞ Board		$43,477.00	$64,347.00	$118,129.00	$114,759.00	$340,712.00
⊞ Boots		$17,390.00	$18,659.00	$44,010.00	$67,120.00	$147,179.00
⊞ Clothes		$16,865.00	$26,474.00	$66,710.00	$84,910.00	$194,959.00
⊞ Electronic		$144.00	$644.00	$2,354.00	$2,966.00	$6,108.00
⊞ Glasses		$164.00	$335.00	$747.00	$2,011.00	$3,257.00
⊞ Poles		$782.00	$832.00	$1,440.00	$1,880.00	$4,934.00
⊞ Rack		$884.00	$1,931.00	$2,306.00	$913.00	$6,034.00
⊞ Ski		$48,966.00	$87,448.00	$94,057.00	$136,683.00	$367,154.00
⊞ Unknown		$186.00	$204.00	$809.00	$1,075.00	$2,274.00
⊞ Wax		$165.00	$135.00	$318.00	$282.00	$900.00
Grand Total		$129,023.00	$201,009.00	$330,880.00	$412,599.00	$1,073,511.00

Introductory Data Analysis

Activity: Analyze Time-Series Data

Most database systems do not provide sophisticated statistical analysis and data mining as part of the base system. In general, you will have to purchase specialized software to perform the analysis that you want. Some companies sell data mining tools that perform a variety of analyses. Most of these tools are stand-alone and can extract data from various sources. In addition to performing a wide variety of functions, they are also optimized to handle large sets of data.

However, if you do not have these tools available, you can still use Microsoft Excel to perform some fundamental analysis. Excel is somewhat limited by the amount of data it can handle, but it is relatively easy to use, and managers can use typical Excel tools to interact with the results. For other problems, you could write your own data mining tools within the Visual Basic programming language, but you should also consider hiring an expert in statistics and numerical analysis.

The data for the All Powder case is small enough that it can be used within Excel. To illustrate the basic capabilities available, the following analyses rely on the same query that powers the PivotTable (qryMonthlyPivot). Begin with a time-series analysis that examines total monthly sales for some of the main product categories. Ultimately, managers want a chart with time on the horizontal axis, sales on the vertical axis, and lines for two or three product categories. To create this chart, it is best to have a table of data that shows the months as rows, and the columns as the product categories. This table is similar to the PivotTable built in the previous section, but with the rows and columns switched. To create this chart, start Excel and create a new PivotTable, using the same qryMonthlyPivot query already saved in the database. On the Excel menu, choose Data/PivotTable. In the wizard, select the option for External data source, then click the Get Data button. Choose the MS Access Database, click the OK button, and then search for the All Powder database. Find the qryMonthlyPivot and move it with all of its columns to the right window. Do not worry about filtering or sorting the data, just return it to Excel. Create the PivotTable on the main page, and you will see a layout screen similar to the one in the previous section. For the time-series analysis, drag the SaleMonth field to the row location, drag the Category field to the columns, and finish by dragging the Value field onto the detail section.

Once the data is in Excel, you can use Excel tools to analyze it. For the time-series analysis of sales, right-click on the PivotTable and select the PivotChart option. Excel will create a chart on a new worksheet. You need to modify several properties to make this chart useful. First, remove some of the categories. Click the drop-down arrow on the legend box and uncheck the minor categories, leaving only Boards, Skis, Boots, and Clothes. Second, right-click on the main chart, choose the Chart Type option, and select Line Chart. Each of the categories

> **Action**
>
> Create a new Excel spreadsheet.
> Choose Data/PivotTable and PivotChart.
> Select External data source.
> Click the Get Data button.
> Browse to your database and select the query built in the previous section.
> Create a PivotTable with the SaleMonth field as rows, the Category field as columns, and Value as the Detail.

> **Action**
>
> Right-click on the PivotTable and select the PivotChart option.
> In the PivotChart worksheet remove all categories except Boards, Skis, Boots, and Clothes.
> Right-click to set the Chart Type as a Line Chart.
> Right-click each series and Add Trendline.
> Choose a linear trend and forecast it for three periods ahead.
> Set properties to improve the chart's appearance.

FIGURE 8.15

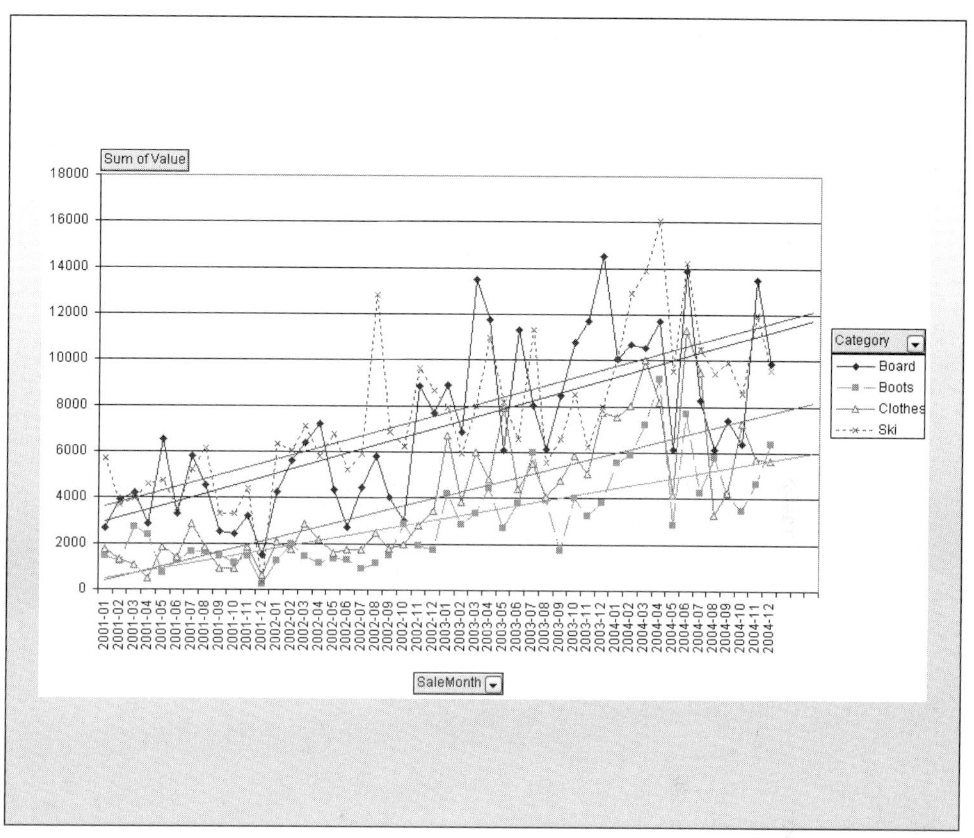

appears to show an upward trend. To verify that, right-click on one of the data lines and select the Add Trendline option. Choose the linear method, then click the Options tab and forecast it ahead for three periods. Follow the same procedure for each of the four data series. You should also go back and set the properties of each trend line to match the color of the underlying series.

Figure 8.15 shows the time-series chart with the properties modified to make it readable on paper. The trend lines provide some interesting insight into the sales. First, notice that the overall trends for snowboards and skis are almost identical. Second, observe that although all four categories exhibit increasing sales over time, the sales for boots are not increasing as fast as sales for snowboards and skis. In looking at the properties for the trend lines, notice that you can also display some of the statistics used to generate them. Excel provides several statistical tools to analyze data. For example, managers might be interested to compare the sales of boards and skis more carefully. You can use a T-test to see if there is a significant difference in the means of the sales. Note that you have to install several data analysis add-ins when you install Office. Also, you have to activate the add-ins by selecting them from the Tools/Add-Ins menu option. Once the tools are installed, you can use Tools/Data Analysis to perform the T-test on the two data series. Try it and you will find that because of the large variance in sales, the means are

Action
Make sure the Data Analysis Add-Ins are installed in Excel (Tools/Add-Ins). Choose Tools/Data Analysis. Select T-Test Two-sample with unequal variances. Compare the Board and Ski sales.

not significantly different. The Data Analysis add-in also provides tools for regression computations and some time-series analyses, such as moving average smoothing.

Activity: Analyze Geographic Data

The Office 2000 version of Excel contained a mapping tool that made it possible to display some geographic relationships. Its main advantage is that it was bundled with Office. Unfortunately, Office XP does not contain that tool, but Microsoft does ship the MapPoint software that performs even more sophisticated graphs (for a fee). Other companies sell even more sophisticated geographic information system software (notably ArcInfo from ESRI). Although you might not have this software available in your lab, it is worth seeing the steps and the maps to learn some of the capabilities and how it can be used to analyze and explore data.

Figure 8.16 shows that a PivotTable is used to retrieve the desired data and format it into rows and columns. Recall that a simple SQL query would not separate the categories into separate columns. Also, the PivotTable data is copied onto a second worksheet that does not include the first row of the PivotTable. This row tends to throw off the MapPoint data wizard and needs to be

> **Action**
>
> If you have Microsoft MapPoint start a new Excel worksheet.
> Create a PivotTable with rows for ShipState and columns for Board, Boots, Clothes, and Skis.
> Create a second worksheet that copies the main data and titles from the PivotTable without the first title rows.
> Save the file.
> Insert a MapPoint chart.
> Follow the wizard instructions to add a North American map with pie charts.

FIGURE 8.16

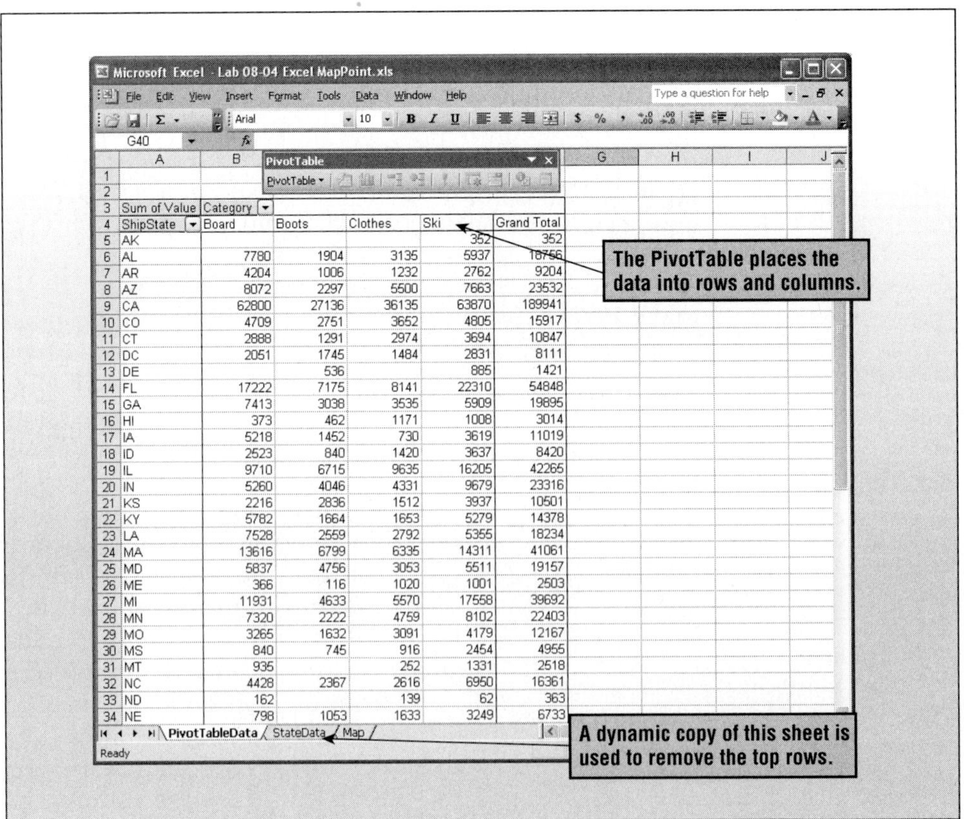

Sum of Value	Category				
ShipState	Board	Boots	Clothes	Ski	Grand Total
AK				352	352
AL	7780	1904	3135	5937	18756
AR	4204	1006	1232	2762	9204
AZ	8072	2297	5500	7663	23532
CA	62800	27136	36135	63870	189941
CO	4709	2751	3652	4805	15917
CT	2888	1291	2974	3694	10847
DC	2051	1745	1484	2831	8111
DE		536		885	1421
FL	17222	7175	8141	22310	54848
GA	7413	3038	3535	5909	19895
HI	373	462	1171	1008	3014
IA	5218	1452	730	3619	11019
ID	2523	840	1420	3637	8420
IL	9710	6715	9635	16205	42265
IN	5260	4046	4331	9679	23316
KS	2216	2836	1512	3937	10501
KY	5782	1664	1653	5279	14378
LA	7528	2559	2792	5355	18234
MA	13616	6799	6335	14311	41061
MD	5837	4756	3053	5511	19157
ME	366	116	1020	1001	2503
MI	11931	4633	5570	17558	39692
MN	7320	2222	4759	8102	22403
MO	3265	1632	3091	4179	12167
MS	840	745	916	2454	4955
MT	935		252	1331	2518
NC	4428	2367	2616	6950	16361
ND	162		139	62	363
NE	798	1053	1633	3249	6733

PivotTableData / StateData / Map /

Ready

FIGURE 8.17

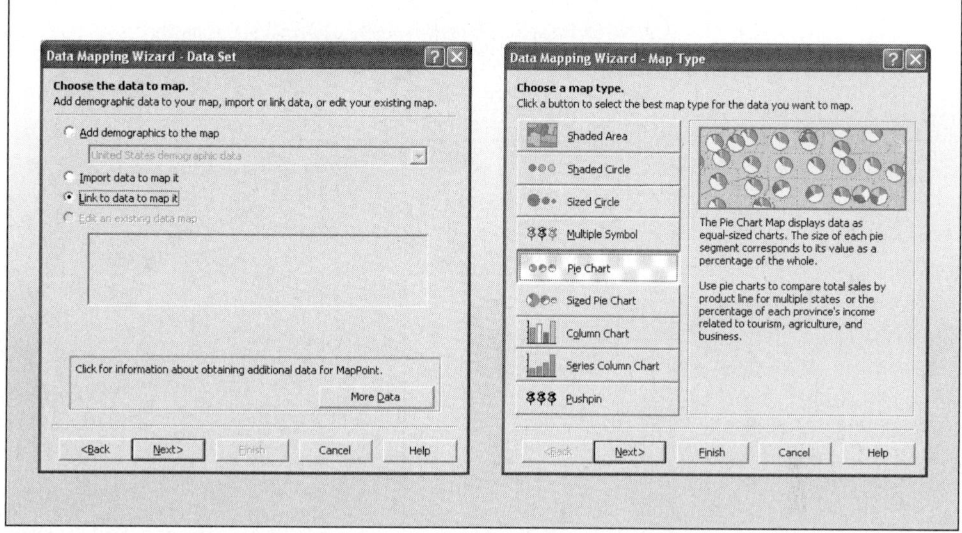

removed, but the PivotTable has no mechanism to remove it. Be sure you save the entire worksheet file.

To create the map, you insert a MapPoint chart onto a third worksheet file, and start the Data Mapping Wizard from the toolbar. Figure 8.17 shows that the wizard enables you to dynamically link to the worksheet file. You are then asked to browse and find the spreadsheet and select the worksheet and columns you need. The next step is to select the type of chart you want on the map. To display only a single series at a time, choose the Shaded Area option. This choice draws the states in darker shades that represent higher levels of sales. To show multiple series on the same state, you need either the pie or column chart.

Figure 8.18 shows the resulting chart. The shop managers are probably most interested in looking for differences between sales of skis and boards. With more realistic data, perhaps there would be a geographic pattern, but no regional trends leap out of this chart. A few states seem to have a substantially higher portion of sales in snowboards, but they are randomly scattered across the country. These cases might be important, or they might be due to random fluctuations. Either way, it would be worthwhile to talk with customers in these states.

Wyoming stands out as unique because only clothes have been shipped there. This piece of information could be highly important, or it might be due to a limited number of customers from Wyoming. Observations of this type often arise in data mining applications. One of the goals of data mining is to highlight patterns and unusual situations. It is up to the analyst to determine if the relationships are important. It is up to the managers to decide how to use the results to increase sales and profits.

Activity: Analyze Data with Regression

Linear regression is a tool that is relatively easy to use and is supported by a variety of platforms, including Excel. Again, with Excel, you need to install and select the Data Analysis tools. Linear regression can be used for many things, and many options and features exist in high-end tools. Its primary

FIGURE 8.18

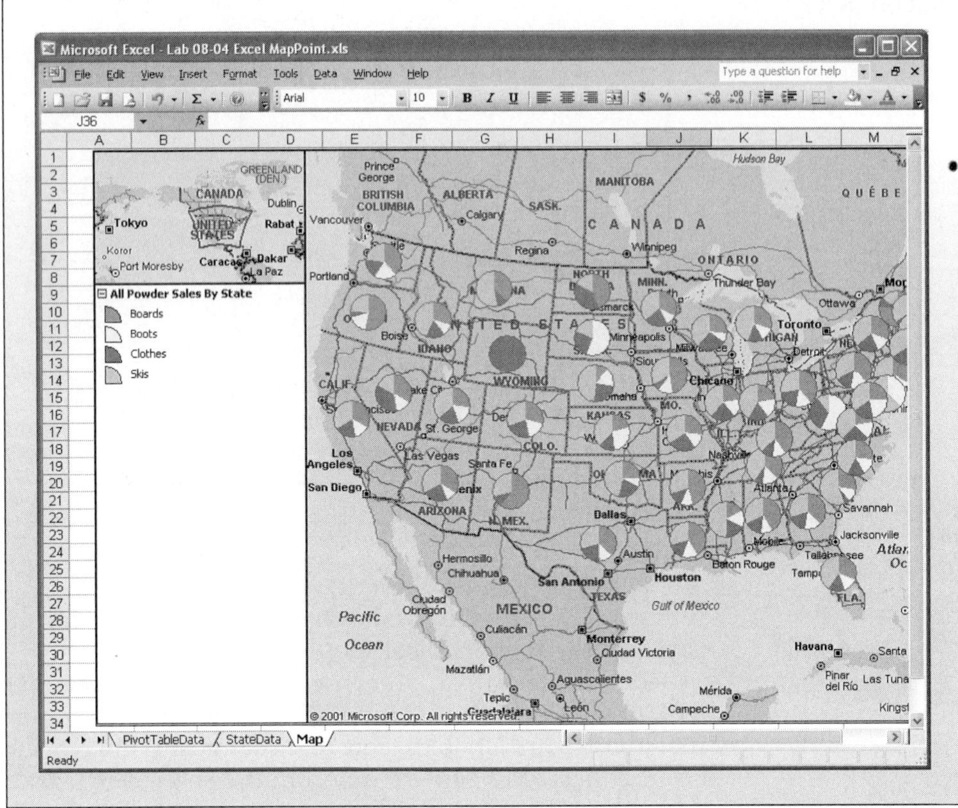

<table>
<tr><td>

</td></tr>
</table>

purpose is to compare sets of data in terms of closeness. The classic two-dimensional example is illustrated in Figure 8.15 where the best line is found that fits the set of points. In multidimensional terms, it is commonly used to determine how a set of exogenous (independent) variables influence an endogenous (dependent) variable.

In the All Powder case, the managers would like to analyze the state data and see if the total sales within a state are heavily determined by the population or income level of the state. In this case, the population and income are exogenous variables (predictors), and the sales total is the endogenous variable to be predicted. As a data mining tool, regression has some strengths and weaknesses. Its main strength is that it has been heavily analyzed and applied for many years, and the results are relatively easy to understand and interpret. Its main drawback is that the results are largely determined by averages, so the conclusions apply to the average or general group, but not necessarily to the outliers. Sometimes the most valuable insights come from understanding the outliers—such as the people who do not buy certain items, or the few leading-edge customers who pursue new sports before the crowd arrives.

Demographics and economic data on states and counties can be found in the federal government publications. The http://www.fedstats.gov site contains links and search engines to an enormous amount of data. For this

FIGURE 8.19

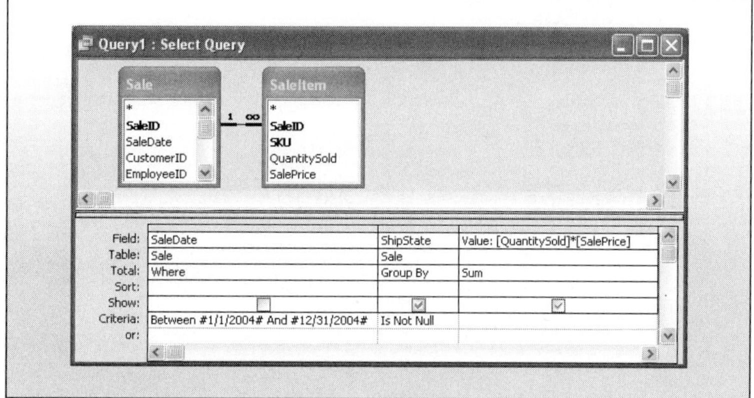

exercise, the 2002 population and 2001 total personal income by state have been saved in an Excel spreadsheet. As shown in Figure 8.19, a basic query can be used to compute the total sales by state for the year 2004. But if you look closely at the results of the query, you will spot a problem. Only 47 states are represented in the sales data. The spreadsheet file contains data on 51 states (counting the District of Columbia as a state). You will need to match the rows from the query with the data in the spreadsheet and discard the states for which your sales query has no data. Fortunately, SQL makes this process easy. Simply import the spreadsheet data into a temporary table, join it to the sales query rows, then save the resulting data into a new worksheet. In Access, use the File/Get External Data/Link Tables command to open the spreadsheet. This way, you can link directly to the worksheet without copying the data into a new table. Create a new query that joins the SalesByState query and the new StateDemographics table. Run the query, highlight all of the rows, copy and paste them into a new Excel spreadsheet.

Start the Excel regresison wizard with Tools/Data Analysis/Regression. As shown in Figure 8.20, you will have to select the Y (dependent) variable as the Value column, as well as the X (independent) variables as the Population and Income columns. To make the results easier to read, when you select the data, you should also include the top row that contains the label for the column. Then make sure you check the Labels box in the wizard so it knows the first row is not part of the numeric data. Most of the time you will want to accept the default option to place the results in a new worksheet.

Figure 8.21 shows the results of the regression for this example. Notice that the R-square value is relatively high, indicating that this simple model describes a little under 90 percent of the variance in the sales. Second, notice that only the population coefficient is significantly different from zero at a 5 percent level of significance (P-value less than 0.05). The coefficient value is positive, indicating that states with higher populations tend to purchase more items from All Powder. In fact, the company receives about $1.76 in sales for every thousand people. In general, this population result is not too surprising. Larger states with more people mean that there will be more boarders and skiers. The lack of significance on the income term is a little more interesting. There is a question of whether or not it really is insignificant, or if there is simply too little data or too few variables in the model. These questions should always be examined for insignificant variables. But, if it is true, it means that the sport has changed. Historically, because of the

FIGURE 8.20

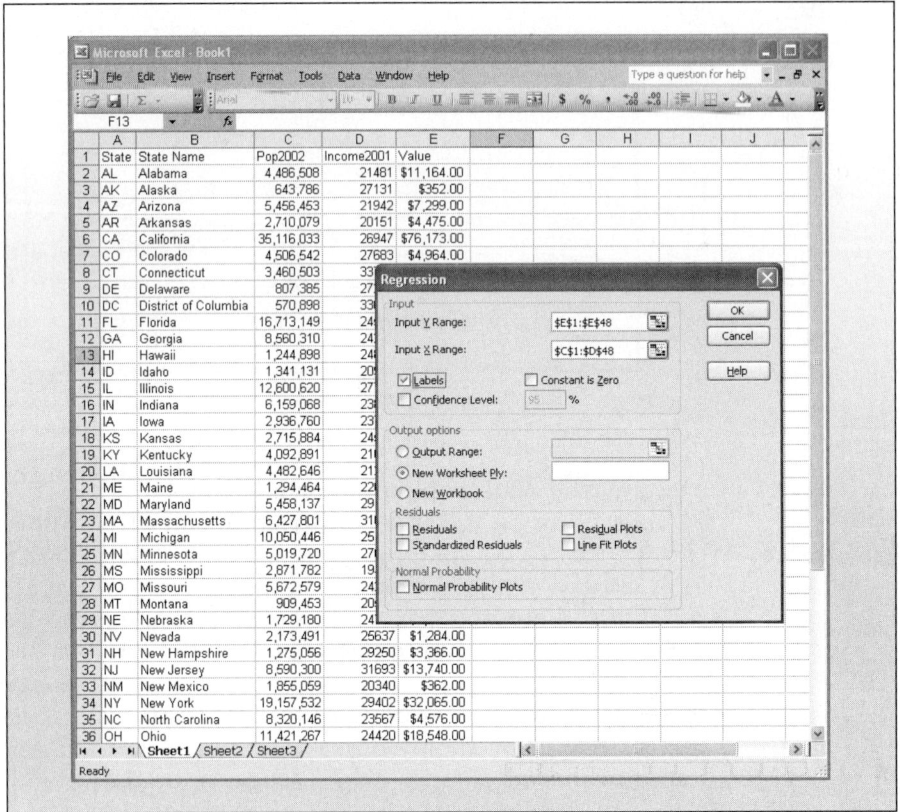

costs, snow sports have generally appealed more to wealthier people. In terms of the business and marketing, it would mean the company should consider a major shift in advertising and promotion if the sports now appeal to all income levels. Of course, considerably more data would be needed before making this commitment, but it is worth investigating. In truth, for

FIGURE 8.21

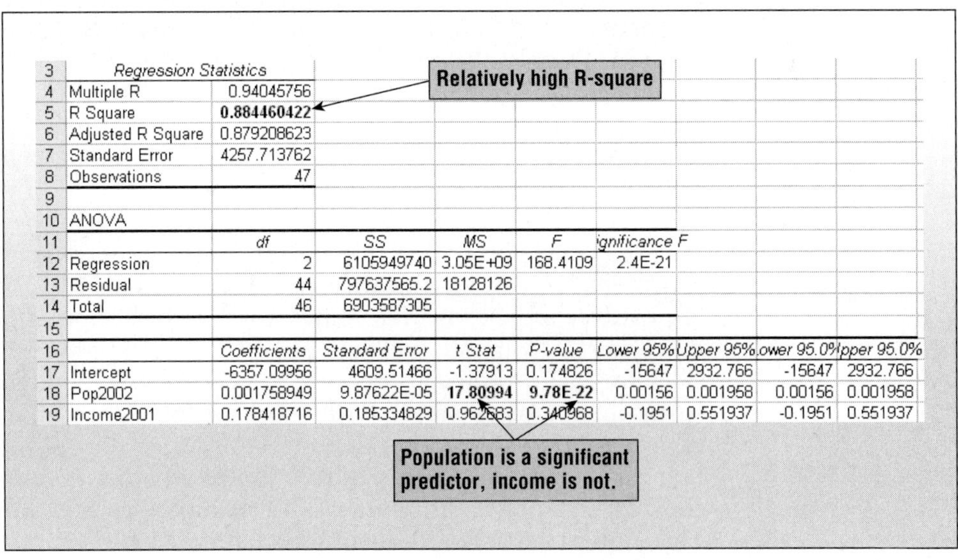

	Regression Statistics				
3	*Regression Statistics*				
4	Multiple R	0.94045756			
5	R Square	**0.884460422**			
6	Adjusted R Square	0.879208623			
7	Standard Error	4257.713762			
8	Observations	47			
9					
10	ANOVA				
11		*df*	*SS*	*MS*	*F*	*Significance F*
12	Regression	2	6105949740	3.05E+09	168.4109	2.4E-21
13	Residual	44	797637565.2	18128126		
14	Total	46	6903587305			
15						
16		*Coefficients*	*Standard Error*	*t Stat*	*P-value*	*Lower 95%*	*Upper 95%*	*Lower 95.0%*	*Upper 95.0%*
17	Intercept	-6357.09956	4609.51466	-1.37913	0.174826	-15647	2932.766	-15647	2932.766
18	Pop2002	0.001758949	9.87622E-05	**17.80994**	**9.78E-22**	0.00156	0.001958	0.00156	0.001958
19	Income2001	0.178418716	0.185334829	0.962683	0.340968	-0.1951	0.551937	-0.1951	0.551937

this case, the customers were generated based on city populations, so the statistical results match the underlying data model. Actual sales data would provide more interesting results, but the process is the same.

Exercises

Crystal Tigers

The Crystal Tigers club does not have a huge amount of data to analyze within the organization. However, they are interested in comparing their service data and the organizations they work with to see if they are serving the needs of the community. Periodically, they survey people in the surrounding areas to determine if they have heard of the club, if they know what charities the club supports, and their overall opinion of the club. In the process, they also ask citizens about the events and problems that most affect their lives. A substantial part of the survey is a listing of support organizations with which the club is considering partnering. Crystal Tigers has collected this survey data every six months for the last three years, and they get several hundred responses each time. All of the data is stored in Excel spreadsheets.

1. Create two sample spreadsheets with the survey data. Create tables in Access to hold the normalized data. Write the SQL statements to transfer the data. Build this code into a form and button that will automate the transfer.

2. Create a query and a PivotTable that will enable managers to analyze the survey data.

3. Create a PivotTable that will enable managers to analyze the existing club service data. Use two possible fact fields: hours worked and money raised. Include all of the dimensions you think managers might need.

4. Do a time-series analysis of the money raised. Managers are particularly interested in trends and in identifying the months that raise the most money.

5. Assume you have data on money raised for several years (make up monthly totals if necessary). Obtain personal income data for your state or metropolitan area over those years and see if the income level is correlated with the money raised.

Capitol Artists

The managers of Capitol Artists are primarily interested in identifying the best employees and the most profitable customers. The job tracking system ultimately generates a considerable amount of data—at the hourly and daily level. Note that all employee tasks are supposed to be recorded in the system based on client, job, and the task involved. The firm has considerable information on clients, including a size classification (tiny, small, medium, and large), and type of company (such as print shop, marketing, retail, and medical). This additional client information is currently stored in a spreadsheet, with one page devoted to each client.

1. Create three sample client worksheets with sample data. Modify the Access tables as needed to handle this new data. Create a form that will enable a clerk to find the worksheet and transfer the data to Access.

2. Create a PivotTable that will enable managers to analyze the hours worked and revenue generated by employees, day of week, client, client size, and so on.

3. Create a PivotChart that compares employees based on billable hours by day during the past month.

4. Assume that you have approximate sales numbers representing the size of each of the clients (make up the data). Create a categorical variable for the client industry (for example, 1 = print shop, 2 = marketing, and so on). Perform a regression to see if the client size or industry influences the amount of sales revenue Capitol Artists generates.

5. If you have mapping software available, analyze the client revenue by location.

Offshore Speed

Inventory control is critical for Offshore Speed because it has to stock thousands of small parts for different engines and drives. All of these parts are grouped into categories in terms of the manufacturer, and the location within the engine or boat. Lately, the owners think there has been an increased demand for oil pump impellers, but they are not certain because there are several different brands. They also suspect that sales of electronic navigation devices have tapered off. Although they have the sales data available, they are not sure how to analyze and compare it. Of course, the sales data for the past three years is stored in Excel spreadsheets. One sheet for each month of sales, and each line contains a sale number, date, part number, quantity, and price. Unfortunately, the part numbers do not match the new ones entered into the database. However, there is a separate spreadsheet that maps the two numbers. The first column lists the old number and the second column contains the new number.

1. Create at least two sample spreadsheets for the older sales, and the spreadsheet that maps the old numbers to the new ones. Create a form that can be used by a clerk to pick a spreadsheet and import the data into the new database.

2. Create a PivotTable that will enable managers to analyze sales by category, manufacturer, and time. Note that category should be a hierarchy. For example, managers might want to see detailed parts, or just the parts that are used in engines (or drives, or steering, and so on).

3. Create a PivotChart that analyzes sales of the major categories over time based on monthly sales.

4. For some reason, an employee of the company has kept records of the weather for the last three years. She has a spreadsheet that contains the date, the amount of rain on that day, and the high temperature for the day. Create a regression to see if there is a relationship between the weather and your sales. (Make up some sample weather data, or find it on the Internet for your area.)

5. If you have mapping software available, analyze the client revenue by location.

6. If you have access to software that performs association or market basket analysis, this case would be a good application to see what types of parts might be purchased together.

Final Project

The main textbook has an appendix with several longer case studies. You should be able to work on one of these cases throughout the term. If you or your instructor picks one, perform the following tasks.

1. Identify at least one primary fact attribute that managers would want to track, along with several dimensions. Create the query and PivotTable to analyze the data.

2. Identify any data that could be analyzed over time, and create a PivotChart and an Excel spreadsheet to forecast the data.

3. Identify any data that could benefit from market basket or association analysis. If you have access to the software, create the queries and analyze sample data.

4. Identify any data that could benefit from geographic analysis. If you have access to the software, create the queries and analyze sample data.

5. Identify any correlations or regression analysis that might help managers better understand the operations and effects of various attributes. If possible, collect sample data and analyze it.

Database Administration

Chapter Outline

Objectives
Database Administration Tasks in Access
Case: All Powder Board and Ski Shop
Lab Exercise
*All Powder Board and Ski Shop
Security and Privacy*
Exercises
Final Project

Objectives

- Evaluate and improve the application performance.
- Establish backup and recovery methods and plans.
- Install simple security controls to provide basic protection of the data.
- Protect the forms, reports, and code from unauthorized changes.
- Protect the data with user-level security controls.

Database Administration Tasks in Access

One of the appealing features of Microsoft Access is that it is easy to use and does not require complex administration chores. On the other hand, the lack of sophisticated administration tools makes it less valuable for large-scale applications. Although Access does not have the powerful tools to support thousands of users, it does have some useful features to help developers and database administrators.

Every DBMS maintains an internal list of all of the database objects, such as table, query, and report names. Only recently has the SQL standard proposed a common method to obtain these names. Consequently, most systems have proprietary tables and columns for the metadata tables. In Access, you rarely need to deal with these tables directly. Instead, it is easier to use the visual administrator and simply select the items you want to modify. Someday you might need to examine a list of the tables from within your code, however, so you should learn about the system tables.

For safety and to reduce clutter, the metadata tables in Access are normally hidden. Figure 9.1 shows that you can use the Tools/Options menu item to make the system tables visible. All system table names begin with MSys, and the MSysObjects table contains a list of all tables in the database. You can open the table to see its structure, but do not change any of the data. The Type column is set to 1 to indicate it is a table object, so you could run a query against the system table to see a list of all tables in the database.

FIGURE 9.1

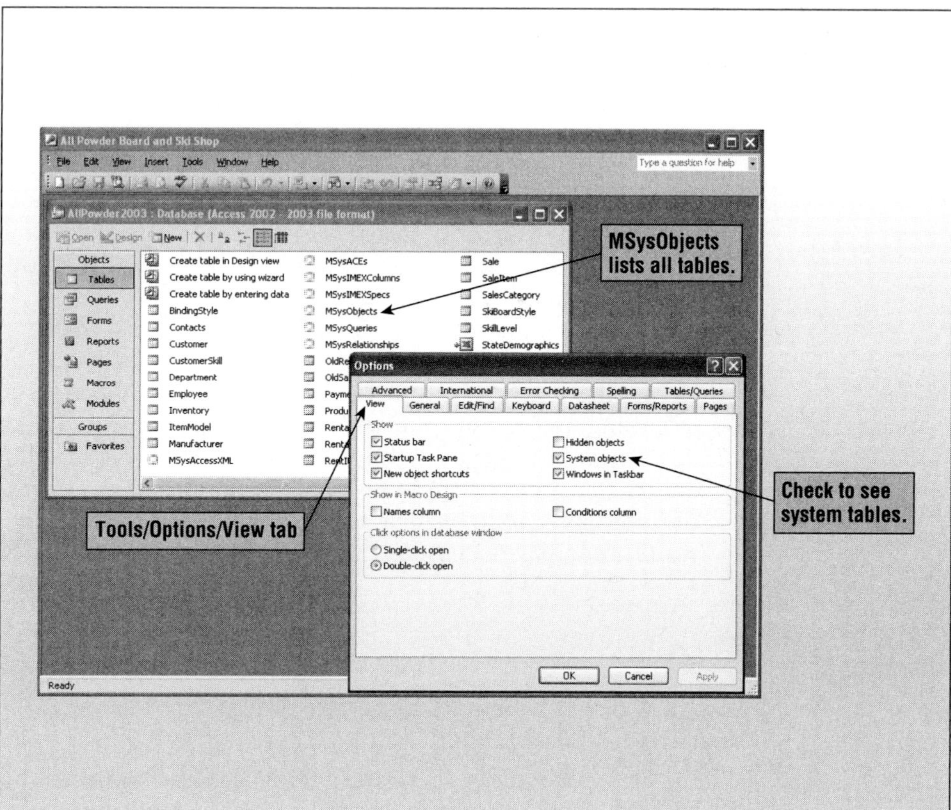

Microsoft also provides the Active Data Object Extensions (ADOX) control to provide programmatic access to the metadata in an underlying DBMS, and you can read the Microsoft documentation to learn how to use ADOX to read the list of tables in a DBMS. For now, return to Tools/Options and uncheck the box to show the system objects.

Performance is always a tricky issue in a DBMS. Small tables with a limited number of joins and a handful of simultaneous users rarely encounter performance problems. Also, with hardware improvements, Access has been able to handle even larger applications without experiencing performance problems. However, you will encounter some databases that will need changes to improve performance.

Backup and recovery are relatively simple in Access since it does not write a transaction log or journal. You can back up an Access database simply by copying the file. Also, Access does not really provide recovery facilities, so if the system crashes in the middle of an application, few steps are needed because most of the data in transition will be lost.

Security is more complex. By default, Access is completely open and everyone has full access to the data, forms, reports, and code. The assumption is that generally only trusted users will be given access to the database, and then they have the ability to use any part of the database. Microsoft now provides several security features to provide different levels of protection. It is even possible to set up user accounts and assign separate permissions to access individual tables, queries, forms, and reports. Once you set up user-level security, someone needs to be assigned to handle the user accounts.

Case: All Powder Board and Ski Shop

Ultimately, the owners of All Powder want to assign individual user permissions. Although the shop trusts its employees, it often hires students to work as clerks, and the owners would like to limit what the clerks can do with the application. The issue is only partly a matter of trust: It is also useful to protect the database so clerks and other users cannot change form layouts or accidentally delete items.

The managers are also somewhat concerned about performance, particularly at the checkout machines. Sometimes the store's checkout lines get hectic, so the application has to be fast. Some of the issues can be handled by installing more computers. The salesperson can enter the basic customer data immediately, and the checkout clerk simply selects the customer and enters the product numbers. Of course, having more computers means that the company will need a network. It also means that more people will be simultaneously accessing the data, increasing the risk of collisions and locks.

Lab Exercise

All Powder Board and Ski Shop

DBMS developers learned early that indexes can significantly improve the performance of a relational DBMS. Key columns and join columns are almost always indexed because they often represent single-item lookups.

Without an index, the computer has to search each row sequentially to find a match. An index can exponentially reduce the number of lookups in a search. On the other hand, indexes have to be updated whenever data is changed, deleted, or added. As a result, placing too many indexes on a table can result in even worse performance.

Activity: Evaluate the Application Performance

Your job is to find the balance with enough indexes to improve performance for key tasks, but not so many that other portions become too slow. This balance is unique to each application and can be difficult to find. Ultimately, you will have to fine-tune the application over time. A few simple rules help you begin: (1) All primary keys should be indexed; (2) Join columns should be indexed—particularly in large tables; (3) Heavily searched or sorted columns should be indexed; and (4) Transaction tables that are constantly changed (such as SaleItem) should have few indexes. The first rule is so strong that Access automatically builds the index for every column in a primary key.

> **Action**
>
> Choose Tools/Analyze/Performance.
> Select all objects.
> Run the analysis.
> Add indexes if they are reasonable.

Access provides a tool to help you determine which columns should be indexed and other ways to improve performance. Use the Tools/Analyze/ Performance menu option to start the analyzer wizard. Figure 9.2 shows the first step of the wizard. You can select the items that you want to examine for performance. You can select individual items, groups of objects (such as all tables), or choose the tab for All Object Types to select everything in the database. Selecting all objects is a good way to cover all possibilities, but it might be overwhelming. Try it first, if there are too many suggestions to scroll through, start over and do one group at a time. At a minimum, you need to analyze the queries.

Figure 9.3 shows sample analyzer results. It attaches a level of importance to each recommendation, and you should seriously consider the higher-level recommendations. Notice that many of them involve indexes. The index for LastName, FirstName makes sense because customer data is often sorted that way.

At this point, you have three methods to create the recommended index. (1) Click the Optimize button and the wizard builds the index for you. This is by far the easiest method. (2) Open the table in Design view and choose

FIGURE 9.2

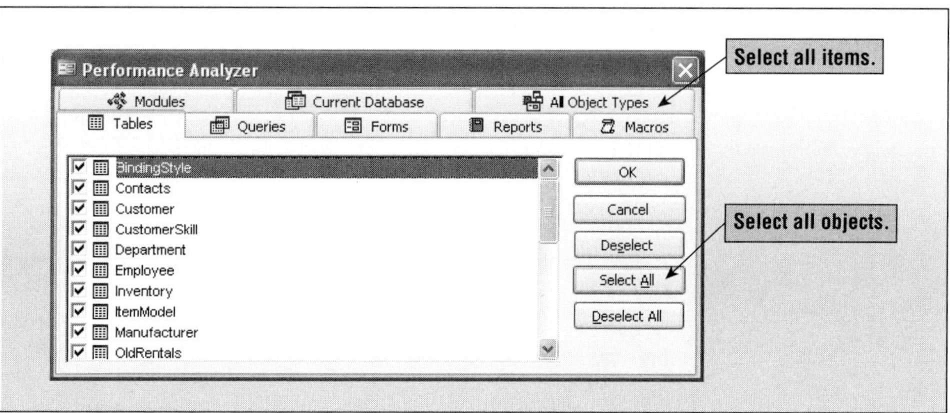

FIGURE 9.3

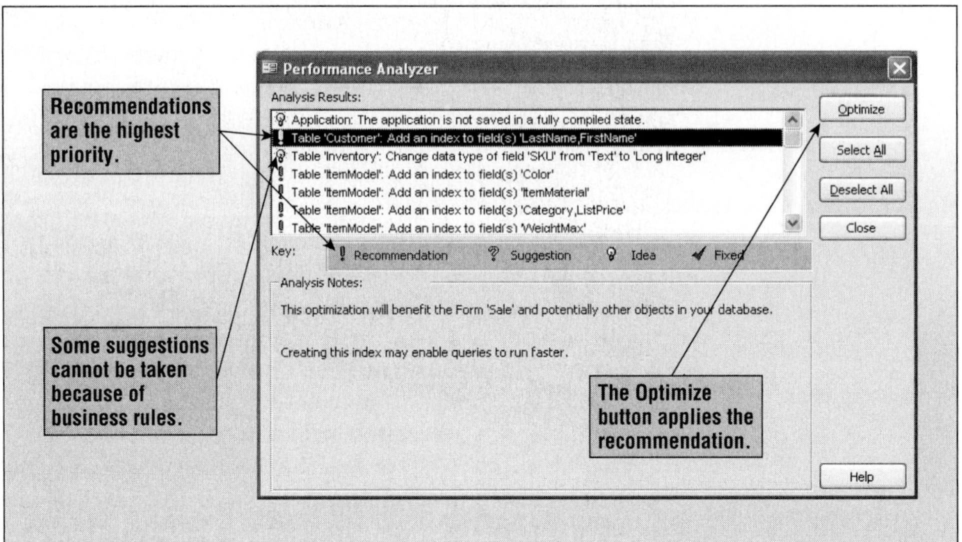

the View/Indexes menu option. Add an index name along with the columns to be indexed. Generally, you will use this method to check to see that the wizard correctly built the requested index. Figure 9.4 shows the index list with the newly created index. (3) You can use the SQL command: CREATE INDEX LastFirstName ON Customer (LastName, FirstName). While this

FIGURE 9.4

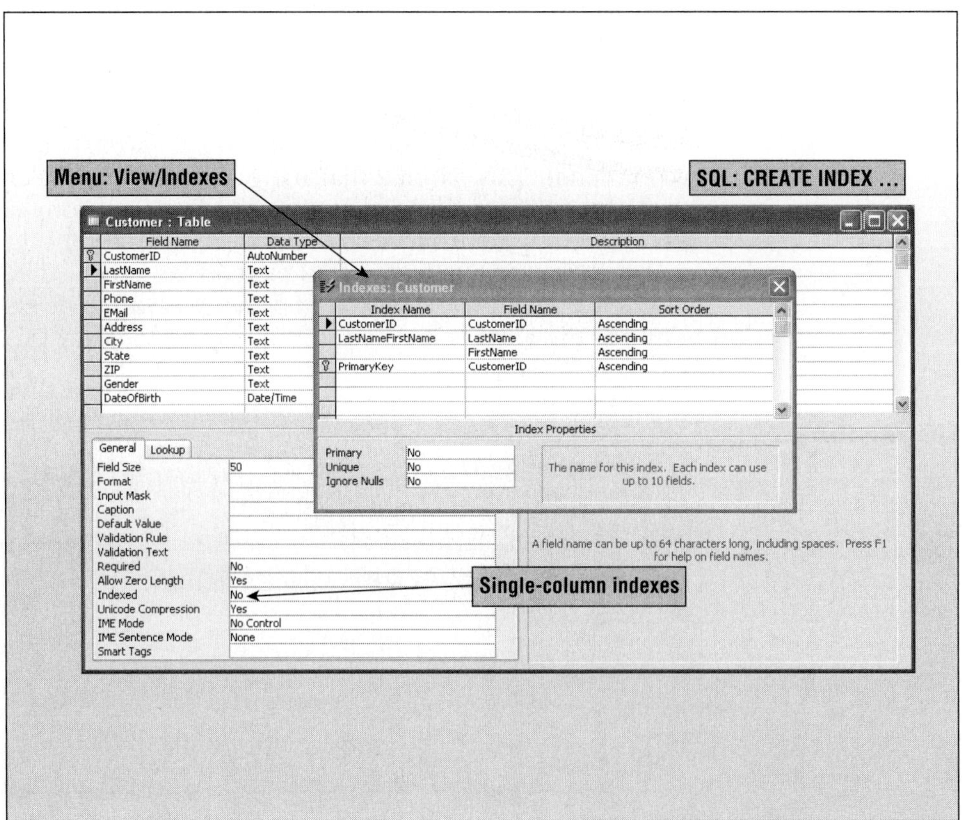

method might seem cumbersome, it is a useful way to write down the indexes and store them in a file. This list could be used to re-create the database on a different machine and to document database definition in case of a disaster.

Again, remember that you will rarely want to accept all of the analyzer's recommendations. If you know that a table is heavily involved in transactions, you want to avoid creating too many indexes on it. If in doubt, test the application both ways for a few days and carefully observe the performance. If an application is too slow, remove the associated indexes and test again. Also, some of the recommendations cannot be taken because it would violate the business rules. In the example, SKUs are currently numeric, so the wizard will suggest converting that column to a Long Integer instead of text. But the managers are planning to implement new SKUs with alphabetic characters, so you should avoid the wizard's recommendation—unless the performance gain is so large that it becomes necessary to talk the managers into always using simple numbers.

Activity: Backup and Recovery

Access does not really provide backup and recovery tools. About the only solution is to use Windows to back up the database file. Several tools are available to make backup copies of regular files, and all of these work on the

<table>
<tr><td>

Action

Choose Tools/Database Utilities/Compact and Repair Database. Close the file but not Access. Run Compact and Repair again; this time enter a new name for the compacted database to use as a backup copy.

</td></tr>
</table>

Access mdb database file. One useful technique is to compress the file using a Zip format. Windows XP and above have a built-in capability to create a compressed (zipped) folder. Just create the folder and drag the database file into it to compress it. The compressed folder is often small enough to e-mail or copy to a secure tape or drive that can be moved offsite.

One catch with the Windows approach is that you should make sure that no one else is using the database when you make the backup copy. For small businesses that shut down over night, this requirement is easy. For operations that run 24 hours a day, it is more complicated, and a key aspect of backup is setting a schedule and notifying everyone of the backup time. Although it might slightly interfere with the business, a full copy provides the advantage of ensuring that you have a clean, consistent copy of the database.

There is an important tool that you need to run on a regular basis in Access databases. To see the effect of this utility, first go to Windows, browse to the folder that holds the main database file, and write down the size of the file. Then select the Tools/Database Utilities/Compact and Repair menu option. After a few moments, the database will close and restart. Return to the Windows folder and check the size of the database. It should be substantially smaller. The main effect of this process is to completely remove the items that have been deleted. Remember that to save time Access simply flags an item as deleted. It is not actually removed from the database until you run the compact and repair utility. This utility is also useful if the system crashes while the database is open. It fixes some basic index issues and can repair common damage issues.

The compact and repair utility cannot repair databases with large errors— particularly those caused when disk drives fail. Keeping full backup copies is critical. However, in an emergency, it is sometimes possible to recover data and perhaps even forms and reports from a damaged copy of Access. The trick is to create a completely new, blank Access database. Then use the File/Get External Data/Import utility to import whatever pieces you can obtain from the damaged file.

Security and Privacy

Activity: Simple Access Security Controls

Setting and maintaining detailed lists of users and access rights can be a time-consuming job. In many small applications, it is not necessary to provide this level of control. In these cases only a few people may need to use the database, and you simply need to restrict access to those selected people and prevent others from using it at all. You can use the simple security controls provided within Access and avoid the management task of setting full security controls.

Figure 9.5 shows the steps needed to assign a database password. The one trick is that you must open the database in Exclusive mode—which means that no one else can be using the database when you set the password. To open a database in exclusive mode, you have to use the Open command and browse to the location of the database file. Then carefully select the Exclusive option at the bottom right of the browser screen. Once the file is open, use the Tools/Security/Set Database Password menu option, and use the pop-up box to enter the new password. When you close the database and reopen it (it no longer needs to be opened exclusively), you will be asked for the

FIGURE 9.5

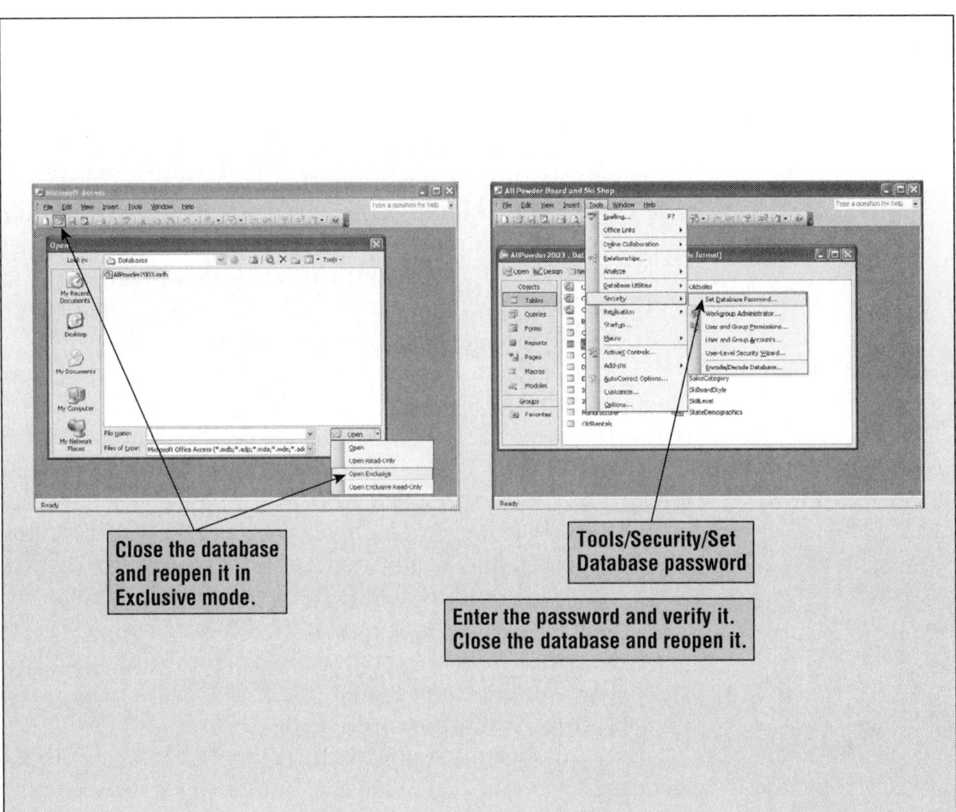

password. Without the password, no one else can open the database. You can use the same process to remove or "unset" the password. Keep in mind that the database password is all or nothing. Anyone who knows the password has full control over everything in the database. Many times, this level of protection is sufficient, but make sure you have backup copies in case things are accidentally deleted.

> **Action**
>
> Choose Tools/Security/Set Database Password.
> Enter test as a password.
> Choose Tools/Security/Encrypt.
> Close the database and reopen it.

There is one more issue with the simple password approach. Technically, someone could use a utility program to open the database file and examine or change the data without ever starting Microsoft Access. Since Access is never started, this attacker does not need the password. There are two ways to control this type of attack: (1) Use the Windows network security controls to allow only approved users to read the mdb file, and (2) encrypt the database file. In practice, you should use both methods. Attackers will then have to circumvent two security blocks instead of one to get to the file. The network access rights are set within Windows by right-clicking on the file-name and following the options on the security tab.

The option to encrypt the database is straightforward, and you do not have to open the file in exclusive mode. Choose Tools/Security/Encrypt/Decrypt Database on the menu. Then browse to a folder and enter a new filename for the secured database. Figure 9.6 shows the result of encrypting a small database. The simple debug utility opens the file in raw form and allows an

FIGURE 9.6

attacker to see the data and even change it outside of the DBMS. The encrypted file is essentially gibberish so no one can find the specific data. However, they can still destroy data by writing random bytes into the file, or even delete the entire file. You still need the Windows security controls to remove write and delete access to the file to prevent these problems.

Activity: Create an MDE File to Protect Forms and Reports

Access provides another useful utility that you can use to protect your forms, reports, and code. This option is particularly useful when you are hired to create a database for a client and you do not want the client to see or modify your proprietary code. The client still needs access to the data and to use the forms, so securing the database is not enough. You need to lock down your forms and reports. Simply choose the Tools/Database Utilities/Make MDE File from the menu. This option creates a completely new file with an mde suffix. Figure 9.7 shows that when you distribute this file to the client, no one can open the forms (or reports or modules) in Design view. They will not be able to change the layouts or to see or modify your code. It is a convenient way to protect your trade secrets and to prevent accidental changes.

When you create MDE files, be extremely careful. No one can edit forms, reports, or modules in an MDE file—including you! Make sure that you keep your original mdb file in several safe locations. When you need to ship a new

> **Action**
>
> Choose Tools/Database Utilities/Make MDE File.
> Close the database and open the new MDE database.
> Try to edit a form.

FIGURE 9.7

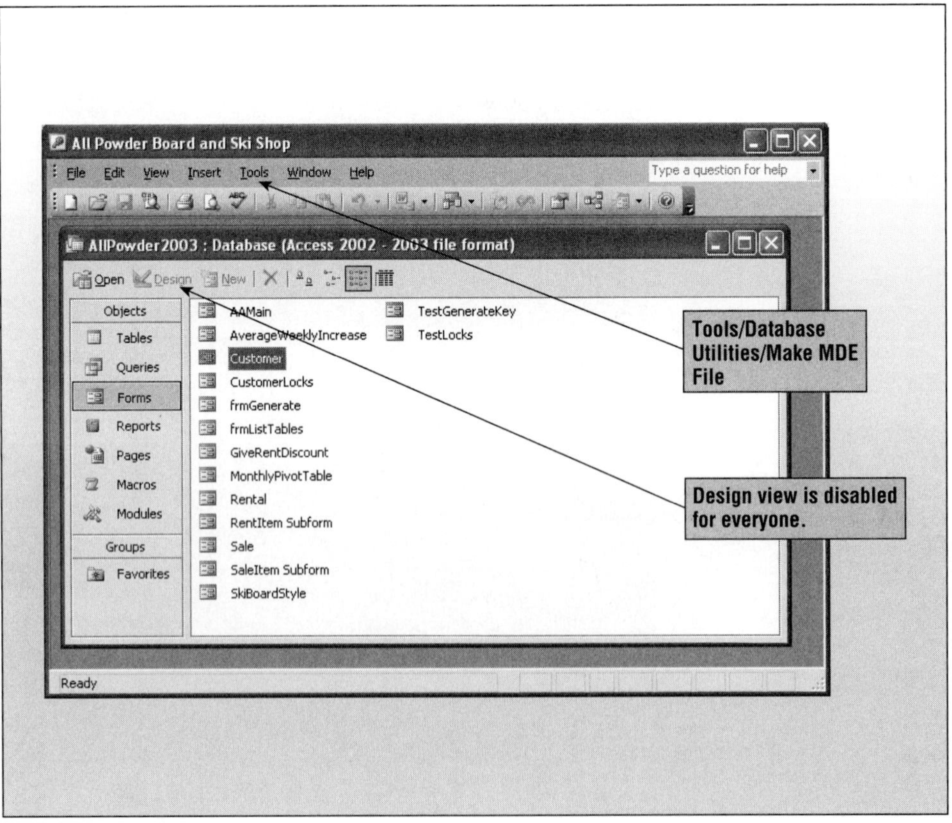

version to the client, you have to make the modifications in the original mdb file, and then rebuild a new mde file.

Activity: Setting User-Level Security Controls

Sometimes a business application requires you to control access to individual tables, forms, and reports for specific users. In this situation, you need to convert the database to implement full user-level security controls. The steps are a little tricky, but the security wizard handles most of the work for you. To understand the steps and questions asked in the wizard, you need to understand the overall process.

The first issue to face is that Access needs to be able to identify the individual users. Figure 9.8 outlines the basic process. The main database application contains forms, reports, and tables. As the database administrator (DBA), you want to assign individual permissions to separate users for each object. For instance, sales clerks would be able to read some supplier data, but not change it, and probably would not need access to the main supplier form. But, before you can assign any permissions, the database application needs to be able to identify the user. Access identifies users by setting up a separate workgroup database that contains usernames and passwords. The main application is associated to this workgroup database. When the application is opened, users must enter a correct username and password. Obviously, this workgroup database must be secure so that no one can alter data. Access handles this issue by automatically encrypting the workgroup database. Of course, someone has to maintain the workgroup database and handle problems such as users forgetting their passwords. From an enterprise perspective, the workgroup database approach has some problems. Mainly, it requires companies to maintain separate lists of users and passwords for applications. Although workgroup databases can be reused in other applications, they rarely are configured that way. Consequently, users end up

> **Action**
>
> Choose Tools/Security/User-Level Security Wizard.
> Create a new workgroup.
> Select the Backup Operators group.
> On the users screen, set a password for your username.
> Add three users.
> Make sure you are in the Admins group.
> Close the database.

FIGURE 9.8

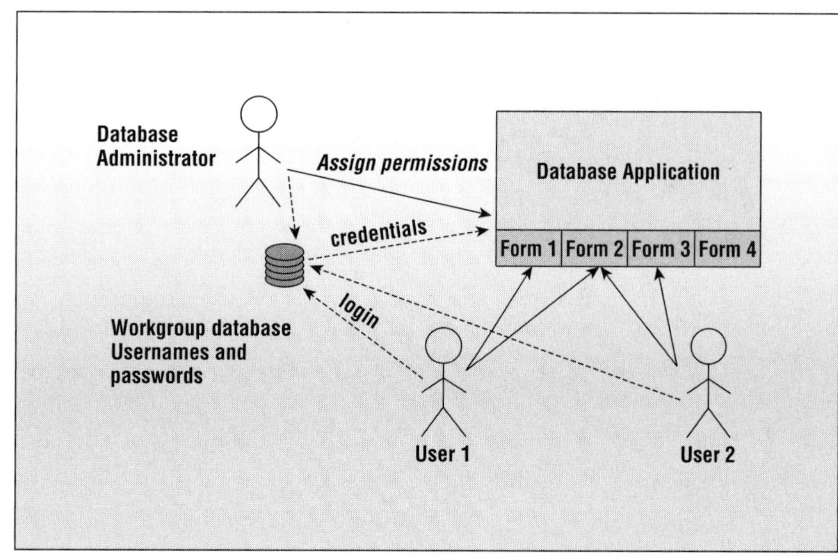

FIGURE 9.9

	Sales table	Customer table	Item table
Sales clerks	S,U,I	S,U,I	S
Sales managers	S,U,I,D	S,U,I	S
Rental managers		S,U,I	S

needing to know dozens of usernames and passwords. For small companies with one or two applications, this issue is less important.

Before running the security wizard, you should write down a list of user-names and initial passwords that you will be asked to enter into the work-group database. While you are identifying users, you should also classify them in terms of tasks or groups. You almost never want to assign permissions to individual users. Instead, you place users into groups and assign database permissions to the groups. Figure 9.9 illustrates the main concept. By assigning permissions to the groups, you should only have to set permissions one time. As individual users are added to or removed from groups, their permissions automatically change.

Before running the security wizard, you should have a list of groups and a list of users and the groups they should be assigned to. You should also have an initial start on the permissions matrix that lists the various resources and the group permissions for each item. Start the wizard with the Tools/Security/User-Level Security Wizard menu option. Most times, you will create a new workgroup—unless you have already developed similar projects and want to use the same list of users. Figure 9.10 shows an important step

FIGURE 9.10

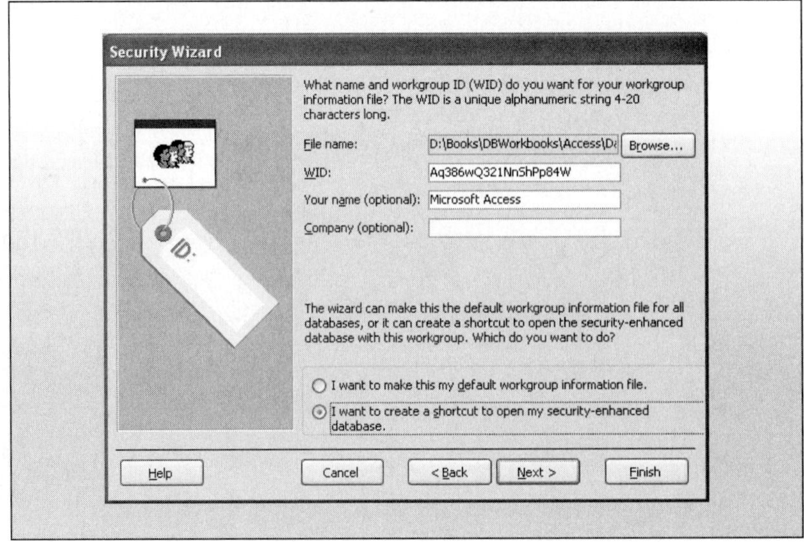

FIGURE 9.11

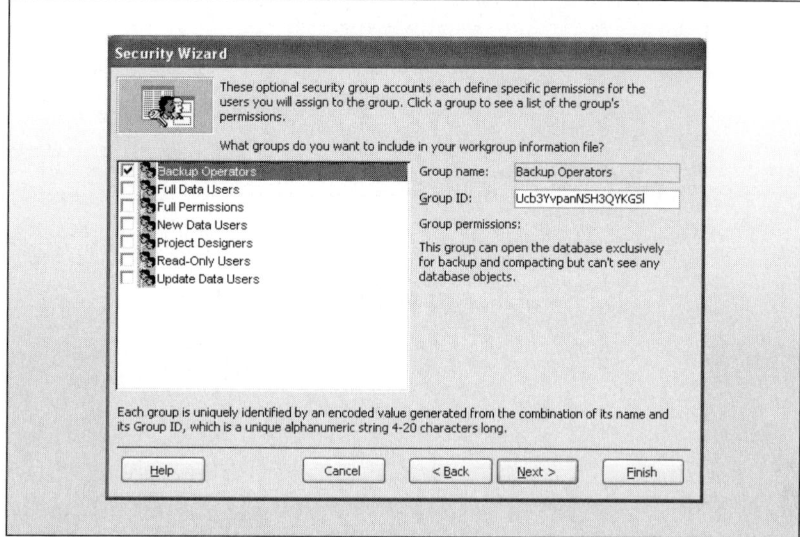

in the wizard that sets up the workgroup file. Generally, you should avoid making the workgroup file the default. If you do, you will be asked to log in every time you open an Access database. You should certainly never pick this option in a shared computer lab.

For the most part, you can select the default options in the security wizard. However, Figure 9.11 shows some options that you should carefully consider. The wizard can create some predefined user groups that might be useful. In particular, the backup user group is a good idea, since it automatically sets permissions properly for someone to make copies of the data, but still prevents them from modifying anything. You might also want to use some of the other groups—such as the Full Permissions group. Keep in mind that there is also an internal Administrators group that you will want to use for the DBA, but it is always created automatically.

Figure 9.12 shows that eventually you reach another important screen in the wizard, where you need to enter your list of users. By default, the wizard picks up the current user on your system (you). Make sure that you assign a password to your username. If you forget, the password will be blank, so you can still log in, but so could any attacker. You will have to add all of the users and passwords from your list. Note that it is possible to add users later, but it is slightly easier to enter them now. Note that you are entering users, not groups.

Figure 9.13 shows the screen that enables you to assign users to groups. Again, this task can be performed later. And you will have to add your application groups later and assign people to those groups. However, it is critical that you assign at least one user to the Admins group now. By default, the wizard will assign the current user (you) to the Admins group. To be safe, select the option to see the list by group and double-check that (1) there is at least one name in the Admins group, and (2) only people who need this high-level permission are in the group. The Admins group always has full control over all objects in the database, including the ability to reassign permissions and change group memberships. You should keep this list as small as possible. But keep in mind that you could use

FIGURE 9.12

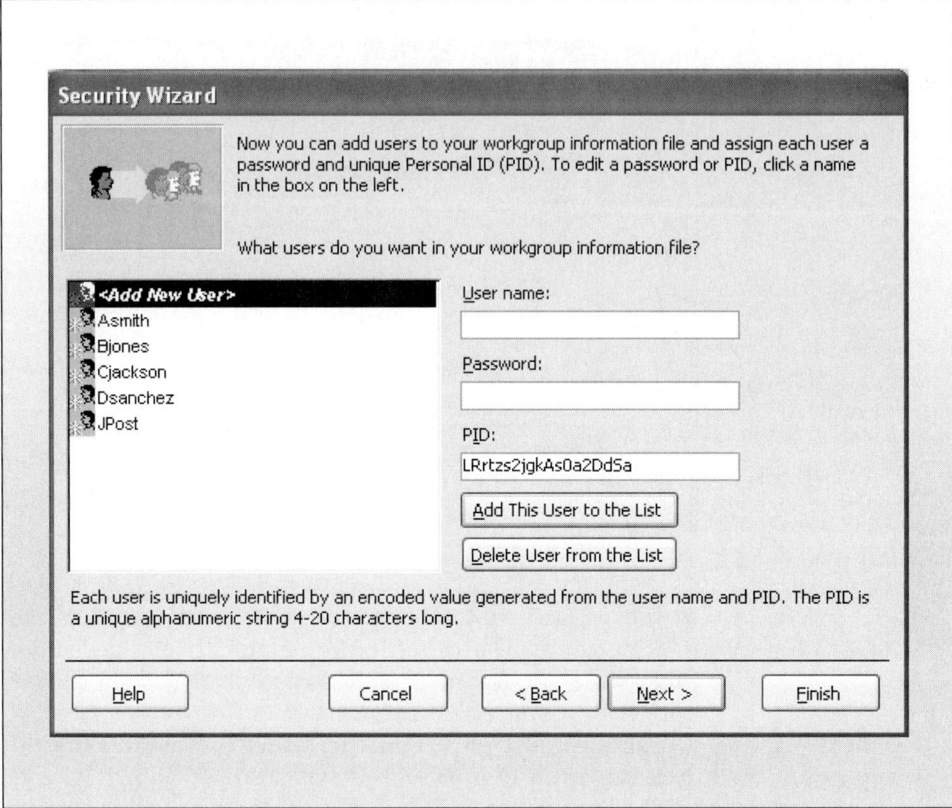

two people in this group in case one person is on vacation or sick and someone needs a password changed. When the wizard finishes, it displays a report that lists the filenames and the workgroup ID. Keep this report in a safe place: It can be used to re-create the workgroup file if it is damaged.

FIGURE 9.13

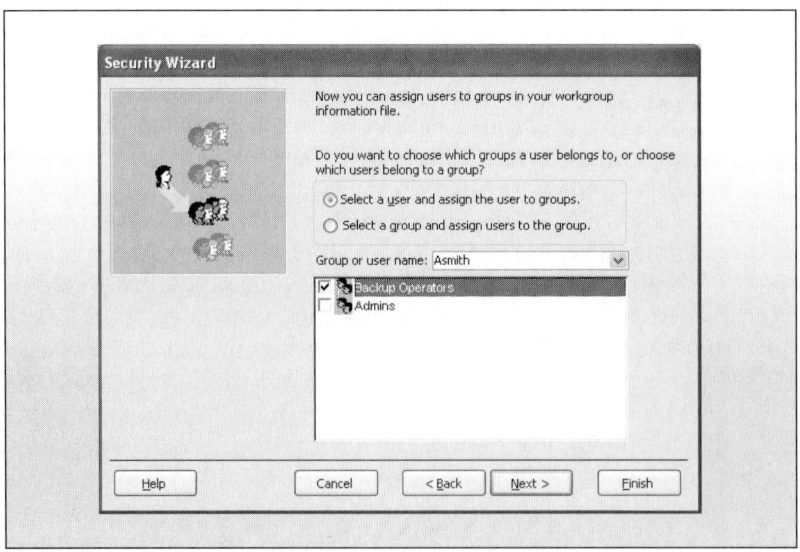

<table>
<tr><td>

Action

Open the database using the desktop link.
Log in with your username and password.
Choose Tools/Security/User and Group Accounts.
Select the Groups tab and add SalesClerks and SalesManagers groups.
Add one of your new users to each group.
Choose Tools/Security/User and Group Permissions.
Grant specified permissions for the two groups to the Sale, SaleItem, Customer, and Inventory tables.
Assign appropriate permissions to the database and the forms.
Close the database.
Log in as a sales clerk and test the permissions.

</td></tr>
</table>

When the wizard is finished, close the database. Because it is encrypted and tied to the workgroup file, you cannot open the database directly. Instead, click on the link that the wizard created. If you examine the properties of the link, you will see that it associates the workgroup file with the database application. When the database starts, you will be asked to log in using the username/password pair that you created earlier. Since you still have some administrative tasks to perform, log in using an account that is a member of the Admins group.

The next step is to create the customized groups and assign users to them. Use the Tools/Security/User and Group Accounts menu option. Use the Groups tab to enter the custom group names. Simply click the New button and enter the group name and an ID value. The ID value should be random so that no one can guess it. If you ever need to re-create the workgroup file, you should write down the personal IDs that are created. But in general, it is easier and safer to keep backup copies of the workgroup file. For now, at least create the SalesClerks and SalesManagers groups. Figure 9.14 shows the screen used to assign users to groups. Simply select the user, then add the desired group to the right-side window. You can also add new users from this screen with the New button.

Once the groups and users have been created, you need to assign the desired permissions within the database. Note that unless you changed the access for the Users group during setup, users will have no access to any of the database objects. So you have to grant all of the permissions that each group will need. Use the Tools/Security/User and Group Permissions menu option to assign permissions. One of the first permissions that you will have to grant to all of the groups is the ability to open the database.

FIGURE 9.14

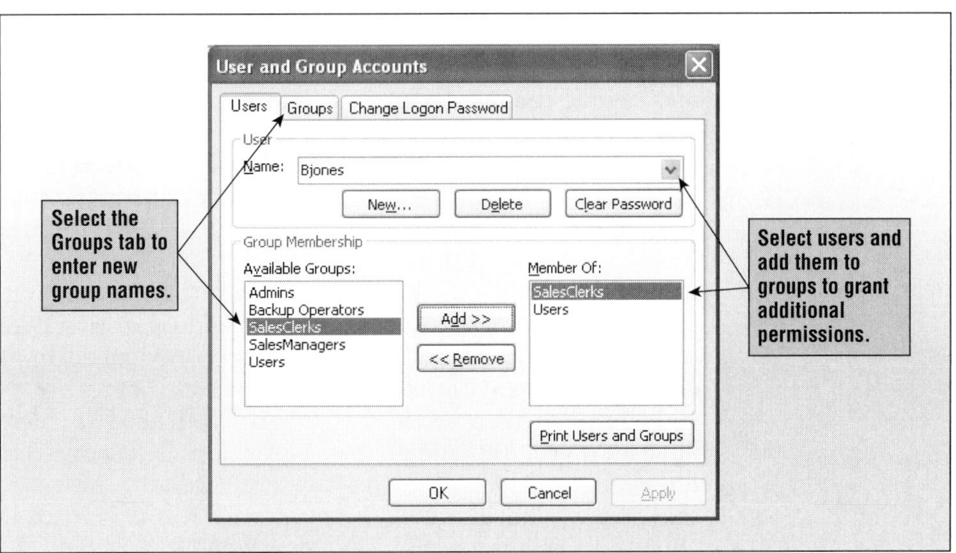

FIGURE 9.15

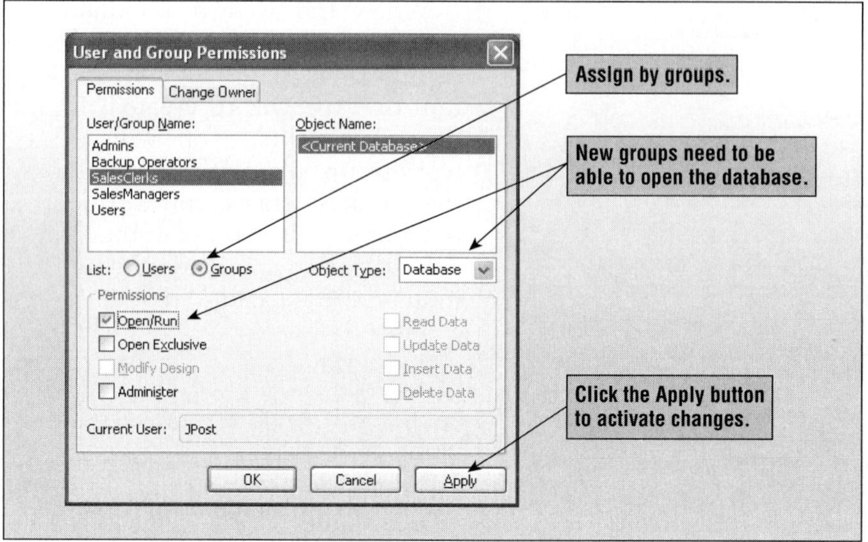

Figure 9.15 shows the basic process. Make sure you select the Groups option to assign permissions to groups and not to individual users. Selecting the object type (Database) displays a list of permissions available for that object. In this case, you need to assign Open/Run to the groups for SalesClerks and SalesManagers.

Other permissions are assigned using the same method. Examine your permissions matrix for the SalesClerks group and customers. Sales clerks need to be able to read, update, and insert customer data. But they should not have the ability to delete customers; that permission is reserved for the sales managers. Select Table as the object type, then click the Customer table in the right-side window. Set the check-boxes to give the appropriate permissions for the SalesClerks and SalesManagers groups. Then switch the object type to Form, and make sure both groups have Open/Run permission for the Customer form and for the startup form. Eventually you can assign the other permissions needed by each group.

For now, reopen the database using the shortcut link. This time, log in as one of the sales clerks and make sure the user can open the customer form and update the data but not delete any rows. Close the database and reopen it as an administrator. Now you can set all of the access rights listed in your permissions matrix. Keep in mind that you need to test all of the permissions. Check to ensure that users can perform their jobs without receiving security notices, and that the users do not have too many permissions. It is time-consuming to test all of the permissions, and you should eventually enlist the help of the actual users to do the final testing and adjustments. To speed up the testing process, you should open two copies of the database— one logged in as a user for testing, and one logged in as an administrator to change the permissions.

To implement a secured database, you need to copy the actual database file (AllPowder2002.mdb), the workgroup file (Secured.mdw), and the startup link (renamed to be StartAllPowder2002.mdb). Moving the databases means that you will have to edit the properties in the startup link so it points to the correct locations on the new machine. Right-click the link and select the

FIGURE 9.16

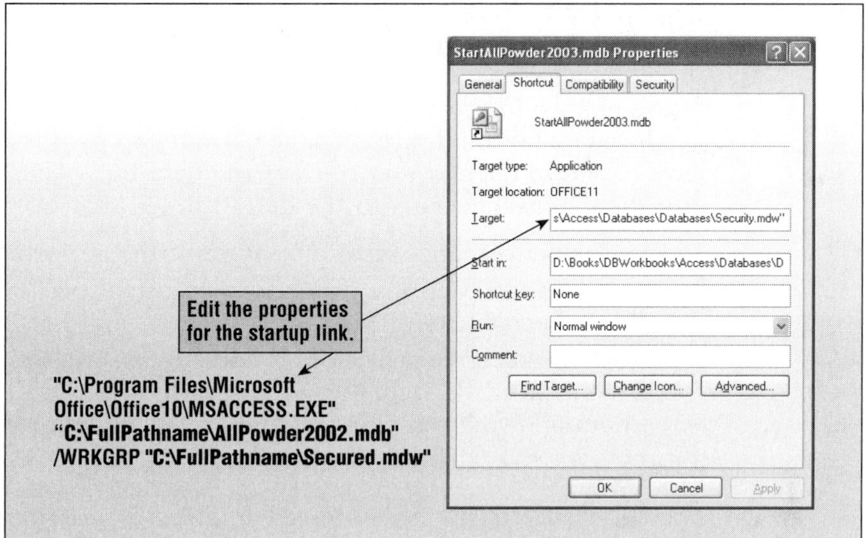

Properties option. As shown in Figure 9.16, you will have to set the Target and Start-In folder. The target contains the names and full pathname location of three files: (1) The Microsoft Access executable file, usually installed to its default location; (2) the full pathname of the secured database (this one you will usually have to change); and (3) the full pathname of the workgroup database (you will also have to change this path). You should generally set the start-in folder to be the same as the location of the main database.

Exercises

Many Charms

Samantha and Madison do not believe that security will be a critical issue at Many Charms. The database will run on one machine, and rarely be used by anyone except the two of them. On the other hand, they do need a system for which it is easy to create backup copies. For some security, they are willing to use the single database password. On the other hand they are concerned about performance. Although they do not expect too many orders to arrive at one time, they do want to examine some lengthy reports to evaluate sales trends.

1. Run the performance wizard to improve the performance of the database—particularly in terms of the reports and queries needed.
2. Create a backup option that makes it easy for the managers to create a backup copy. As much as possible, keep it down to one button. But provide some notices about moving the backup copy offsite in case of fire.
3. Add the security provisions needed by Samantha and Madison.

Standup Foods

Security is a serious concern for Laura. The database contains a large amount of data about employees—and movie star preferences. Managerial employees will need access to the database to enter a considerable amount of information regarding other employees and the status of the event.

Consequently, employee access has to be carefully thought out. Managers should have the ability to enter data on employees who report to them, but should not be able to even see most data on other employees. You will have to use queries to provide this level of security. Assigning access to the entire employee table would give managers too much permission. Instead, you will have to set up queries that retrieve the data for specific managers and then give the managers access to the data through that query.

1. Run the performance wizard to improve the performance of the database.
2. Create a backup option and a written set of procedures that Laura can follow to ensure the data is protected.
3. Create the security provisions needed by Laura. Concentrate on the permissions needed to handle evaluation of employees by a manager—without allowing the manager full access to data for all employees.

EnviroSpeed

The knowledge in the EnviroSpeed database is a major strategic asset to the company. This data represents experience gained over several years and enables the company to be considerably more productive and profitable than its competitors. Tyler and Brennan believe it is critical to protect this asset. On the other hand, it is also critical that employees and hired experts have immediate access to all of the knowledge during a disaster cleanup. Security controls need to be set carefully to protect the database from outside hackers. Fortunately, Brennan and Tyler can trust all of the employees and experts, and do not believe it is necessary to track the exact usage by each person to prevent theft.

1. Run the performance wizard to improve the response times of the database.
2. Create a backup option and a written set of procedures to follow to protect the database.
3. Create the security provisions needed. Concentrate on protecting the data from external attacks.

Final Project

The main textbook has an appendix with several longer case studies. You should be able to work on one of these cases throughout the term. If you or your instructor picks one, perform the following tasks.

1. Run the performance wizard and improve the responsiveness of the application. Identify the main areas that will be stressed as loads increase.
2. Create a backup option and a written set of procedures to protect the database.
3. Identify the main risk factors and implement the security provisions needed to protect the data, but still ensure users have the access needed to perform their jobs efficiently.

10

Distributed Databases and the Internet

Chapter Outline

Objectives
Location, Location, Location
Case: All Powder Board and Ski Shop
Lab Exercise
  All Powder Board and Ski Shop
  The Internet
Exercises
Final Project

Objectives

- Split a database and link the parts for use on a LAN.
- Replicate a database and synchronize the changes.
- Create Web pages to edit data over the Internet.
- Export and import data as XML files.

Location, Location, Location

Even small companies often need to access data in multiple locations. This distributed access generates several issues in database management. The most important question you will face is where to store the data. The answer depends on how the database is used, how fast the connections are, and whether everyone needs 24-hour access to immediately current data. The first step in designing a distributed system is to answer these questions and determine the most efficient method for handling data updates in the various locations. Note that efficiency also includes cost issues.

Microsoft Access provides some support for distributed databases, but does not have as many options as SQL Server or the other big (expensive) systems. The two main techniques supported are linked files and data replication. However, with some additional tools Access can also be used as a database server for small websites. Internet connections are rapidly becoming a useful way to handle distributed access to data. Interestingly, with most Internet database approaches, the data itself is actually centralized in one location. The browser and Internet protocols provide users access to the database from any location with an Internet connection—including wireless devices.

Case: All Powder Board and Ski Shop

Initially, you might think that All Powder, having only one store, would not care much about distributed databases. Certainly if the owners consider adding a second store, the issues become more complex. This situation will be examined in a second lab exercise. In the meantime, even with one store there are some simplified distributed issues to address. The distributed aspect arises because there will be several locations within the store that need access to the database—the checkout stations, the rental desk, and a couple of offices. Figure 10.1 shows that each of these locations will have a computer that needs to run the forms and share the data.

FIGURE 10.1

Distributed questions within a single building are much easier to solve than those spreading across wide geographic areas. The reason is because of the speed of local area networks (LANs). Within the store, it is relatively easy to install a high-speed LAN that can transfer data as quickly as a typical computer can transfer data to an internal hard drive. Consequently, it is possible to store the database in one location and share it with all of the other computers—with no noticeable delays.

Lab Exercise

All Powder Board and Ski Shop

Consider the in-store situation with a high-speed LAN and the need to run the database on several computers at the same time. Currently, you have a single mdb file (plus the security workgroup file if you are using the secured copy). How would you use this single file on six different computers at the same time? You could copy the file to all six machines, but remember that the file contains all of the forms, reports, and data. Any changes to the data on one machine are not going to be available to the other computers.

With a LAN, you could put the single copy of the database on the server on a shared folder. Each workstation would open the same copy of the database. This way, everyone is using the same copy of the data, so all changes are available to everyone. The drawback to using a single file for the database is that all of the forms and reports are also shared—which places a load on the network. Each time a form is opened, it has to be transferred across the network. Another problem is that you cannot make design changes to forms or reports until everyone has closed the database. Even if you simply need to tweak a report that only one person needs, you have to wait until everyone closes the database—because all users are sharing the same forms and reports file.

Activity: Split and Link the Database

One solution to these issues is to split the database into two components: (1) the data tables with relationships, and (2) the forms, reports, queries, and modules. The main data file will reside on the shared server. The file containing the forms and queries can be copied and placed on each individual machine. With this approach, forms and reports load quickly—even if they contain graphics. Minor changes can be made to the files on individual workstations, although at some point you have to copy the changes to all computers. Figure 10.2 shows the concept of the split database. The key to making it work is that the forms database contains links to the actual data tables stored on the shared server. These links are shown as virtual tables in the forms copy of the database, and can be referenced the same as a native table.

> **Action**
>
> Choose Tools/Database Utilities/Database Splitter.
> Choose the name and location for the back-end database.
> Examine the contents of the two databases.

Splitting the database into these elements has an additional impact that can be useful later as the company expands. At some point, the data can be transferred to a more powerful DBMS. The forms and reports will still work! You generally just have to change the links to point to the new, larger DBMS.

To illustrate the process, it is best to use the unsecured database. The process will work on the secured database, but either way, you will have to rebuild the security conditions. In practice, you would build the split

FIGURE 10.2

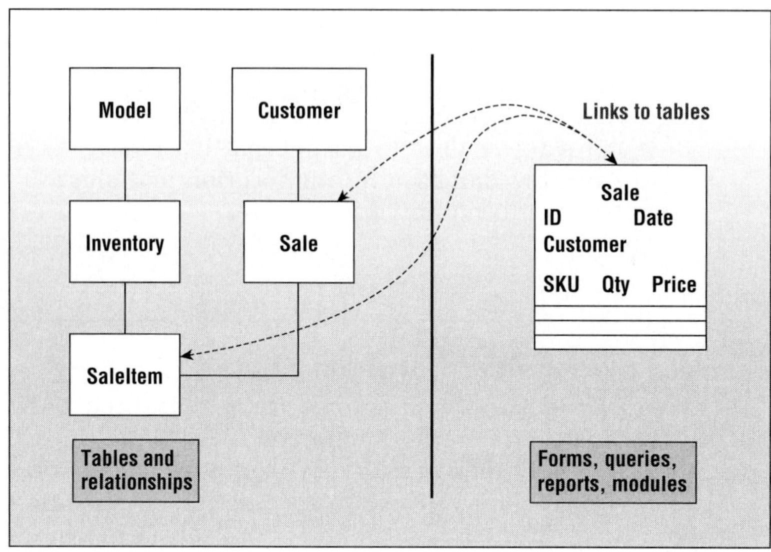

database first and then set the security conditions. You could split a database manually; the process is not too difficult. You simply create a new database and import all of the tables from the original. Then you delete the tables from the original database and build links into the new back-end database. To make the process even easier, Access contains a database splitter wizard. To use this wizard, open the main database and choose the Tools/Database Utilities/Database Splitter menu option. There are no options, but you will be asked to select a name and location for the new back-end database that will contain the tables. Figure 10.3 shows the results. You end up with two mdb files, one for the front end, one for the back end. You should open both files and see what pieces exist. The back-end database contains only tables. The front-end database contains links to the tables, but not the actual data. It also contains all of the forms, reports, queries, and modules. Run the forms in the front-end database to verify that they work.

Once the tables are linked, you can treat them as if they were local tables. When Access needs data, it automatically goes across the network and retrieves it. In the All Powder store, you can place the back-end database on the server, and then put copies of the front-end database on each machine. Be sure you set security permissions in both the back-end and front-end databases first. One issue does arise with linked databases: What happens if you move the back-end database? The front-end forms will not be able to find the tables to establish the link. Access contains a Linked Table Manager to solve this problem. As shown in Figure 10.4, right-click on the linked tables in the front-end database and select the Linked Table Manager. Then select (check) all of the links and click the OK button. At this point, Access will prompt you for the new location of the back-end database. Simply browse to its location and select it. The Linked Table Manager will rebuild all of the links.

Activity: Replicate and Synchronize a Database

Linked tables are an efficient and easy solution when all of the computers are connected by a high-speed LAN. If the company decides to open a second store, even if it is in the same city, it is usually too expensive to link the

FIGURE 10.3

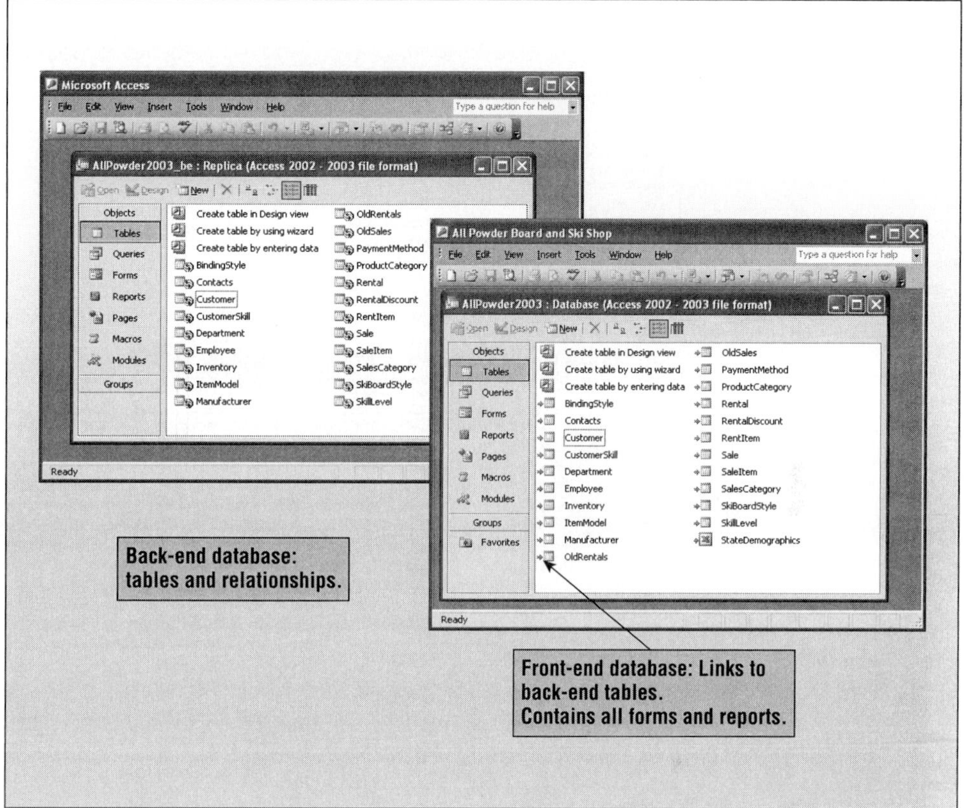

Action
Choose Tools/Replication/Create Replica.
Make a change to a customer name in the master database.
Add a new customer in the replica.
In the master database, choose Tools/Replication/Synchronize Now.
Verify that both databases now contain the same data.

stores with a high-speed network. Within each store, the LAN probably runs at 100 megabits per second (Mbps), but connections between stores are expensive and pricing is based on the transmission capacity. Even relatively low-speed simple T1 connections at 1.544 Mbps can cost $1,000 to $2,000 per month. No one will be happy with linked tables at that speed, and faster links can be substantially more expensive. With slower connection speeds, you need to distribute the data so that most of the accesses remain within each store. In this case, you will have two separate copies of the data tables. Then you need to synchronize the data so the two copies of the database exchange updates until they both contain the same data. How often the databases need to be synchronized depends on the use of the data. If sales clerks routinely need to know the inventory status of items in the other store, the synchronization will have to occur several times throughout the data. However, in most cases, daily synchronization will be sufficient, and the databases can be exchanged over night when there is less traffic on the network.

The first step is to create a replica of the database. You cannot simply copy the mdb file. A true replica contains information that enables it to connect back with the master database and synchronize the data changes. For the case of the All Powder database, each store would run split copies of the database. Each store would contain a back-end database that contains only

FIGURE 10.4

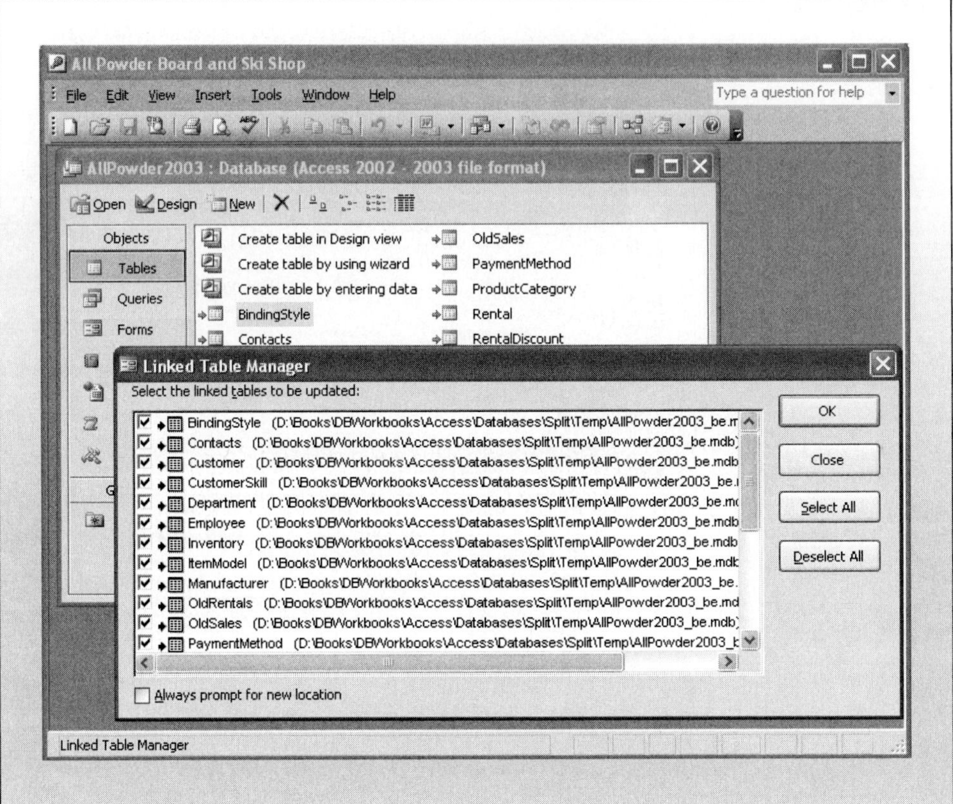

the tables. This database is the one that would be replicated and later synchronized. The front-end database could simply be copied and loaded onto the individual user machines.

To create a replica, open the back-end database and choose the Tools/Replication/Create Replica menu option. The process is almost automatic. Stick with the default choices and make sure you include the backup copy of the original database. When the wizard finishes, you will have the original master copy of the database and a replica. If desired, you can create additional replicas from the master. Figure 10.5 shows the result of the process. Initially, it appears that little has changed except for the new icon. However, several changes were made to the master database internally. Check the file size and you will see that it has doubled.

AutoNumber keys present one of the more visible issues in replicated databases. When managers are simultaneously adding new customers in different stores, how does the database ensure that the generated keys are unique? It can no longer use a simple increment approach. Instead, Access essentially randomly assigns values for AutoNumber keys. A more sophisticated approach would be to assign the values with a component added for each copy. Purely random numbers are not guaranteed to be unique—but with over 2 billion possibilities, the chance of simultaneously generating exactly the same value is fairly small.

To see how the replicated database works, open the Customer table in the master database and change one of the names slightly (for example, Jones2). Close the database and open the Customer table in the replica. This copy

FIGURE 10.5

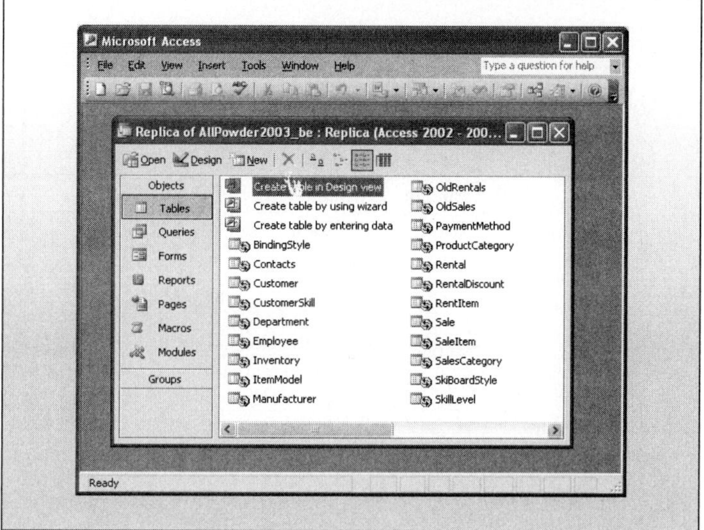

still has the original name because the databases have not been synchronized yet. Add a new customer in the replica database, and observe the generated AutoNumber key. Again, this new row exists only within the replica database until it is synchronized to the master. Figure 10.6 shows a partial version of the two Customer tables and the changes.

To synchronize the replica to the master database, close the replica and open the master database. Choose the Tools/Replication/Synchronize Now menu option. If necessary, browse to find the replica. The process is largely automatic. Open the Customer table in the master database. The modified name is still intact. Scroll to the end of the table and notice that the row added to the replica has been transferred to the master. Open the Customer table in the replica database. Notice that the modified name has been updated in the replica. Figure 10.7 shows that all changes are made in each table.

FIGURE 10.6

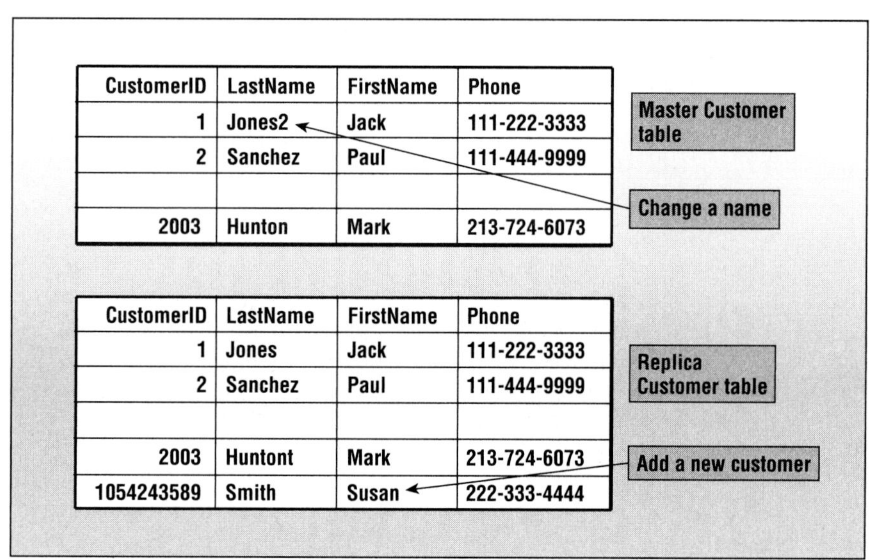

CustomerID	LastName	FirstName	Phone
1	Jones2	Jack	111-222-3333
2	Sanchez	Paul	111-444-9999
2003	Hunton	Mark	213-724-6073

CustomerID	LastName	FirstName	Phone
1	Jones	Jack	111-222-3333
2	Sanchez	Paul	111-444-9999
2003	Huntont	Mark	213-724-6073
1054243589	Smith	Susan	222-333-4444

FIGURE 10.7

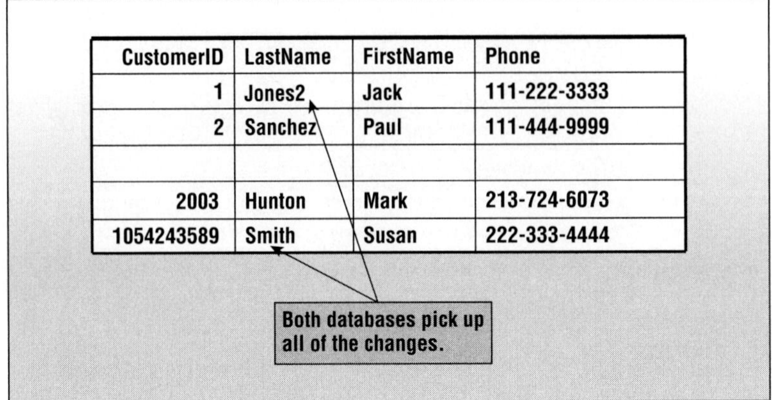

What about concurrency? With replicated databases, it is possible for two people in different locations to modify the same piece of data at essentially the same time. For instance, both could be changing an address for the first customer. Try it by modifying the address for the first customer in the master database and then making a different change for the same address in the replica. Then reopen the master database and synchronize it with the replica. You will receive a message that a conflict exists and an option to resolve the conflict.

Figure 10.8 shows the analysis by the Resolve Conflicts wizard. It indicates that the same row was changed by two different operations and shows

FIGURE 10.8

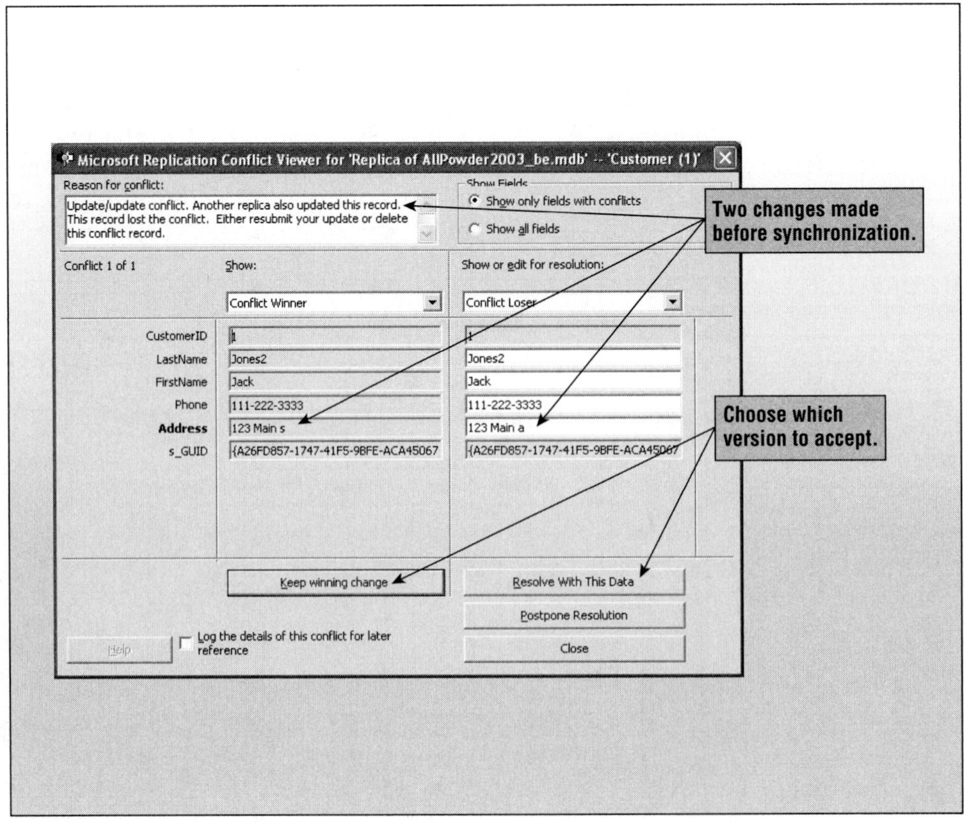

the two values that were entered for the Address. In this case, the values on the left were entered into the master database. By clicking the button beneath the desired set of values, you can indicate which data should be kept and which discarded. You can also postpone the decision, while you talk with others to find out which change should be kept. With replicated databases, this manual process cannot be avoided. There is no good way for the computer to decide which change to accept when two changes occur at the same time. You could make an argument that the most recent change should be kept, but that decision might not be the best in every case.

The Internet

Activity: Web Pages with Access

Web-based applications are becoming the preferred method of building systems—particularly when users need distributed access. With relatively simple browsers, users can access the data and the applications from anyplace that has an Internet connection. With the increasing availability and features of wireless devices such as cell phones, managers will want even more access to data remotely. Unfortunately, the technologies and infrastructure are still immature, and Web-enabled applications can require intricate coding and time-consuming debugging.

As shown in Figure 10.9, Access provides a wizard to create Web-based forms. The database and Web pages are

> **Action**
>
> In the Pages section, create a data access page by using the wizard.
> Select the Customer table with all columns.
> Save the page as Customer.html.
> Open the page and test it.
> Test the page by opening it outside the database using a browser.

FIGURE 10.9

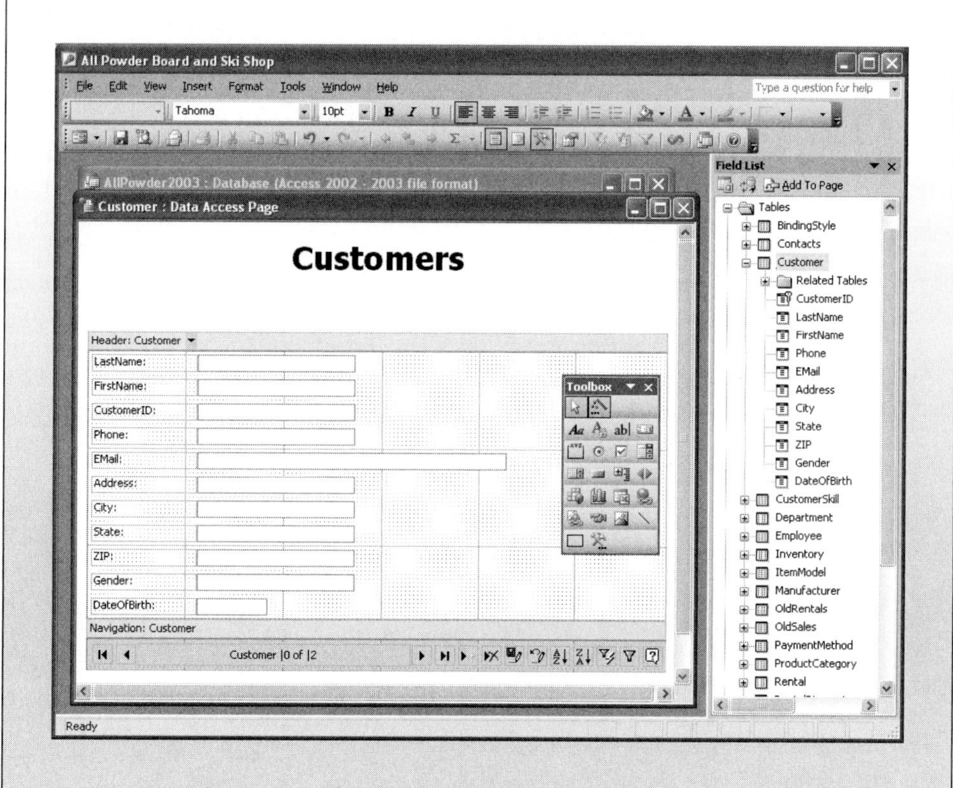

placed on a Web server with appropriate security controls. Managers use a browser to connect to the site and open the pages. They enter data much as they would with a Windows-based form. Most of the detailed programming controls are missing, but it is possible to quickly build a usable page. However, it is critical that you understand a fundamental drawback to the Access approach. It requires that users have special Office components installed on their machines to use the forms. This issue can be solved if the application is built for internal company use, and managers generally use the company computers. Even in this situation, managers will not generally have access to the forms when they are traveling and need to use a computer not furnished by the company. More importantly, you cannot use this technology for applications that will be used by outsiders, such as customers and suppliers.

To test the Web form wizard, switch to the Pages section on the main database window. Select the option to Create a New Page using the wizard. Choose the Customer table in the drop-down list box. Use all of the columns in the Customer table by moving them to the right-hand window. Since you want a simple main form, do not use any grouping options. You can select a sort order if desired. Close and save the form as Customer.html. You can open the form from the page window, or through the Windows browser. If you copy the form and the database to a Web server, you will have to edit the HTML forms, search for the mdb file, and enter the correct path location.

Activity: Transferring Data with XML

One issue you will face with distributed databases is the need to transfer data among differing database systems. For example, a supplier might send you product information electronically. Since the supplier does not know what type of database system you have or how your database is organized, it can be difficult to provide the data in a format that your system can read. The process is complicated when suppliers have thousands of customers just like your shop. Suppliers have no desire to create thousands of different electronic files. Instead, they should be able to send one file in a standard format, and your system should be able to identify the necessary data, select it, and import it into your database. This dream is not quite reality, but XML (eXtensible Markup Language) was created to make it easier to exchange data among disparate systems. If you need to transfer data to someone outside the company, you can use File/Export and select XML as the file type. An XML file is a text file that contains tags that describe the data. You should select the option to create a schema file (xsd) that defines the structure of the data file.

Importing data is generally not much more difficult, but your original source file might not have all of the data that you need. You might have to edit the file to add or modify some of the data. For example, a vendor might send you a file that lists some new skis and snowboards. This data can be imported into the ItemModel table, but this table has a column for ManufacturerID. You will have to add that column to the XML file because your vendor is not going to know what number you use. Alternatively, if you are careful, you can import the data with a blank ManufacturerID and use SQL to update those new rows. You have to be careful with this method, because you need a way to identify which rows should be updated.

<table>
<tr><td>

Action

Highlight the Employee table name.
Choose File/Export.
Set the type as Text/csv.
Save the file with a csv extension.
Select comma delimited and include the field names on the first row.
Save the file and close the database.
Open the file in Excel.

</td></tr>
</table>

FIGURE 10.10

Action

Open the ModelSample.xml file with Wordpad and verify that the fields match your column names.
Edit the file if needed and save it.
In the database, choose File/Get External Data/Import.
Select the file and append the data to your ItemModel table.

Figure 10.10 shows that you can open XML files using the Internet Explorer browser. This approach highlights the individual data records and makes it easy to see the structure of the data. You can expand or contract individual segments to focus on individual areas. This example has three new items, with basic data about the products. Notice the tags used to indicate the purpose of the data items. These tags could have any names, but choosing names that are understandable to humans makes the file easier to read and to edit. This file was generated by an Access export, so it uses the existing column names.

Figure 10.11 shows a portion of the same XML file as it would appear in a text editor. Notice the tags are there to help you, but the text editor lacks the formatting and highlighting of Internet Explorer. Nonetheless, the text-based data is easy to edit, and you could quickly change the ManufacturerID

FIGURE 10.11

```
<ItemModel>
<ModelID>BQQ-333</ModelID>
<ManufacturerID>23</ManufacturerID>
<Category>Board</Category>
<Color>Black</Color>
<Cost>137.50</Cost>
<ModelYear>2005</ModelYear>
<ItemMaterial>Composite</ItemMaterial>
<ListPrice>224.99</ListPrice>
<Style>Downhill</Style>
<SkillLevel>6</SkillLevel>
<WaistWidth>159</WaistWidth>
<EffectiveEdge>1021</EffectiveEdge>
<BindingStyle>Strap</BindingStyle>
<RentalRate>20</RentalRate>
</ItemModel>
```

FIGURE 10.12

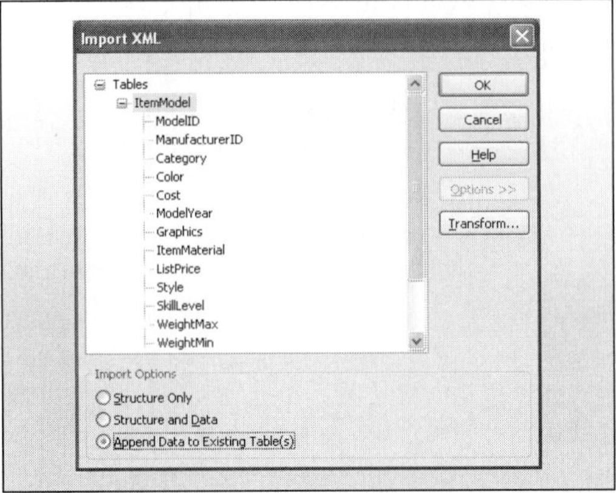

data. However, be careful if you have to add new tags. It is easy to add the tags into an XML file, but most files are also transferred with a schema file that lists the tags that can be included in the XML file. If you add sections or tags to an XML file, you will also have to modify the accompanying XSD file.

Once the file is acceptable, you can import the data into Access. Use the File/Get External Data/Import menu option. Figure 10.12 shows that you are given the option to append the data directly to the end of an existing table. If the data and tags in the XML file match the table definition, you can use this option. It will still work if columns are in a different order. On the other hand, if the XML file is missing key columns, or needs additional cleanup, it would be wiser to import the file into a new table. Then use **SQL** to extract and clean up the data and transfer it to the desired database table. If you look closely at the data being imported, you will see that there are many opportunities for problems. For instance, what happens if the manufacturer does not use exactly the same style and binding descriptions that are in the main database? The inconsistent rows will not be appended because they would violate the integrity constraints. When there are many rows of data, and many of these situations, you will need to import the data into a separate table and clean it up first. Many times you can write a sequence of **SQL** statements to do the cleanup, making the process easier next month when you receive a new file from the same vendor. For these reasons, even XML cannot solve all of the data transfer issues.

Exercises

Crystal Tigers

Most of the information for the Crystal Tigers club can be maintained on one computer run by the club secretary. However, the secretary sometimes needs assistance entering all of the data during special events. Although he brings the database on his laptop, it would probably be easier if two or three people brought laptops and handled specific tasks. At the end of the day, the data could be synchronized and available for analysis. It would at least speed up the data entry and give more people access to the critical information needed during the day.

1. Replicate the database and test it on three separate computers, then synchronize the changes a few times to see if this approach will work for the club.
2. The club has talked about making some data available to members over the Internet. Although many of the members do not have Microsoft Office installed, the club would prefer to provide read-only access. Set up a page that generates activity lists for an upcoming event so members can check the schedule.
3. One of the charitable organizations the club works with is impressed with the database and would like some of the data. Create a query and export an XML file that lists the members and the hours worked for a particular event.

Capitol Artists

Because the system for Capitol Artists collects data from many employees at the same time, the main database needs to run on a central server. All of the computers are connected by a high-speed LAN, and based on the company growth rates, you need to plan ahead for possibly moving to a larger back-end DBMS. It makes sense to split the database and link the forms to the data tables. The company is unlikely to open a second office; however, many of the employees have suggested that they would be more productive if they worked from home. The managers have suggested testing this idea by using the database work-tracking system. A few employees would install the database on their home systems. As they completed client tasks, they would fill out the work table as usual. This data could then be synchronized with the company database at the end of the day. After a month, the managers could see if the employee productivity declined or improved.

1. To handle the internal LAN, split the database. Install the back-end database on one machine, and install at least two copies of the front-end database on other machines. Get someone to help you test the system for performance.
2. Create a replica of the database that could be checked out by telecommuting employees. Test the work-progress forms and synchronization.
3. One of the owners travels often and wants to check on daily progress reports over the Internet using her laptop. Create a Web page that displays the work done for the current day and lists the hours and expense of the employees for each project.

Offshore Speed

The Offshore Speed company has some aspects in common with All Powder. In particular, the store needs several computers running the application to handle sales, orders, and management reports. For some reason, the company owner is leery about splitting the database. To satisfy him, you should test the application both ways, so you will need two or three people to assist you in loading and running the forms at exactly the same time. Because of the huge number of parts, the company is particularly interested in obtaining XML product files from vendors. With 20 primary vendors and changes every month, you need to find a way to automate the imports of this data.

1. Install the single copy of the database on one computer. Get two or three other students to simultaneously open the application across the network and enter some basic sales data. Time the process. Split the database, putting copies of the forms on each computer. Repeat the test and see if there is a difference in performance. Make a recommendation to the owner.
2. Create at least three different XML files that might arrive from vendors with product details. These files should not contain VendorID and other specific information that exists only in your database. Create a system that will automate these imports whenever a file arrives.
3. One of the managers wants to bring a copy of the database home to look through reports and the PivotTables at night. Create a replica and set up a synchronization process that is easy for the manager to use at the end of the day, so that his laptop will have up-to-date data.

Final Project

The main textbook has an appendix with several longer case studies. You should be able to work on one of these cases throughout the term. If you or your instructor picks one, perform the following tasks.

1. Split the database into a back-end and front-end database. Test the applications.
2. Create a replica; test all of the forms and reports on both copies. Test the synchronization.
3. Export at least one table into an XML file that could be sent to an outside firm such as a customer or supplier.
4. Create a basic Web page to enable workers to enter data using a browser.
5. Create a more complex Web page to handle a main form/subform situation such as Sales. Be sure to create drop-down lists for foreign key columns. *Hint:* You will have to first create a query for the data displayed in the drop-down list because a Web page combo box can use at most two columns.